Alambrista
AND THE U.S.-MEXICO BORDER

Alambrista

AND THE U.S.-MEXICO BORDER

Film, Music, and Stories of Undocumented Immigrants

Edited and with an introduction
by Nicholas J. Cull and
Davíd Carrasco

UNIVERSITY OF NEW MEXICO PRESS ■ ALBUQUERQUE

10 09 08 07 06 05 04   1 2 3 4 5 6 7

CD: *Alambrista:The Director's Cut Soundtrack* ©2004 by Dr. Loco, Inc.
DVD: *Alambrista:The Director's Cut* ©1997, 2004 by Bobwin Studios.
Special features, interviews, commentary and musical journey ©2004 by the
Alambrista Project, Moses Mesoamerican Archive, Harvard University.

LIBRARY OF CONGRESS CATALOGING-IN-PUBLICATION DATA

Alambrista and the U.S.–Mexico border : film, music, and stories
of undocumented immigrants / edited and with an introduction
by Nicholas J. Cull and David Carrasco.
p. cm.
Includes bibliographical references.
ISBN 0-8263-3375-3 (cloth: alk. paper)
ISBN 0-8263-3376-1 (pbk. : alk. paper)
1. Alambrista. 2. Mexican American migrant agricultural
laborers—Social conditions—20th century. 3. Illegal immigrants—
United States—Social conditions—20th century.
I. Title: Alambrista and the United States-Mexico border.
II. Cull, Nicholas John. III. Carrasco, David.
PN1997.A317A43 2004
791.43'72—dc22
2004004308

*This publication has been supported in part by a generous grant
from the Ford Foundation, and from Tobias Durán, Director,
Center for Regional Studies, University of New Mexico.*

Book and cover design and composition: Kathleen Sparkes
All photographs by Andrew Young ©Bobwin Associates, 2003.

Type in this book is set in Minion 10.5 / 14
Display type is Architectura and Berthold Akzidenz Grotesk

Contents

INTRODUCTION

Footsteps in the Wind

Nicholas J. Cull and Davíd Carrasco

At 11.42 P.M. on the night of Tuesday May 13th, 2003, an emergency dispatcher on duty in the small southeastern Texas town of Kingsville, about 75 miles north of the U.S. border with Mexico, received a 911 call from a cellular telephone. A desperate male voice speaking in a mixture of English and Spanish pleaded: "We're asphyxiating. Help me, help me. We're asphyxiating.... We're in a trailer. We're illegals.... There are ten down." Before the dispatcher could summon a bilingual assistant to help, the call ended. Within a few hours the context of this call for help had become horribly clear. At around 2.30 A.M. on the morning of May 14th sheriff's deputies from Victoria, Texas, about 175 miles north of the border, found an abandoned trailer at a truck stop on U.S. route 77. In and around the truck lay seventeen dead bodies. An eighteenth and nineteenth victim died shortly afterward. The dead included a five-year-old boy, later identified as Marco Antonio Villaseñor Acuña, and his father, José Antonio Villaseñor Leon, aged thirty-one, from Mexico City. As other officials began to pick up badly heat-exhausted survivors in the surrounding area the full story became clear. Around eighty-five would-be immigrants from Mexico, Honduras, and Guatemala had been packed into the insulated trailer to cross the border into the United States. Trapped for hours without fresh air and in record heat for the time of year they had begun to die. In despair some had clawed holes into the side of the trailer for air and to attract attention. The driver—one Tyronne Williams of Schenectady, New York—had panicked when he realized that his human cargo had begun to die. He unhooked his trailer and fled the scene in his cab. He was arrested some hours later along with accomplices. He told investigators that he had been paid the sum of $5,000 to haul the migrants from Harlingen, Texas (near the border town of Brownsville) to Houston. Although other arrests followed, the masterminds behind the smuggling operation remained at large.[1]

As journalists reporting this case soon noted, this incident was not unprecedented. In October 2002 the decomposed bodies of eleven Mexican immigrants were discovered in a railway car in Iowa, while in 1987 U.S. authorities found eighteen young Mexicans dead in a boxcar in Sierra Blanca, Texas. Moreover, these mass deaths were just the most extreme examples of innumerable individual stories of suffering, exploitation, and death connected to the illegal crossing of the border between the United States and Mexico.[2] Such cases are not unique to the United States. Similar stories of death on the border can be found in the newspapers of Western Europe and wherever people from the have-not portions of the world are prepared to risk everything for a better life in the have portion.[3] Yet however familiar the headlines, the human stories behind such reports are seldom told. These experiences seem to disappear as swiftly as the footprints left in the desert sand during their border crossing: wiped by the first stiff breeze. Whether in the United States or Western Europe the migrants who slip through the official net become faceless statistics in newspaper columns or the speeches of generally unsympathetic politicians. It was a desire to give a human face to such statistics and to draw attention to the horrendous conditions faced by such migrants after crossing the border that motivated the film that is at the heart of this collection of essays: Robert M. Young's *Alambrista*.

Approaching *Alambrista*

When *Alambrista* first appeared in 1977 there had been little or no discussion of the exploitation of undocumented migrant farm workers in American film or television. The best-known exception to this was a famous CBS documentary from 1960 called *Harvest of Shame*. Fictional movies had evolved little in their representation of Mexican Americans since the stereotyped "greasers" of Hollywood's silent era. To be the subject of a Hollywood movie it certainly helped to be White and speak English. Robert M. Young, a White American filmmaker who had moved from documentary into politically engaged independent feature filmmaking, sought to plug this gap. He worked with the Californian public television station, KCTV, which was eager to address one of the most significant social issues in the state. The finished film did not quite match Young's hopes for the project, and after a distinguished career on the festival circuit and showings on TV in the US and abroad, *Alambrista* dropped from view.

The relevance of *Alambrista* did not diminish in the quarter century following its release. People continued to risk their lives in large numbers to win the dubious privilege of forming the lowest rung on the economic ladder of life in the United States. No other film emerged addressing their story as eloquently or compassionately as Young's original work. Mindful of the value of Bob Young's film in its own time and its potential as a teaching resource in today's classrooms, around the turn of the millennium a group of academics mainly working in Chicano and American studies resolved to work with Young to create a new print of *Alambrista*. In discussions with Davíd Carrasco, who had met Young while the two were assisting Edward James Olmos in the production of the film *Americanos: Latino Life in the United States,* Young raised the possibility of a new soundtrack and the restoration of scenes deleted from the original version. Carrasco felt immediately that he knew just the musician and scholar to assist them in the new project, namely the anthropologist-musician Professor José Cuellar. Cuellar, also known for his musical and performance virtuosity as "Dr. Loco" of "Dr. Loco's Rockin' Jalapeño Band," knew and respected Young's work in *Alambrista* and joined in the discussion with Carrasco and Young. Together they realized they could produce a real "director's cut" of the film. Carrasco and Cuellar set out to form a team of writers, interpreters, and activists who could be part of a project they called "Alambrista 2001." It soon became apparent to this group that the film's value as a teaching tool would be much enhanced if it were accompanied by a collection of essays to both provide the historical and political context for the events depicted in the film and to analyze the film itself. As part of this phase of reflection and writing, members of the group screened the film at two farm-worker communities, first in Southern

California's Coachella Valley and later in Gettysburg, Pennsylvania, in the shadow of the infamous battlefield. Discussions with present-day farm workers who critically commented on the film's power and relevance to their lives assisted the group in both the composition of the director's cut and in the writing of an anthology of essays. The creation of such an anthology became a core element of the Alambrista project and this collection is the result. At the end of this introduction you will find a selection of questions raised by *Alambrista*, intended to provoke lively classroom debate. There are no easy answers to these questions but incidents like that on U.S. highway 77 underscore the need to ask them.

■

This collection is divided into two main portions. The first part, "*Alambrista* Footsteps: Context in History, Politics, and Lived Experience," provides detailed background to the social situation depicted in the film: essays to help the student or interested scholar acquire an informed overview of the subject. First, Albert Camarillo provides an account of the history of Mexican migration into the United States in "*Alambrista* and the Historical Context of Mexican Immigration to the United States in the Twentieth Century." Next, Richard Griswold del Castillo's chapter "*Alambrista*'s Inspiration: César Chávez and Migrant Farm Workers" surveys the life of César Chávez, the Chicano rights activist whose campaign first attracted Bob Young's attention to the subject of undocumented Mexican labor. Daniel Groody presents oral testimony collected from migrant farmers whose experiences match those depicted in *Alambrista*. His essay "The Drama of Immigration and the Cry of the Poor: The Voices of *Alambrista* Yesterday and Today" demonstrates the authenticity and relevance of Young's film. The final two essays bring the story into the present day. Bill Ong Hing's "Operation Gatekeeper: The War against the *Alambristas* of the 1990s" provides an account of a Clinton-era initiative to keep out migrants and its tragic results. On the other hand, Teresa Carrillo's "Watching Over Greater Mexico: Mexican Initiatives on Migration and the *Alambristas* of the New Millennium" documents the more positive recent responses of the Mexican government to address the needs of Mexican people living beyond its borders.

The second half of this anthology is entitled "*Alambrista* Sights and Sounds: Film Criticism and Analysis." Articles here engage the fabric of the film directly. The contributors discuss Young's career and the making and remaking of *Alambrista* and analyze and interpret Young's achievement in *Alambrista*. In the first piece in this section, Cordelia Candelaria's "Tightrope Walking the Border: *¡Alambrista!* and the Acrobatics of Mestizo Representation" investigates the multiple meanings of the film's title, which can be translated as "high-wire artist." In the border slang of the 1970s it became an ironic comment on the precarious life lived on the ultimate high wire: that separating the United States from Mexico. In the next essay, "Border Crossings: The Cinema of Robert M. Young," Nicholas J. Cull sets *Alambrista* in the context of Young's wider body of work. The collection is then enhanced further by the film critic Howie Movshovitz's essay "Robert M. Young and *Alambrista*," which provides both personal reminiscence and critical views of Young's achievement and contribution to understanding the "strangers" among us. José Cuellar's "*Notas en el Viento*: The Musical Soundtrack of *Alambrista*—Director's Cut" provides a firsthand account of the creation of the soundtrack to the director's cut, and adds complete texts for the songs heard in part in the film. In a final chapter, "Dark Walking, Making Food, and Giving Birth to *Alambristas*: Religious Dimensions in the Film," Davíd Carrasco considers the religiosity of the film and the way in which *Alambrista* touches on the universal themes of human experience and mythic imagination.

The reader will note that many of the contributions to this book—like the classic study of border culture, Gloria Anzaldua's book: *Borderlands—La Frontera: The New Mestiza* (1987)—draw on personal experience. Groody presents the testimony of the migrants themselves; Cuellar and Candelaria relate their own encounter with the film as musician and teacher/critic respectively; Camarillo's piece includes his own family history and the corridos, the ballads that served as the repositories of collective experience for the community of the border. This emphasis on the personal and community-generated sources reflects the degree to which the story at the heart of *Alambrista* frequently lies outside the limits of American written discourse. Carlos Fuentes once said that "the unwritten part of the world is much greater than the written part of the world" and this project also shows that "the unfilmed part of the world is immensely larger and more significant than the filmed part of the world." It also reflects the degree to which there is no fixed border between the authors and their subjects. They are themselves made by or caught up in the world of the border.

Unlocking *Alambrista:*
Some Questions for the Reader/Viewer

1) *Alambrista* and contemporary American life
Robert Young made *Alambrista* in order to show American people the story behind the food they eat. In what ways does contemporary life in North America depend on cheap labor from undocumented and other immigrants?

2) *Alambrista* and the missing voices of the border experience
Considering both the film and Daniel Groody's collection of voices from the immigration drama, which voice is new to you? Which challenges you most? Are any voices missing?

3) *Alambrista* heroes and villains
Every movie has heroes and villains: to what extent is Roberto a hero? Did he risk too much in making his journey to the United States? Can the breaking of immigration law be justified by need? Who is the villain?

4) The conclusion of *Alambrista*
At the end of *Alambrista* an undocumented Mexican woman gives birth clinging to a border post and rejoices that her child won't need papers to live in the United States. To what extent does birth in the United States resolve the problems depicted in the film? Where—if anywhere—do you find hope in *Alambrista*?

5) The politics of *Alambrista*
Although *Alambrista* was inspired, in part, by the work of César Chávez it does not endorse his chosen method of reform and resistance as documented by Ricardo Griswold: the trades union. Does Young offer any other solution?

Why do you think the U.S. immigration authorities cooperated in the making of *Alambrista*?

6) *Alambrista* and policy
Reading the essays by Hing and Carrillo, compare and contrast the responses of recent U.S. and Mexican governments to the problem of undocumented migration. Which strategy do you feel would do most to address the problems highlighted in *Alambrista*?

7) *Alambrista* and authenticity
Alambrista was created by a White American filmmaker. In what ways can it be considered an authentic document of the undocumented migrant experience? Does the addition of a soundtrack by the Chicano artist José Cuellar make a difference to this work's authenticity? How does Cuellar's music contribute to your experience of the film?

8) *Alambrista* as fiction/myth
Cull and Carrasco identify certain universal elements within *Alambrista*. The protagonist, Roberto, is a hero seeking to be reconciled with his father (not unlike Luke Skywalker in *Star Wars*), while his friend Joe functions as a trickster (not unlike *Brer Rabbit* in African American folklore). Do these universal elements deepen the meaning of the film by making it "true" to the deepest stories in human culture, or do they work against the sense of authenticity by over-generalization and requiring supporting plot devices?

9) Stylistic border-crossing in *Alambrista*
Young's film *Alambrista* crosses borders in terms of its style: mixing documentary and fictional techniques. What are the elements of each style? Which do you believe to be dominant in the final film? Why do you think Young included the revival-meeting scene in the film?

10) *Alambrista* and other border films
Robert M. Young's *Alambrista* is not the only film to depict either the life and culture of the Mexican border or conditions of Mexican workers in the United

States. Some other films that can be usefully compared and contrasted with Young's film include:

John Sayles (dir.) *Lone Star* (1996) and

Ken Loach (dir.) *Bread and Roses* (2000).

What do these films add to your understanding of the border?

11) *Alambrista* and history

Alambrista was set in the late 1970s. How different would Roberto's story be if set earlier in the long history of Mexican migration or more recently? If you were remaking *Alambrista* in the present day, what elements would you develop further?

■

On 21 May 2003 the bodies of eleven of the dead from highway 77 were transported back to Mexico City by air. From there they were returned to their hometowns. Mexico's Foreign Relations Department issued a statement on their deaths: "This lamentable incident shows the need for and importance of achieving safe conditions on the border for migrants, and the need for safe, legal and orderly migration. The Mexican government reiterates its commitment to fight gangs of immigrant traffickers, and those who seek to profit at the expense of undocumented migrants." Barely two weeks later Texas authorities found the decomposed bodies of three more migrants found in a railway freight car near Baytown, Texas. They had concealed themselves in a hopper wagon as a cheap way to get from one harvest to the next within the United States, in much the same way as the protagonist of *Alambrista*.[4] The director's cut of *Alambrista* and these supporting essays cannot provide an answer to the problem of undocumented migration, but they are offered in the belief that the undocumented migrants of the world have a history that needs to be told, have a present that needs to be understood, and will be part of the future of the developed world, whether the developed world wishes it or not.

■

Notes

1. "18 Migrants found dead in trailer at Tex. Truck stop," *Washington Post*, 15 May 2003; "'I have just seen the most horrible thing of my life': Truck's airtight trailer became a death trap," *Houston Chronicle*, 18 May 2003; "List of Victims," *Houston Chronicle*, 21 May 2003; "Immigrants' bodies on journey home," *Houston Chronicle*, 22 May 2003.

2. "18 Migrants found dead in trailer at Tex. Truck stop," and "'I have just seen the most horrible thing of my life.'"

3. On 18 June 2000, in a case similar to that of Victoria, Texas, British officials in the port of Dover discovered 54 men and 4 women of Chinese origin dead in back of a lorry. On 18 June 2003 Italian newspapers reported the death of over 70 illegal immigrants in a shipwreck south of Sicily.

4. "Immigrants bodies on journey home," *Houston Chronicle*, 22 May 2003; "Stifling near Baytown hot trip ends," *Houston Chronicle*, 4 June 2003.

PART ONE

Alambrista Footsteps

Context in History, Politics, and Lived Experience

Alambrista and the
Historical Context of
Mexican Immigration to the
United States in the
Twentieth Century

Albert Camarillo

Roberto, the protagonist in the film *Alambrista,* is a young family man who works the land in his native state of Michoacán on the southwest coast of Mexico. In the film, set in the 1970s, Roberto makes his decision to leave his wife, baby, and mother in search of wage labor in *el norte.* His decision is given additional meaning and significance because his father had departed many years before to follow the same path north to the United States. Although his father never returned, Roberto makes the journey nonetheless. About sixty years earlier, another young man from rural Michoacán, Benjamín, also decided to leave his family's small plot of farmland

to make the trek north to find work and to follow his father, who had also abandoned the family and remained in the United States. Benjamín, like Roberto
many decades later, worked the fields moving from crop to crop and from state
to state in search of employment. Unlike Roberto, however, Benjamín never
returned permanently to Mexico, and instead planted roots in California, where
he and his brother eventually earned enough money at unskilled, low-wage jobs
to send for the other members of the Camarillo family, reuniting all in Los
Angeles in 1916. Though time, space, and circumstance separated the experiences of Roberto and Benjamín—one fictional and one real—these two young
Mexican immigrants represent a basic human story that is repeated time and
time again throughout the twentieth century by millions of others, women and
men, old and young alike. Their stories are part of one of the largest and continuous international migrations in U.S. history. This essay provides a general
overview for understanding the history of immigration and migration from
Mexico to the United States over the past one hundred years.

The Movements North

For nearly four hundred years since the establishment of Spanish colonial settlement in New Mexico in the early seventeenth century, mestizo people from
Mexico have traveled north into the region that today borders the United States
and Mexico. Hardy frontier people—soldiers, missionaries, and civilians, men
and women—settled the sparsely populated far northern borderlands, first for
the Spanish crown and later for the Republic of Mexico (1821–1848). After the
U.S.-Mexican War in 1848, the once northern provinces were annexed by the
United States and a new international boundary line separated the two nations.
About a hundred thousand former Mexican citizens opted to remain in their
native land, as they became Americans by virtue of the treaty that settled the war.
For nearly seventy years after the war, Mexicans could freely cross the Rio Grande
river into Texas or travel without interference across the largely imaginary line
in the desert between Mexico and the United States elsewhere in the region.
Though no mass migration of Mexicans took place in the nineteenth century—
with the exception of thousands of Sonoran "forty-niners" who rushed to
California's Sierra Nevada foothills after the discovery of gold at Sutter's mill—

movement back and forth was common, especially among those Mexicans who lived in border towns such as El Paso/Juárez and Brownsville/Matamoros. It was not until the first decade of the twentieth century that Mexicans began to come to the United States in large numbers, the first great wave of what would become a century-long movement of people north from Mexico.

Four periods of immigration mark the history of movement of Mexican people to the United States: the first "Great Migration" (1910s–1920s), the "Bracero Era" (1942–1964), the so-called "Los Mojados" period (1950s), and the "Second Great Migration" (1970s–present). Regardless of the period of migration, one unifying theme binds the story of Roberto and Benjamín to the vast majority of people who opted in the past, and who continue to cross into the United States today: the search for opportunity. Though circumstances have changed greatly over time for those seeking to enter the United States, most have done so for a chance to work and to earn a fair wage before returning home. For the millions who decided to remain in the United States over the past century, a search for stability and a better life for themselves and their families motivated them to cross the border, *la frontera*. A variety of additional reasons hastened the departure from *la madre patria* for millions of Mexican immigrants. In the first Great Migration, for example, escape from the turmoil caused by the Mexican Revolution was uppermost in peoples' decision to leave Mexico. For the Mexican men who signed on as Braceros (those who work with their *brazos,* or arms) during World War II and the two decades that followed, opportunity to earn American dollars for a few months each year as part of the binational labor contract agreement offered advantages over the meager wages they received in Mexico. For many hundreds of thousands of other Mexican immigrants—both legal and undocumented—over the past fifty years, the prospect of reuniting with family members and relatives provided the primary reason for crossing *al otro lado,* to the other side. Some immigrated with the intention of staying a short while and others traveled north with whatever belongings they could carry, knowing that a permanent return to Mexico was not likely. Still others crossed back and forth between both countries, and those with work permits (green cards) developed a lifestyle of working by day in the United States and returning at night to their homes across the international line. Many came as *solos,* or individuals, while others arrived as part of nuclear or extended family units.

Robertos and Robertas continue to come to the United States either as documented immigrants or *sin papeles,* without legal immigration documents. Their movement north to the United States has revitalized and remade existing Mexican American communities many times over during the past century. And despite the increasingly difficult physical barriers they must cross on the border and the restrictive U.S. immigration policies governing their movement, they continue to come. The people crossing the border at this moment are part of a long historical legacy.

The First Great Migration

The first mass movement of people across the U.S.-Mexico border occurred during the early decades of the twentieth century, especially after 1910. During these years perhaps as many as 1.5 million people—about a tenth of the entire population of Mexico—crossed the border to the U.S. side of the international boundary. But even before the human tidal wave swept north, a result of the destructive effects of the 1910 Mexican Revolution, the movement of many thousands of immigrants north from Mexico had already begun. Lured by abundant employment opportunities and the prospects of earning higher wages in the American Southwest, Mexicans from primarily the northern and central states, mostly younger males, followed the corridors of Mexico's new railway system that connected with the major U.S. railroad lines at several points along the border in Texas (El Paso, Eagle Pass, Laredo, and Brownsville) and in Arizona (Nogales and Yuma). American employers and labor contractors in need of large numbers of unskilled workers for the growing economy in the West actively recruited Mexican workers. Some recruiters ventured into the interior of Mexico to entice people to head north while others stationed themselves at border cities waiting as more and more Mexicans traveled the rails in search of better jobs and higher pay.[1]

The civil war that erupted in Mexico in 1910 emerged from long simmering discontent among reformers, anarchists, and revolutionaries who ousted dictator Porfirio Díaz in 1911. Rather than some orderly accession to power among revolutionists, conflict between contending political forces and revolutionary armies resulted in a broadening of warfare and political chaos. The spread of military conflict throughout the south central states of Mexico soon engulfed the northern states as well; the already teetering economy lay shattered in the wake of the internecine conflict as inflation soared. Urban economies virtually came to a halt, and as unemployment became widespread, desperate workers looked elsewhere. Rural villagers, caught in the crossfire of hostile revolutionary armies, and clinging tenuously to bare subsistence during a period of great uncertainty, were forced to consider limited options. One of those options was to sell off what they could of their meager possessions, pack those belongings they could carry, and move. As the Mexican Revolution intensified, so too did the movement of individuals and families who made the big decision to head toward *la frontera.* Lyrics from a corrido ("El Deportado," 'the deportee'), a Mexican folk ballad of the era, captured the feelings of thousands of immigrants who left their native Mexico for the United States:

Adios mi madre querida,	Goodbye my beloved mother,
Héchame su benedición,	Give me your blessings,
Ya me voy al extranjero,	I am going abroad,
Donde no hay revolución.	Where there is no revolution.[2]

"El Corrido de Inmigrante" (Ballad of an Immigrant) also conveyed the lament of the masses of Mexicans that left because conditions had deteriorated so much that there were few alternatives to immigration.

Mexico, my homeland, where I was born Mexican,
Give me the benediction of your powerful hand.
I'm going to the United States to earn my living;
Good-bye, my beloved country, I carry you in my heart.
Don't condemn me for leaving my country,
Poverty and necessity are at fault.
Good-bye, pretty Guanajuato the state in which I was born.
I'm going to the United States far away from you.[3]

They came mostly from the central and northern plateau states of Mexico, especially from Michoacán, Guanajuato, Jalisco, Durango, Sonora, Chihuahua, Zacatecas, and from *el Distrito Federal* (Mexico City). Typically, single men made the journey first and after they secured work, they either returned to Mexico for other family members or sent them money orders for the train ticket north to the border. As the revolution spread, more and more of the immigrants came as family units hoping to reestablish households in the United States until conditions in Mexico were settled enough for them to return. Most of the immigrants during this period crossed the border through Texas, the great majority of whom entered through El Paso, the Ellis Island for Mexican immigrants. Texas was the favorite destination as the immigrants headed to cities such as San Antonio and Houston while others opted to work in the growing agricultural areas of south Texas. Seasonal farm labor and work on *el traque* (the railroads) employed the largest number of immigrants. Employment in these growing sectors of the regional economy in the Southwest carried tens of thousands of the *mexicanos* west to California, north through the Great Plains to the Great Lakes states, as far east as Pennsylvania, and east from Texas into the South. Not surprisingly, about 90 percent of all Mexican immigrants remained in the states that border Mexico, especially Texas, California, and Arizona.[4]

Once at the border, finding work was not difficult. They could sign on with a labor contractor, who would consign a group of workers to agricultural jobs in Texas or somewhere in the Midwest. Or, they could hire directly on with a railroad contractor for work on the section gangs that roamed the rails maintaining the thousands of miles of tracks across the West. The work was hard, the wages were poor, and the living conditions primitive. The corrido of "Los Betabeleros" (the beet-field workers) conveys the difficult times workers encountered.

Año de mil novecientos	In the year 1923
Veinte y tres en el actual	Of the present era
Fueron los betabeleros	The beet-field workers went
A ese "michiga" a llorar	To that Michigan weeping,
Por que todos los señores	Because all the bosses
Empezaban a regañar	Began to scold,
Y don Santiago les responde	And Don Santiago says to them:
"Yo quiero regresar	"I want to return
Por que no nos han cumplido	Because they haven't done for us
Lo que fueron a contar."	What they said they would."
Aqui vienen y les cuentan	Here they come and they tell you

Que se vayan para allá,	That you ought to go up there,
Por que allá tiene todo	Because there you will have everything
Que no van a batallar	Without having to fight for it,
Pero son puras mentiras	But these are nothing but lies,
Los que vienen y les dicen.	And those who come and say those things are liars.[5]

Those who contracted with the railroads instead of farm labor also found the work very difficult with low wages and long days on the section gangs. Often, at first opportunity, immigrant workers would use the transportation provided by the railroads to reach other destinations where they would leave *el traque* with the hope of finding better jobs for higher pay. They traveled between cities and countryside working in seasonal harvests and then migrating to find jobs in the cities during the winter months. By the 1920s, both the agricultural and railroad industries had become dependent on Mexican immigrant labor in the West.

By the hundreds of thousands, Mexican immigrants fanned out across the Southwest and Midwest, sometimes settling in cities where historic Mexican American barrios existed, such as in Los Angeles, Tucson, San Antonio, and El Paso. Others settled in the small rural towns in south Texas, southern California, Colorado, and in various midwestern states such as Kansas, Nebraska, and as far north as Wisconsin and Minnesota. Some left the agricultural work in the Midwest and headed to the large cities, especially Chicago, where they worked in the meatpacking houses and in other industrial jobs.[6]

During and after World War I the demand for Mexican labor surged as the volume of European immigration slowed greatly because of the war. With immigration from Asia already cut off and immigration from Europe effectively halted by U.S. immigration restriction policies in 1921 and 1924, the need for Mexican workers increased. Though there were efforts to include Mexicans in the 1924 National Origins Act, the policy that slammed the door closed on immigration from every part of the world except the Americas, the clamor by agribusiness concerns and industrialists in the Midwest kept the borders open between the United States and Mexico. Indeed, the border before 1917 was more a fictional line than a guarded international boundary. Mexicans could come and go with

little trouble. Only if one wanted to register at one of the few immigration stations in border cities was it necessary to delay entry. Relatively few bothered to enter the United States as official immigrants because the open border did not require this formality. Beginning in 1917, a new immigration law requiring all immigrants to pay a head tax and prove they were literate upon inspection by officials was largely skirted along the U.S.-Mexico border. More immigrants from Mexico did enter the United States legally during the 1920s, but a much larger number probably didn't bother and instead merely walked over to the other side or waded across the river border, a boundary line that in most places did not exist. The need for labor in a booming economy and the decline in European immigrant workers combined with increased desire among Mexicans to travel north. Despite the end of revolutionary battles in Mexico in 1921, economic impoverishment and political uncertainly in the republic and the lure of higher wages in the United States drove Mexican immigrants across the border in record numbers during the 1920s. Between 1920 and 1930, nearly half a million Mexicans officially entered the United States and probably an equal or greater number arrived without stopping to pay a head tax and registration fee for entry.[7]

The masses of Mexicans who settled in the United States provided the labor necessary to make Southwest agriculture a major industry. Employers that depended on Mexican labor could extol the hard-work ethic of their employees and, at the same time, categorize them as a group of workers who could be treated differently than White workers. A farmer in the South Platte Valley in Colorado in the late 1920s stated, for example:

> The Mexicans want to work and aren't looking for other kinds of work.... The Mexicans are like the plantation Negroes in improvidence, lack of foresight, or desire to do other tasks. I get the doctor for them, advise them, call on the police for them to help straighten out cases of auto accidents, etc. The Mexicans help me with the milking, and in return I supply them with milk. The Mexicans appreciate these things, and it established a plantation-like relationship.[8]

Another farmer interviewed by labor economist Paul S. Taylor in the area claimed that "A Mexican is the best damn dog any white man ever had."

He will do lots more for you than any white man would. If you are doing something heavy he will come and help you. Of course you can't kick him and cuss him around any more than you would a dog. He is more loyal to you than any white friend.[9]

Mexicans also helped build the region's transportation networks and irrigation projects. Likewise, the construction industry and new manufacturing industries in southwestern cities were all increasingly dependent on the labor of Mexican workers. The food-processing plants and canneries and the emerging garment industry were jobs sites where *mexicanas* predominated. From city to countryside Mexican immigrants were the foundation upon which the regional economy was built, an economy that could not have grown without legions of low-wage immigrant workers from Mexico.

The work performed by Mexican immigrants in the early twentieth century provided a meager cushion of stability for a group of people displaced from Mexican society and adjusting to life in a foreign land. But Mexicans were often subject to exploitation and abuse at the hands of employers, some of whom believed Mexicans didn't deserve better or that they could live with less than Americans were used to. Mexicans, for example, often received less pay for the same work performed by other workers because of so-called "racial-wage differentials" and were assigned to "Mexican work," jobs no American was willing to accept. During the prosperous years through the 1910s and 1920s Mexicans were wanted to fill unskilled, low-wage jobs, but when times were bad, as they were in the 1930s, immigrants from Mexico became pariahs.

As the Great Depression took hold across the nation, U.S. and Mexican authorities encouraged Mexicans to return to Mexico. However, when fewer than expected repatriated voluntarily, the U.S. federal government embarked on a program to deport Mexicans. Between half a million and 750,000 Mexican immigrants and their American-born children left the United States during the 1930s. A large majority decided to stay in the United States as they rode out the worst years of the depression. Immigration slowed to a trickle during the 1930s, but by the start of World War II, the need for Mexican immigrant labor ushered in a new phase of movement across the border.[10]

The Bracero Era

A different type of immigration from Mexico began in 1942 when the United States and Mexico agreed to a guest worker program commonly referred to as the "Bracero Program." This binational agreement was forged during World War II as Mexico cooperated with its northern ally to help provide temporary workers to southwestern farmers. Growers clamored for the guest worker program because of a labor shortage that threatened productivity of agricultural products during the years of war emergency. The agreement called for Mexico to recruit a certain number of workers for temporary, seasonal employment in the United States. American employees promised to provide housing and transportation for the workers. Though a much smaller and different type of guest worker program was first implemented during the First World War, the Bracero Program was unprecedented because of the number of workers involved and because of its longevity.

American agribusiness concerns were eager to replenish a dependable supply of farm workers during years when tens of thousands of Mexican immigrants and Mexican American farm workers were either inducted into the armed forces or moved to cities to take advantage of better jobs in the war-related economy. With war production levels for American agriculture in full gear, growers worried that without additional workers seasonal crops could neither be planted nor harvested. President Roosevelt and President Camacho agreed to what was a war-emergency measure allowing for periodic, but temporary workers from Mexico to enter the United States for agricultural harvests first in California and later in other regions of the nation. The number of workers during the war years was modest, beginning with a mere 4,200 in 1942 and growing to slightly fewer than 50,000 by the end of the war. Though the program was designed specifically for agricultural workers, some braceros were permitted to work in the railroad industry in the West.[11]

Through informal agreements between growers, the U.S. government, and Mexican authorities, the program continued after the war. But beginning with the Korean War, the powerful western agribusiness lobby convinced Congress to pass Public Law 78 reauthorizing a guest worker program based on the earlier Bracero Program. The number of Mexican farm workers who entered the United States for temporary work increased significantly during the early 1950s to about 200,000 per year. After the war, growers mustered enough political clout to have Congress extend P.L. 78 on an annual basis until it was terminated in 1964. Southwest growers, especially in Texas and California but elsewhere in the West, had obviously grown dependent on bracero labor for crop production. By 1956 the number of braceros that arrived each year was well over 450,000, a number that began to tail off in the early 1960s before Congress decided not to reauthorize the program.[12]

Obviously, there were hundreds of thousands of Mexican men eager and willing to sign contracts for temporary work in the United States. Over the twenty-two years it operated, the program brought nearly five million workers to the United States for periods usually from three to six months. Though no numbers were kept, many thousands of braceros left the program, married Mexican American women, and legalized their status. Importantly, the stories about working in the United States told by braceros when they returned home circulated among friends, families, and village and town folk, and these stories played a critical role in the development over time of a pattern of cyclical migration carried out by millions of Mexicans since the 1950s. Ramón "Tianguis" Pérez, a young man from the state of Oaxaca, recalled how he and others in his village first heard about life in "el norte" and how this influenced two generations of his countrymen who immigrated to the United States for work.

> My townsmen have been crossing the border since the forties, when rumor of the *bracero* program reached our village, about ten years before the highway came through. The news of the *bracero* program was brought to us by out itinerant merchants.... One of them came with the news that there were possibilities of work in the United States as a *bracero*, and the news passed from mouth to mouth until everyone had heard it.[13]

When two merchants went to investigate the rumor at the U.S. Embassy after they returned to Mexico City, they signed up as contracted workers and spent several months in the United States. "From the day of their departure," Pérez recounted, "the whole town followed the fate of those adventurers with great interest."

After a little while, the first letters to their families arrived. The closest kins-men asked what news the letters contained, and from them the news spread to the rest of the villagers. Afterwards, checks with postal money orders arrived, and their families went to Oaxaca City to cash them. The men's return home, some six months later, was a big event because when they came into town they were seen carrying large boxes of foreign goods, mainly clothing. Their experience inspired others, but not all of them had the same good fortune. . . . I, too, joined the emigrant stream.14

In post-revolution and post-depression Mexico, pent-up demand for employment enticed many more Mexicans who could not be accommodated through the Bracero Program to enter the United States illegally. By the early 1950s, a large migration of undocumented workers was underway.

The 1950s and Los Mojados

As the number of braceros working in the United States temporarily increased during the 1950s, so too did legal immigration as the number of permanent visas issued totaled nearly 300,000 by 1960. But the great numbers of Mexicans who wished to work in the United States in the post-war decades could neither be met by the Bracero Program nor by the expansion of legal, or "green card" (in refer-ence to the color of the visas) immigrants. There were several reasons why great demand for work in the United States occurred during this period, leading to large-scale undocumented immigration. First, the land redistribution program of the Mexican government, the key rallying cry of the revolution, never met expectations. Even after plots of land were given to farmers little was done to pro-vide them with equipment and other resources to make living off the land sus-tainable. In addition, as Mexico's economy in its urban sectors grew in the 1950s and attracted hundreds of thousands of rural people to the cities, those who benefited most were the middle classes. The growing ranks of underemployed and unemployed urban poor created a large labor pool seeking opportunity where it could be found. And, after irrigated farming was introduced in the north-ern Mexican states, tens of thousands of Mexicans traveled north to work in the fields, but their numbers were far larger than could be employed in the agricul-tural economy. Many drifted to border cities where populations exploded in the two decades following World War II. Here, again, a large pool of laborers looked north for job prospects. These factors, together with the relative ease of crossing the border during this period, resulted in a huge spike in the number of illegal entries during the 1950s and early 1960s. For example, in 1953, 875,000 Mexicans were apprehended and deported by the Immigration and Naturalization Service (INS). Alarmed by the growing number of illegal Mexican immigrants in the Southwest, the INS launched "Operation Wetback," the term commonly used to refer to undocumented immigrants in the period. (The term "wetback" was a pejorative term not used by immigrants themselves. They instead often used the term "mojados," the 'wet ones', to refer to those who crossed illegally, made in reference to crossing the Rio Grande river.) The deportation program resulted in raids and sweeps that netted about one million immigrants in 1954, who were returned to Mexico. As the border patrol became more aggressive in its techniques to thwart illegal crossing, the *alambristas* came to rely more on a small army of smugglers, known as *coyotes* or *polleros* (literally poultryman, but this term refers to smugglers who bring in the undocumented immigrants, or *pollos*, 'chickens'). Those who were caught and returned to the Mexican side of the border often found a way to return soon thereafter. A story told by Maclovio Medina was probably told by countless unknown immigrants from the period. After finding a *coyote* to take him and his friends across the border, Medina recalled:

> We passed in the night, without problems. But later there were problems, because the immigration came to where we were working and they threw us out. They sent us to the other side, but just to Mexicali, and we came back. We came back through some hills called El Centinela and we crossed over a bridge that was there. We passed, and it wasn't far. We were working in a pueblo called Silas. That's where we were on a ranch. They caught us in the morning when we were working and sent us back because they didn't have very many jails. Well, we returned before noon. We arrived in time to work. But after awhile, it began to get more difficult and eventually we returned to Mexico. The first time we stayed six months.[15]

As immigrants grew more concerned than ever about being apprehended by *la migra* (the INS's border patrol), a clandestine existence began to define the lifestyles of hundreds of thousands of Mexican immigrants in the United States who crossed over each year to secure work. Employers eagerly made jobs available and paid *los mojados* low wages for work Americans were unwilling to perform. Despite the growing difficulty of crossing and staying out of the reach of *la migra*, undocumented workers continued to arrive in the United States with the intent of earning wages substantially higher than those they could earn in Mexico.

Mexico's booming population, growing unemployment (especially among younger adults), and large number of poor people created pressures for more and more Mexicans to attempt the crossing and to find work in *el norte*. After the Bracero Program was not reauthorized by Congress in 1964, thus eliminating a source of work for about 178,000 contracted Mexican laborers, and as Mexico's economy in the 1960s could not absorb the great numbers of new workers, an unprecedented volume of illegal immigrants entered the United States beginning in the late 1960s, precipitating one of the largest sustained immigrations in American history.

The Second Great Migration

The trials and tribulations of *Alambrista*'s Roberto were set in the 1970s and his experiences in the United States were part of a much bigger picture of undocumented immigration over the past three decades. Longstanding problems in Mexico combined with new developments that spurred border crossings to new heights. Mexico's overall economic status in the post–World War II decades was quite impressive, but its average GNP growth rate of about 5 or 6 percent produced a growing inequality of wealth in the nation. National policies to increase agricultural output geared to export markets and industrialization resulted in a growing disparity between those who benefited from economic growth and those who didn't. Two major problems resulted: underemployment and growing income inequality. In 1970, for example, about half of Mexico's workers were either underemployed or earned so few *pesos* that they could not make ends meet. In addition, by the 1960s, so many Mexicans had some firsthand or secondhand knowledge about working in the United States that the act of migrating north for wage labor was becoming the rule rather than the exception for millions of Mexicans. So many individuals, families, villages, and towns had become dependent on money earned during temporary or full-time work in the United States that cyclical migrations north became an expectation for economic survival. For many, a binational lifestyle was shaped as movement back and forth across the border became commonplace. Though the majority immigrated from small towns and rural areas of central and northern Mexico, a large number of people migrated from cities and other industrialized urban areas, adding to the diversity of Mexican immigration in the contemporary period. Mexico's inability to absorb its growing, young workforce combined with other reasons to produce a massive migration. The devaluation of the *peso* in the 1980s worsened the economic destabilization of the working classes and resulted in pushing millions more across the border. The vast majority of Mexicans entered as economic refugees hoping to work in the United States.[16]

Immigration from Mexico to the United States in the twentieth century is not only the most prolonged movement of people in American immigration history, it is also the largest sustained international labor migration in the world. Since 1942, when the Bracero Program was initiated, over 6.3 million Mexicans have crossed the border into the United States, with the greatest numbers of immigrants arriving during the 1980s and 1990s. Both legal and undocumented immigration increased during these decades. For example, the total number of legal immigrants from Mexico grew to 680,000 during the 1970s, but in the 1980s the number climbed to an amazing 3 million. It has been estimated that during this same decade some 800,000 Mexicans entered without papers. In the first half of the 1990s, 2.2 million Mexican immigrants entered the United States legally, a figure that surpassed the unprecedented numbers established in the 1980s. Illegal crossings kept apace. The INS estimated over half (54 percent) of the approximately 5 million undocumented immigrants in the United States in the mid-1990s were from Mexico.[17]

The millions who entered the United States as undocumented immigrants over the past thirty years have lead "shadowed lives," a description offered by an anthropologist who studied the lifestyles of the "indocumentados." The fear of detection and apprehension by the INS looms over those who live in the United States without papers, some for short periods of time and others for decades. The fear of *la migra* is a real one. Enrique Valenzuela, a resident of San

Diego, the city where he has lived for over fifteen years, compared his experience as an undocumented person with life in a prison.

> In all these 16 years I feel like I've been in jail. I don't feel free. I came to this country to work, not to do things on the street that you shouldn't do. That's not what I mean by freedom. I'm referring to the feeling of being in a prison because if you go out, like when we got out for fun, it's always in the back of your mind, will immigration show up? Or when you go to work you think all the time, from the moment you walk out of your home, you think, "Will immigration stop me on the way or when I'm at work?" So I do feel like I'm in jail.[18]

In the mid-1970s, as the pace of illegal crossings into the United States increased significantly, so too did the apprehension and deportation of Mexicans, reaching 750,000 people in 1975. The number of deportations increased through the 1980s and 1990s. In 1987, for example, the INS apprehended 1.2 million deportable immigrants, 97 percent of whom were Mexican.[19]

Despite the constant threat of deportation, Mexicans in great numbers have shared a familiar general experience of departing from their home town or village, crossing the border typically with the assistance of a paid smuggler, and finding work on the other side. Martín left his native town of Meoqui, located about 150 miles south of El Paso, Texas, in the state of Chihuahua, when his brother Alberto, who had left for the United States three years earlier, sent him bus fare and an invitation to join him in the small Texas panhandle town of Dalhart. A Mexican American named Paco from Dalhart, who owned a small business in Meoqui that he visited routinely, moonlighted as a smuggler on his return trips to Texas.

Martín told a story about his first attempt to cross into the United States:

> When Paco came by the house, he had two other men with him, Ramon and Chelito. I already knew Ramon, because we had gone to school together. Paco drove us up to the border, and then took us down to a little shack on the Mexican side. He told us to wait until nightfall, then to cross the river and walk up to the first highway. He said he would flash his turn indicators

as he drove along the highway and that we should come out of the bushes when we saw him. Then he took our money and left.[20]

Martín and his two fellow travelers encountered the border patrol and decided they could not make the crossing at that time. Later, however, they made arrangements with Paco who made good on a second attempt to get the men to the U.S. side. After dropping the other men off in Odessa, Paco delivered Martín to his brother's house.

Ramón Pérez also decided to join the migrant stream with a group of other men who paid a smuggler to get them across the border from Nuevo Laredo. After successfully crossing the river, he was taken with a group of other immigrants to a safe house to await travel to Houston. After five long days of waiting, Ramón was finally picked for the car ride to Houston. Stuffed in the trunk of the car with two others for the suffocatingly hot journey, the car was suddenly stopped by border patrol agents. Pérez recounts:

> A half hour later, we find ourselves in the Immigration offices in the little south Texas town of Hebbronville.... Nine of us are locked in a cell in one of the buildings. Inside the building are ten agents, most of them Mexican-Americans, who go back and forth from outside into the office.... A bronze-skinned agent with a sparse moustache comes up to our cell and recites the following words: "You are detained for having illegally entered the country...[21]

"In less than half an hour," Pérez recalled, "they discharged us at the entrance to the international bridge in Laredo" where the men walked across in silence to the Mexican side. Though Pérez gave thought of returning to his village in the state of Oaxaca, he decided to make another crossing aided by his friend who lived in Houston. Once in Houston, his friend took him to the old Magnolia barrio section of the city where he eventually rented a room, paid $5 for a counterfeit social security card, and began to look for work.

In 1988, Maria De Jesús Ordaz Viuda de Vásquez decided to cross for the first time so she could work in an Oakland restaurant owned by her *compadre,* who had promised her a job if she came north. Maria's husband had died of cancer and left her with the care of ten children, from age nineteen to eight months. The decision to leave was difficult, but for the sake of her children, she needed to make more money than she was earning in San Juan, Mexico. Borrowing money from friends and her oldest children, the thirty-four-year-old set out with one of her sons for *el norte*. She told a story filled with pain but with promise of work in the San Francisco Bay Area.

> How should I begin? I wanted to go to work. I had been offered work and I had the desire to go to the United States. It was very difficult, because the Immigration caught me two times, the first time before arriving at San Ysidro and the other in San Clemente [cities just north of the border city of Tijuana]. They wanted to put me in the trunk of a car, but I didn't fit. The man was very mad and bawled me out because I didn't have makeup on and wasn't dressed nice. Well, I was all dirty. What do you think, without water, without clothes, without anything?...This was the *coyote* that was going to pass us when they caught us in San Clemente.[22]

On her third attempt Maria finally made it to San Diego, where she made arrangements for someone to drive her to Oakland. After many months, she returned to San Juan with clothes for her children and a little money in her pocket, having worked as a kitchen helper in the restaurant and as a house cleaner in Fresno.

The opportunity to earn wages higher than those in Mexico continued to motivate countless others who were willing to take risks to enter and live in the United States. Jorge Díaz left his family in Guadalajara, first in 1970 and then again in 1972. "It was a difficult decision," he remembered, "because I had to leave my family."

> But I had decided I had to change my life because I realized that life in Mexico was too difficult. There is much poverty. The jobs were very difficult to obtain. If you had family members that were involved in politics, then you would have a good job. If not, and if you are not well educated, then you do not have a good job.[23]

Isabel left her home state of Oaxaca in 1988 out of desperation. She left behind two children and ended up in the United States in a shantytown shared with other Oaxacans located in Carlsbad, San Diego County. "I came here because there is no work over there," she said.

> Oaxaca has no factories, no large businesses to employ people. When you do find work it's very difficult. You work from nine in the morning to nine at night for little pay and it's hard to find another job. I was told that there were good wages here and that there was plenty of work for women. Right now I do housekeeping, but sometimes I do that and sometimes I don't. It's not stable [work].[24]

A million unique stories could be told about immigration from Mexico to the United States with similar themes running through most. For some the crossing became a way of life, with seasons spent in the United States and periods spent at home in Mexico. Others involved in cyclical migrations found it increasingly more difficult and more expensive to get across as U.S. immigration policy over the past two decades has sought to control the border with ever more vigilant patrols and apprehensions. In 1986, the newly enacted Immigration Reform and Control Act (IRCA) provided additional resources to the INS's border patrol to stop Mexicans at the border during a period when an anti-immigrant political discourse was gaining momentum. More importantly, in an effort to make it more difficult for undocumented workers to find employment in the United States, IRCA instituted an employers sanction provision making it illegal to knowingly hire a person without official papers. The law also provided for amnesty for those immigrants who could prove they had worked in the United States since 1982. Those who could meet requirements established by the new law had the opportunity to legalize their status and begin the process of naturalization. IRCA also established a legalization status for immigrant agricultural workers who had worked on U.S. farms for a specified number of days, and together this program and the amnesty provision resulted in 2.3 million Mexicans attaining legal status between 1987 and 1990. This trend of legalizing formerly undocumented workers continued into the early 1990s.

Despite the amnesty program, undocumented workers kept coming and, as a result, the chorus of immigrant bashing grew louder as many politicians joined the bandwagon. Blamed for many social problems, the so-called "illegal aliens" were targeted by politicians such as California Governor Pete Wilson, who fanned the flames of anti-immigrant sentiment. The culmination of the anti-immigrant crusade occurred in 1994 when Proposition 187 was passed overwhelmingly by California voters. The law, if enforced, would have prevented undocumented immigrants and their children from attending public schools and would have cut off their access to medical care and welfare programs. Though the law was eventually deemed to be unconstitutional by the federal courts, it represented the high tide of restrictionism and a new xenophobia in California, the state with the largest number of undocumented immigrants in the nation.

More barriers along the U.S.-Mexico border will continue to be erected and greater enforcement of the region by the INS to keep Mexicans from entering is also likely to occur in the near future. The new fences and walls and new policies will obviously make it more difficult for illegal immigrants to enter the United States for work. But the human condition in Mexico and the availability of jobs in the United States that Americans simply will not perform are the two factors that will continue to propel Mexicans to *el norte*. Roberto followed in the footsteps of Benjamín and others such as Maria, Isabel, Maclavio, and Martín are all links in a chain of human migration north from Mexico that has no end in sight.

■

Discussion Questions

1. Roberto is among the millions of undocumented immigrants who have migrated to the United States from Mexico over the past thirty years. How is Roberto's story of immigration both similar and different from that of those who crossed the U.S.-Mexico border in the decades prior to the 1970s?

2.. What is the most appropriate term to use to refer to people who come to the United States from Mexico outside official immigration channels (e.g., illegal aliens, undocumented workers, wetbacks, clandestine migrants)? What does each of these terms imply?

3. In response to the so-called crisis of "illegal aliens" in California, former Governor Pete Wilson supported Proposition 184. Passed by a majority of Californians in 1994, the proposition became law and restricted undocumented immigrants from sending their children to public schools and denied them access to medical care and public assistance benefits. Although Proposition 184 was later found to be unconstitutional by a federal court before it was enacted, do you think such a law was a logical way to respond to the presence of "illegal" immigrants? What other ways might a state government deal with a problem involving large numbers of immigrants?

■

Notes

1. For a general description of the factors leading to immigration from Mexico during the early twentieth century, see Lawrence Cardoso, *Mexican Emigration to the United States, 1897–1931: Socio-Economic Patterns* (Tucson: University of Arizona Press, 1980).

2. *El Deportado,* Texas-Mexican Border Music, Part I, Arhollie Records (Berkeley, 1975).

3. Marilyn P. Davis, *Mexican Voices/American Dreams: An Oral History of Mexican Immigration to the United States* (New York: Henry Holt and Company, 1990), 8.

4. For a contemporary general description of Mexican immigration for this period, see the classic study by Mexican anthropologist Manuel Gamio, *Mexican Immigration to the United States* (Chicago: University of Chicago Press, 1930; Dover Publications edition, 1971).

5. Ibid., 86–87.

6. Paul S. Taylor's classic multivolume study *Mexican Labor in the United States,* vols. 1–7 (Berkeley: University of California Press, 1928–1932; Arno Press and *New York Times* edition, 1970) provides detailed descriptions of conditions faced by Mexican immigrant workers in the Southwest and in the Chicago area.

7. Mark Reisler, *By the Sweat of Their Brow: Mexican Immigrant Labor in the United States, 1900-1940* (Westport, Conn.: Greenwood Press, 1976), 49–76.

8. Taylor, *Mexican Labor in the United States,* vol. 6, 154–55.

9. Ibid., 155.

10. For a good description of the repatriation and deportation program aimed at Mexicans in the 1930s, see Francisco E. Balderrama and Raymond Rodriguez, *Decade of Betrayal: Mexican Repatriation in the 1930s* (Albuquerque: University of New Mexico Press, 1995).

11. Ernesto Galarza's study of the Bracero Program is still the best available book on the subject: *Merchants of Labor: The Mexican Bracero Story: An Account of the Managed Migration of Mexican Farm Workers in California 1942-1960* (Charlotte, N.C.: McNally and Loftin, 1964). See also, Kitty Calavita, *Inside the State: The Bracero Program, Immigration, and the I.N.S.* (London: Routledge, 1992).

12. Leo Grebler, Joan W. Moore, and Ralph Guzmán, *The Mexican-American People: The Nation's Second Largest Minority* (New York: The Free Press, 1970), 67–69.

13. Ramón "Tianguis" Pérez, *Diary of an Undocumented Immigrant* (Houston, Tex.: Arte Publico Press, 1991), 12–13.

14. Ibid., 13.

15. Davis, *Mexican Voices/American Dreams,* 27–28.

16. Alejandro Portes and Robert L. Bach, *Latin Journey: Cuban and Mexican Immigrants in the United States* (Berkeley: University of California Press, 1985), 111–15.

17. Julie A. Phillips and Douglas S. Massey, "Engines of Immigration: Stocks of Human and Social Capital in Mexico," *Social Science Quarterly* 81:1 (March 2000): 33–34: Manuel G. Gonzales, *Mexicanos: A History of Mexicans in the United States* (Bloomington: Indiana University Press, 1999), 225.

18. Leo Chávez, *Shadowed Lives: Undocumented Immigrants in American Society* (Orlando, Fla.: Harcourt Brace Jovanovich, 1992), 157.

19. Dick J. Reavis, *Without Documents* (New York: Condor Publishing Company, 1978), 69; Alejandro Portes and Ruben G. Rumbaut, *Immigrant America: A Portrait* (Berkeley: University of California Press, 1990), 15.

20. Reavis, *Without Documents,* 14.

21. Pérez, *Diary of an Undocumented Immigrant,* 46.

22. Davis, *Mexican Voices/American Dreams,* 184.

23. Chávez, *Shadowed Lives,* 29.

24. Ibid., 32.

Alambrista's Inspiration

César Chávez and Migrant Farm Workers*

Richard Griswold del Castillo

César Chávez rose from humble beginnings as a migrant farm worker to become the founder of a farm-worker union that captured world attention on the plight of America's most oppressed group of workers. César Chávez established the United Farm Workers Union in California in 1965 and, after five years of bitter strife, in 1970, he succeeded in gaining union recognition and labor contracts from grape growers in the San Joaquin Valley. He became the most well-known Mexican American labor or reform leader of his generation, gathering support from organized labor, Protestant and Catholic churches, progressive intellectuals and students, and international labor organizations. His union went on to improve wages and working conditions for all farm workers by setting industry standards. Chávez's struggle to force agribusiness to recognize the basic rights of farm workers continued throughout his life. He remains an inspiring example of a leader who aroused America's conscience regarding the poor in our society.

---

*Note: This essay first appeared in *American Reform and Reformers: A Biographical Dictionary,* ed. Randall M. Miller and Paul Cimbala (Westport, Conn. and London: Greenwood Press, 1996) reprinted with their permission.

The Early Years

César Estrada Chávez was born on March 31, 1927, in Yuma, Arizona, the child of Mexican-born parents, Librado and Juana Estrada, who had settled on a small farm. He grew up, with his four brothers and sisters, nourished by the values of his family and the rural Mexican community. From his mother he learned the importance of nonviolence and self-sacrifice and his grand-mother impressed on him the values of the Catholic faith. As a youth he had experience with racial discrimination in school and he absorbed from the Mexican community the folklore of their struggle against oppression in Mexico during the revolution. In 1939, because of the depression, the Chávez family lost their farm and they had to join the migrant stream flowing west into California. For the next few years they traveled up and down the state following the crops.

For the next ten years, the Chávez family worked as migrants, moving from farm to farm up and down California and taking odd jobs to supplement their income when there was no farm work. It was during this period that César encountered the conditions that he would dedicate the rest of his life to chang-ing: wretched migrant camps, corrupt labor contractors, meager wages for backbreaking work, bitter racism.

In 1942 César's father got in a car accident and was unable to work for a month. It was then that César decided to quit school (he had completed the eighth grade) and work full time in the fields with his brothers and sisters to help support the family. Chávez's migrant period introduced him to labor organizing. While moving from crop to crop, his father had joined several unions—the Tobacco Workers, Cannery Workers, the National Farm Labor Union (NFLU), the Packing House Workers, and the Agricultural Workers Organizing Committee (AWOC). The family participated in many strikes dur-ing the late 1930s and 1940s and was quite active in union activities, although never serving in a leadership capacity.

César joined the navy in 1944 along with thousands of other Mexican Americans, and like them he discovered a wider world. He went to San Diego for boot camp and discovered that Mexicans were not the only ones discrimi-nated against because of their nationality or language. Sent to the South Pacific, he served as a coxswain's apprentice in Saipan and Guam assisting in ferrying ship pilots in and out of the harbor.

When César got out of the navy in 1946 he returned to the family home in Delano and resumed work in the fields. On October 22, 1948, César married Helen Fabela, whom he had first met occasionally when his family had been passing through Delano following the crops. She had been born in Brawley in 1928 of Mexican campesino parents. Her family, like César's, had become migrant workers during the thirties and forties. She became an important partner with César as he began to fulfill his dream of doing something to improve the lot of the farm workers. The Chávezes eventually settled in San Jose and began raising a family of eight children while César worked for a lumber company.

The Education of a Farm Labor Organizer

César's introduction to community organizing began in 1952 when he met Father Donald McDonnell, a Catholic priest who was trying to build a parish in the San Jose barrio of Sal Si Puedes. From Father McDonnell he learned the church's social doctrines on labor organizing and social justice and read the *Life of Gandhi,* a book that made a deep impression on the young Chávez. Mahatma Gandhi's values struck a responsive cord: the complete sacrifice of oneself for others, the severe self-discipline and self-abnegation to achieve a higher good. These values Mexican farm workers could understand, not only in religious terms but also in their own daily experience. Especially important to Chávez's moral development was Gandhi's teaching on nonviolence; these echoed his mother's admonitions and teachings. The philosophy of nonviolence later would become the hallmark of Chávez's leadership of the farm-worker movement.

Another organizer who was at work in the Sal Si Puedes barrio in San Jose also changed young Chávez's life. In 1952 Fred Ross had been sent to find an organizer for Saul Alinsky's Community Service Organization. After he met Ross, Chávez was genuinely impressed by his sincerity and his message. He talked about local concerns as well as the CSO's advocacy of Mexican rights in police brutality cases. That night Fred Ross wrote in his diary, "I think I've found the guy I'm looking for." Chávez recalled, "My suspicions were erased.

As time went on, Fred became sort of my hero. I saw him organize, and I wanted to learn."[1]

Soon Chávez was working full time for the CSO and in it he learned an important lesson that was to be the foundation of his organizing style: helping people and expecting their help in return was a way to build a strong organization. César worked in many of the small towns of the San Joaquin Valley and eventually rose to be the executive director of the CSO in California. While working for this organization he recruited Dolores Huerta, Antonio Orendain, and Gil Padilla, some of his first lieutenants in founding the UFW. As the CSO executive director in Los Angeles, Chávez met and worked with the early founders of the Mexican American Political Association (MAPA), Eduardo Quevedo and Bert Corona. They had founded a political association in 1959 to advance the Chicano community's political interests in the state. The CSO, MAPA, and the Viva Kennedy Clubs in the early sixties became important training grounds for young Mexican Americans who were beginning to self-consciously call themselves "Chicanos," a slang term that for decades had been used by natives to denigrate newly arrived Mexican immigrants.

In 1962 the CSO had its annual convention, where Chávez proposed that the CSO support a union movement for farm workers. The board refused to support his project, arguing that the CSO was a civil rights, not a labor organization. So Chávez decided to resign and devote himself to building an independent farm-workers union. Soon after his resignation, AWOC, an AFL-CIO farm union organization, offered him a job as a paid organizer, but he turned it down because he wanted to be able to work with "no strings attached." In 1962 the Chávez family moved to Delano, a small town in the San Joaquin Valley. For the next three years César slowly built up a membership in a Farm Worker's Association. Using his CSO training, Chávez emphasized the service aspect of his organization. He traveled extensively, talking to the workers to see what they thought about a union and the services it should provide. He went out into the fields and into the camps and colonias where he passed out more than one thousand questionnaires that people could fill out and mail in. He talked personally to thousands of workers.

Prior to César Chávez's full-time commitment to farm-labor organizing there had been a long history of struggle in the fields. One of the earliest agricultural unions, organized by Mexicans in California, was the Imperial Valley Worker's Union (La Unión de Trabajadores del Valle Imperial). In 1928, with more than 2,700 members, the union went out on strike, attempting to increase the piece rate for cantaloupe picking, reform the labor contractor system, and get accident insurance for workers. The growers tried to end the strike by getting court orders against picketing, organizing armed vigilante groups, getting the police to make mass arrests, and by red baiting the union leadership with hysterical media accounts. Within a year the growers defeated the union. In the process they established a pattern for handling future farm-labor strikes that would last well into the 1970s.

Despite this early setback, California became a focus for labor organizing activity in the 1930s. In 1933, for instance, five thousand Mexican berry pickers in El Monte organized a union, the Confederación de Uniones de Campesinos y Obreros Mexicanos (CUCOM), which went on strike to raise hourly pay for pickers. Strikers were joined by a more militant, communist-led labor union that included some Mexican organizers, the Cannery and Agricultural Workers' Industrial Union (C&AWIU), with seven thousand workers. Because the growers were Japanese farmers who feared a nativist backlash, the Mexican union won its wage demands.

The C&AWIU moved on to organize cotton workers in the San Joaquin Valley. The result was a prolonged and violent cotton strike in 1933. In that strike twelve thousand cotton pickers, 75 percent of whom were Mexican, confronted the powerful San Joaquin Valley Agricultural Labor Bureau, representing the cotton growers. Events followed a familiar pattern: evictions, court orders, arrests, and violence. The growers hired goons and strike breakers, who surrounded union meetings at the towns of Pixley and Arvin and killed three farm workers. During the strike, hospitals refused to admit wounded and sick striking farm workers and their families. People starved because there were no relief or charity funds available, and eventually nine infants died of malnutrition. When the violence and suffering could no longer be ignored, state and federal officials intervened to negotiate a compromise settlement. The strike ended.

Throughout the 1930s, hundreds of agricultural strikes occurred. Many were spontaneous walkouts in protest over the numerous injustices. During the postwar years the AFL organized the National Farm Labor Union (NFLU).

Led by Hank Hasiwar and Ernesto Galarza, the union launched a number of strikes throughout California. Along with several thousand Mexican workers, the Chávez family participated in a cotton strike the union organized in 1948. A few months earlier the union had begun a strike against the DiGiorgio Corporation, a family-run corporation and one of the largest fruit growers in the United States. The struggle against the DiGiorgios lasted two and a half years, until it was broken by the use of a government injunction under the Taft-Hartley Act, the recruitment of braceros as strikebreakers, and red baiting by the California Senate Committee on Un-American Activities.

This was the previous history of farm-labor organizing that Chávez sought to reverse during the 1960s. His Farm Workers Association grew, nourished by personal sacrifice and dogged commitment. The Chávez family frequently had to go without food and clothing to pay for union expenses. He felt that the union would be stronger if, in its early years, it relied only on its membership for financial support. César was the only farm-worker union official in the nation whose salary came 100 percent from the farm workers themselves. In 1962 they held their first convention with 150 delegates when they adopted the distinctive union flag, the black eagle on a red field. By August 1965 César's faith in the union was beginning to be rewarded. They had one thousand dues-paying members and more than fifty locals.

The Grape Strike and Boycott

After a series of small strikes that won concessions for agricultural workers in McFarland and Porterville, the UFW had its baptism by fire. They had been asked to join the Filipino grape workers who were on strike for higher wages. After an emotional meeting, on September 15, 1965, on Mexican Independence Day, the members voted to join them. They needed little convincing; the members seemed to spontaneously join a struggle that they had long considered their own.

The Delano grape strike was the largest in the history of California. The region covered a four-hundred-square-mile area and involved thousands of workers. The job of organizing picket lines to patrol the fields fell to inexperienced farm workers and urban volunteers, who worked side by side. The sheer dimensions of the ranches and farms made it impossible to constantly maintain pickets at all the entrances. Inevitably scab workers (called *esquiroles*) found their way into the fields and the union had to find a way of convincing them to come out and join the strike. The picket line then became a noisy place. The picketers cajoled, argued, pleaded, orated, and shamed the scabs in Spanish, Tagalog, and English, trying to get them to join the strike. Picketers walked the dusty borders of the fields holding hand-painted signs "Huelga," "Delano Grape Striker," "Victoria!" accompanied by the NFWA black eagle.

Whatever its practical effect, Chávez saw the picket line as an educational and recruiting experience. It was the place where you could feel the confrontation between the worker and the grower. It became a way of building a strong membership. He would later say, "The picket line is where a man makes his commitment, and it is irrevocable; the longer he's on the picket line, the stronger the commitment.... The picket line is a beautiful thing, because it does something to a human being."[2]

From the beginning of the strike, Chávez had emphasized the importance of nonviolence as a strategy. He exhorted the volunteers and picketers: "If someone commits violence against us, it is much better—if we can—not to react against the violence but to react in such a way as to get closer to our goal. People don't like to see a non-violent movement subjected to violence, and there's a lot of support across the country for nonviolence. That's the key point we have going for us. We can turn the world if we can do it non-violently."[3]

César's main activity during the early months of the strike was to travel around the state to the various college campuses to give speeches to galvanize support for the striking farm workers. The national news media helped in generating support for the strike. Television news crews visited Delano and filmed the drama of the confrontations at the picket line. The 1960 CBS documentary *The Harvest of Shame* depicting the tragic conditions of migrant labor in the United States had begun to make people more aware of the farm worker's plight. Newspaper reporters from the big-city newspapers and national magazines traveled to Delano to interview Chávez and other union officials as well as the growers. Chávez spoke about how the farm workers were fighting for their civil rights and economic justice. This fit in with a growing national concern with civil rights.

Publicity became increasingly important when the union decided to launch a boycott to put pressure on the growers to recognize the union and sign contracts. They targeted the most identifiable grape products from the largest Delano growers. When Walter Reuther visited Delano in December 1965 the grape strike and boycott had become a national news item.

Other dramatic events gave a momentum to the strike and boycott. Three months after Ruether's visit, On March 16, 1966, Chávez organized a march from Delano to Sacramento to dramatize the strike and get the support of the governor, Pat Brown. Chávez marched with the procession as it left Delano. They carried the American and Mexican flags, the NFWA and AWOC banners, and a flag with the image of the Virgin of Guadalupe, the patron Saint of Mexico, who had been the banner of rebellion during the Mexican Wars of Independence in 1810. The march helped recruit more members and spread the spirit of the strike. As they passed through each small farming town, hundreds of workers would greet them. Others would join the march to carry the flags to the next town.

Just prior to the end of the pilgrimage the first grower, Schenley, announced that it was willing to sign a contract with the UFW. On April 7 the agreement was made public. In a triumphant mood, the pilgrimage ended a few days later on the steps of the state capitol. They had won their first victory and demonstrated the power of their cause. This was the first time in American history that a grassroots farm-labor union had gained recognition by a corporation. (In Hawaii, some years earlier, the Longshoreman's Union had gotten a contract for pineapple workers.)

The other large growers remained. The most important was the DiGiorgio Corporation. The DiGiorgios also had thousands of acres of pears, plums, apricots, and citrus trees and marketed their products under the S & W Foods and TreeSweet labels. Robert DiGiorgio, the patriarch of the family, was on the board of directors for the Bank of America. The DiGiorgio family had successfully broken strikes and unions since the 1930s. Steinbeck in his novel *The Grapes of Wrath* (1939) had used DiGiorgio as a model for the grower named "Gregorio."

Chávez was convinced of the power of the boycott and soon hundreds of volunteers who remembered the previous struggles against the DiGiorgios joined the boycott drive. Within a short time the company agreed to enter into negotiations to have an election but Chávez broke them off when company guards attacked a picketer at Sierra Vista. When negotiations finally resumed, Chávez discovered that DiGiorgio had invited the Teamsters Union to recruit among vineyard workers. Thus beginning in mid-1966 the two unions, the Teamsters and the NFWA, began an on-and-off jurisdictional fight that lasted more than ten years and resulted in violence, injury, and deaths.

About this time, in order to consolidate its power, the AWOC and the NFWA formally merged to form one united union within the AFL-CIO. There was some debate about the wisdom of this move, but not a single farm worker voted against it. Under the final merger agreement a new organization, called United Farm Workers Organizing Committee (eventually to become the United Farm Workers of America, AFL-CIO) was formed with Chávez as the director. The UFW became a full member of the AFL-CIO and as a result received millions of dollars of emergency aid during the early years of struggle. This was the first time that a predominantly Mexican union had been incorporated within mainstream organized labor. Over the years the relationship proved to be mutually supportive and the UFW never seemed to be hampered in its independence of action.

From the beginning César had thought of "La Causa" as a movement that would not be motivated by appeals to race or nationality. When he had worked for the Community Service Organization, César had confronted the issue of Mexican chauvinism and had been uncompromising in fighting for the inclusion of Blacks within the organization. While the primary "core" leadership of the NFWA was Mexican American, the staff, and hundreds of volunteer workers, were predominantly Anglo American.

Toward a Victory

During they next four years the UFWOC grew in strength, nourished by the support of millions of sympathetic Americans who sacrificed for the farm workers. Hundreds of student volunteers lived on poverty wages in the big cities to organize an international boycott of table grapes. Scores of priests, nuns, ministers, and church members donated time, money, facilities, and energies to the farm worker's cause. Organized labor donated millions of dollars to the

UFWOC strike fund. Millions of Americans gave up eating table grapes. All this was inspired by the example of César Chávez, the soft-spoken, humble leader who quietly worked to revolutionize grower-worker relations.

In 1967 the union moved from its cramped offices on Albany Street in Delano to some new buildings on some land they had purchased with the help of private donations and contributions from AFL-CIO affiliates. The new headquarters was located near the city dump on forty acres of alkali land. Volunteers had built a complex of buildings, including a service and administrative center, a medical clinic, and a cooperative gas station. It was called "The Forty Acres." It became the center of the farm-workers union movement in California for the next three years until the union moved its headquarters to Keane, a small town just outside of Bakersfield.

On April 1, 1967, the newspapers announced the signing of a union contract between DiGiorgio Fruit Corporation and the UFWOC. The contract contained wage increases for workers and set up a special fund for health and welfare benefits. It provided for unemployment compensation and specified that hiring would be done through the union labor hall. UFWOC strikes continued against other Delano growers and by October seven new wineries had signed contracts with the union.

During one of the strikes against Guimarra Corporation, César began a fast to protest the mounting talk of violence. In characteristic fashion he began the fast without telling anyone. He did not know how long it was going to last. On the fourth day, he decided to hold a meeting of the strikers to announce his intentions. "I told them I thought they were discouraged, because they were talking about short cuts, about violence. They were getting so mad with the growers, they couldn't be effective anymore."[4]

After the meeting with the membership, Chávez walked to the Forty Acres. He set up his monastic cell in the storage room of the service station with a small cot and a few religious articles. Soon hundreds of farm-worker families began appearing at the Forty Acres to show their support for Chávez and to attend the daily mass that he attended. A huge tent city with thousands of farm workers sprang up surrounding the gas station. There was a tremendous outpouring of emotion during the masses. Daily hundreds stood in line to meet and talk to Chávez.

The national media helped make the 1968 fast a major event. As the fast went into its twentieth day letters of support came from congressmen and senators, union and religious leaders. Dr. Martin Luther King Jr. sent a telegram supporting César. He would be assassinated a month later. Robert Kennedy, who had not yet decided to run for the nomination for the presidency, also sent a telegram expressing concern for his health. Chávez would not let a doctor examine him because he felt that "Without the element of risk, I would be hypocritical. The whole essence of penance . . . would be taken away."[5] When Chávez finally decided to end his fast, on the twenty-fifth day, he asked Robert Kennedy to attend. On March 11 they held a mass at a county park with more than four thousand farm workers in attendance along with national reporters from the major papers and television cameras. The mass was said on the back of a flatbed truck. César was too weak to stand and he could not speak but Jim Drake read a message he had written earlier. It was a powerful expression of his spiritual commitment.

> Our struggle is not easy. Those who oppose our cause are rich and powerful, and they have many allies in high places. We are poor. Our allies are few. But we have something the rich do not own. We have our own bodies and spirits and the justice of our cause as our weapons.
>
> When we are really honest with ourselves, we must admit that our lives are all that really belong to us. So it is how we use our lives that determines what kind of men we are. It is my deepest belief that only by giving of our lives do we find life.
>
> I am convinced that the truest act of courage, the strongest act of manliness is to sacrifice ourselves for others in a totally nonviolent struggle for justice. To be a man is to suffer for other. God help us to be men![6]

Over the years Chávez engaged in many other fasts, each one for a specific purpose. His followers soon learned the depth of his commitment to the principle of nonviolence, so that to violate that code was to personally affront César. For the most part his followers remained nonviolent because of Chávez's moral authority.

The challenges of nonviolence in confronting very real exploitation is illustrated in the film *Alambrista* as Robert Young, the director, recreates a dialogue between the poorest of the poor. Roberto witnesses an outpouring of anger by a drunken African American who is waiting, along with other farm workers, in the early morning dark for a job. This scene was enacted using both real farm workers and actors. As two drunks ranted against the workers that slavery is the American way, the verbal attack on the labor system almost provoked a riot among the waiting campesinos while Robert Young was filming the scene.

In the late spring of 1969 the grape harvest was about to begin. To rally support for the strike and boycott César decided to organize a march through the heart of the Coachella and Imperial Valleys to the U.S.-Mexican border. One of the primary purposes of the march was to dramatize the growers' use of undocumented immigrants from Mexico as strikebreakers. On May 10, 1969, César began the march with an outdoor mass celebrated in a labor camp in Indio. As in the 1966 march to Sacramento, the Coachella pilgrimage was a tremendous organizing tactic. Hundreds of farm workers and supporters joined in the colorful procession. Reverend Ralph Abernathy, the heir of Dr. Martin Luther King Jr.'s movement, joined the march on the eighth day, pledging the support of the Southern Christian Leadership Conference. Walter Mondale, a liberal senator from Minnesota who would be a future presidential candidate, joined the march along with famous Hollywood actors and Chicano student activists. The march dramatized the strike to hundreds of Mexican workers who were in the fields as the marchers passed. In the evening masses, speeches and teatros educated them about the issues involved. The march lasted nine days and ended in Calexico, the border town across from Mexicali, Baja California, where Chávez gave a speech calling for Mexican workers to join the strike and support the UFWOC.

By 1969 Chávez had expanded the boycott to include all California table grapes. All over the country volunteers were picketing supermarkets that sold grapes. Shipments of California table grapes practically stopped to the cities of Boston, New York, Philadelphia, Chicago, Detroit, Montreal, and Toronto. Grape sales fell while millions of pounds rotted in cold storage sheds. In reaction the growers filed a lawsuit charging that they had lost more than 25 million dollars since the beginning of the boycott. In desperation they turned to the Teamsters and held meetings to try to work out a contract that would bring peace to the fields. But the Teamsters were leery of entering the fields again given their previous experience when the growers had reneged on a sweetheart deal when the pressure had become too great.

Despite the support of the Department of Defense for grape purchases, the boycott pressures began to be unbearable and gradually in the late spring of 1969 some influential growers in the Coachella Valley came to the negotiating table and signed contracts with the UFW.

By June 1970 the majority of table-grape growers who were still resisting unionization were in the Delano area. Finally, through the intermediations of a committee organized by the National Conference of Catholic Bishops twenty-three companies, including Guimarra Corporation, agreed to begin negotiations to recognize the UFW.

On July 29, 1970, twenty-six Delano growers filed into Reuther Hall on Forty Acres to formally sign contracts. César gave a short speech recalling the sacrifices that so many had made to make this moment possible and they signed the historic agreement. The contract raised the workers' wages to $1.80 per hour. In addition the growers would donate 10 cents an hour to the Robert Kennedy Health and Welfare Fund. The contract provided for all hiring to be through the union hiring hall and for the protection of workers from certain pesticides. The victory in Delano now meant that almost 85 percent of all table-grape growers in California were under a union contract. This was a victory without precedent in the history of American agriculture. Never before in history had an agricultural-workers union managed such a sweeping success.

The Lettuce Strike and the Teamsters

There were indications that the farm workers were facing another formidable challenge, this time from the Teamsters and growers in the Salinas Valley who were conspiring to undercut the UFW's newly won recognition.

The Teamsters organization had several times before threatened to expand their operations to organize field workers. In 1970 the Teamsters and the UFW were both members of the AFL-CIO so this announcement by the Teamsters amounted to a raid on the UFW's jurisdiction. The Teamsters had signed sweetheart contracts giving the vegetable growers almost all that they wanted while sacrificing workers' benefits. There was plenty of evidence of collusion. The Teamsters had signed the contracts without even negotiating wage rates for the workers.

Quickly Chávez moved to counter. He and the rest of the staff moved the headquarters of the union to Salinas and began organizing a strike. He traveled to the AFL-CIO convention in Chicago and attempted, with no success, to get the national organization to publicly condemn the Teamsters. Throughout the month of August César had worked to keep the pressure on the growers with Teamster contracts by selective picketing of the largest corporations. About 170 vegetable growers stubbornly refused to switch from the Teamsters to the UFW. This led Chávez to call for a general strike.

During this struggle with the Teamsters César led the union to fight against a farm labor law passed by the Arizona legislature and signed by the governor. It outlawed the boycott and limited strikes much as had been advocated by Nixon's administration. To raise people's awareness over the necessity of repealing the law and recalling the governor who had signed it, César began a fast. For twenty-four days César fasted and directed the recall campaign from a small room in Saint Rita's Center in a Mexican barrio of Phoenix.

That fall the California growers would also try to pass similar legislation to hamstring farm-labor movement. They sponsored Proposition 22, an initiative that would outlaw boycotting and limit secret-ballot elections to full-time non-seasonal employees. Chávez followed the strategy in Arizona of getting citizens registered to vote as well as informing them about Proposition 22's threat to workers. During the fall the "No on 22" campaign gathered momentum through the use of human billboards. On November 7, 1972, Proposition 22 was soundly defeated by a margin of 58 percent. The UFW had used the boycott organization to mobilize political support. In this election they proved that they were a serious political force.

Meanwhile the lettuce boycott and struggle with the Teamsters continued. On April 15, 1973, grape growers in the San Joaquin Valley announced that they had signed contracts with the Teamsters. César immediately called for a strike and pulled most of the UFW workers from the fields. The Teamsters recruited goons and soon violence exploded, with two union members being killed. Finally on September 1, César decided to call off the strike and resume the boycott, which now included Gallo Winery, which had signed a contract with the Teamsters. The decision to abandon the strike was motivated in part by his desire to avoid future violence but also because he felt very deeply that the boycott would be more effective than a strike. The Teamsters finally gave up their campaign to organize field workers and take over UFW contracts late in 1974. Nevertheless the grape and vegetable growers had contracts in place that were not set to expire for several years. Until then César had to decide on a strategy to keep his union together.

The film *Alambrista* depicts some of the abuses that Chávez fought all his life to end. One of the primary evils has been the use of *"coyotes"* or smugglers to import undocumented workers in unsafe and inhuman conditions in order to break strikes. This is graphically shown in the film—the disregard for the workers' safety, a racist and inhuman attitude on the part of the coyotes and growers, and the feelings of fear endured by farm workers.

The California Farm Labor Act

In 1975 Chávez decided to intensify the boycott against Gallo wines. The AFL-CIO had agreed to support the UFW lettuce and grape boycotts, if the union dropped the secondary boycott of Safeway and A&P markets. Gallo had signed a Teamster contract after their UFW contract had expired and were highly vulnerable. On February 22, César organized a 110-mile march from San Francisco to Modesto, home of the Gallo Wineries. More than fifteen thousand supporters ended the march a week later. The tremendous turnout proved again that the UFW had great popular support.

The message was not lost on the newly elected governor of California, Jerry Brown, a son of the former governor whom some considered to be almost an anti-politician, a perfect type to be successful in the post-Watergate era. Jerry Brown had supported the farm workers' cause and even marched with them in the Coachella Valley. As secretary of state in 1972 he had helped the UFW challenge Proposition 22. His election to the governorship in November 1974 signaled a new opportunity for the UFW.

Late in 1974 César began to think that a state agricultural law might help reverse the decline of the union's strength but only if the law had certain provisions. First, it had to allow for boycotts. Second, it had to allow seasonal workers to vote in elections (under previously proposed legislation, including the Arizona law, only permanent workers were allowed to vote). Third, a UFW-supported farm-labor law had to allow for legitimate strikes. Initially, the growers opposed all of these conditions for a farm-labor law but by 1975, after the years of strikes, jurisdictional violence, and boycotts they were willing to concede these points.

After considerable political maneuvering the California Agricultural Labor Relations Act was passed in May 1975, the first such law in the continental United States governing farm-labor organizing (farm workers in Hawaii had a similar law). The law gave the UFW what it wanted: secret-ballot elections, the right to boycott, voting rights for migrant seasonal workers, and control over the timing of elections. The growers, for their part, were convinced that the law would end boycotts and labor disruptions that had cost them millions of dollars in profits.

The struggle with the Teamsters for representation of farm workers continued under the supervision of the state agency. Governor Brown continued to support Chávez and the UFW by appointing a pro-UFW majority to the Agricultural Labor Relations Board, the body that was to oversee the elections and rule on the complaints. A big controversy arose over the access rules for union. The UFW wanted unlimited rights to enter ranches and farms to talk to workers about the union, while the growers wanted total control over access, giving preference to the Teamsters.

Another problem was funding. The ALRB ran out of money for its daily operation at the beginning of 1976 and suspended operations for five months until the legislature could vote for a regular appropriation. The legislature lacked the necessary majority to pass an emergency appropriation and so the ALRB stopped reviewing and certifying elections.

César decided to attack the issues of funding and access by appealing to the voters. In a massive initiative campaign the UFW sent out its workers and gathered over seven hundred thousand signatures in only twenty-nine days. The initiative, known as Proposition 14, was to be voted on in November. The UFW-sponsored initiative provided for guaranteed funding for the Agricultural Labor Board as well as assuring union organizers access to workers. Due to an advertising campaign funded by oil companies and agricultural corporations Proposition 14 lost by a two-to-one margin. The public seemed to have been convinced that the funding of the Farm Labor Board was already a moot point and that the access provision was a threat to property rights.

Strengths and Weaknesses: Mixed Results

Some regarded the defeat of Proposition 14 in 1976 as a turning point in Chávez's ability to mobilize the public's support for the farm workers and their union. The promise of the ALRB as a means of helping organize farm workers rapidly disappeared. The Farm Labor Board was increasingly controlled by Republican pro-grower interests who consistently ruled against the many grievances that were brought before it by the union.

There were some victories. One was the result of years of lobbying and complex legal maneuvers: the abolition of *el cortito* or the short-handled hoe in 1975. For decades the growers had required field workers to use this tool, which forced the workers to bend over and work for hours on end. Thousands of farm workers permanently damaged their backs and spent the rest of their lives in disabling pain. Chávez and the UFW had opposed the use of el cortito because of its damaging effect on the workers' health. Together with attorneys for California Rural Legal Aid (CRLA) they won its abolishment.

In terms of union building, the period following the passage of the California Farm Labor Act was one of growth in membership and contracts. The UFW had won almost two thirds of the elections after 1975 and the Teamsters admitted in March of 1977 that they were beaten and that they would not contest future elections. The dues-paying membership of the UFW soared to over one hundred thousand by 1978.

It would seem that the union had reached a degree of organizational success. But there were troubling signs that all was not well. A number of long-time staff members quit the union, some expressing their unhappiness with César's leadership and others admitting to being burned out by the long hours at almost no pay. In March 1979, Jerry Cohen, the UFW's chief attorney, left after the executive board defeated his proposal to allow his staff to be paid salaries rather than in-kind benefits. A few months later, Marshall Ganz, who helped organize the lettuce strike, and Jim Drake, another long-time organizer, left the union, along with a number of other union leaders from the Salinas area, over a dispute having to do with the union policy. The newspaper and journal reactions to these resignations were to magnify them as signaling the end of the Chávez-led union.

César had decided to reorganize the union and some left because they disagreed with his strategies. In late 1975 he called for a conference to discuss ideas for modernizing the union and invited several management consultants to La Paz for staff-training sessions. As part of the modernization drive they began computerizing all the union records and purchased a microwave communications system so that they would not be dependent on the public telephones.

Despite these measures, there were indications that the UFW lost momentum. In 1984 only fifteen of the seventy grape growers in the Delano area were under a UFW contract. The union was winning fewer and fewer elections: in 1976 they had won 276 but in the years since they had won only 56. Union membership dropped to less than twelve thousand active members. There were fewer and fewer strikes and the UFW cut down on the numbers of organizers in the fields, hoping to encourage local leadership and initiative.

The reason for the decline, César felt, was that the Farm Labor Board was firmly in the hands of the grower interests. The board now was used to stifling unionization. The ALRB took on the average 348 days to settle disputes over contested elections and about half as long to render a decision whether or not to litigate an unfair labor practice. As of 1984 the ALRB had not rendered any award for violation of the labor law.

As a result of the stalemate promoted by the ALRB César came to the conclusion that the only tactic left was to boycott in order to force the growers to sign contracts. So on June 12, 1984, César announced that the union would embark on a new grape boycott. The UFW had sponsored more than fifty boycotts over the years and the public was confused as to what was and wasn't still being boycotted. There remained a tremendous educational campaign for the union to undertake.

For the next few years Chávez targeted the environmental concerns of the nation's middle class. In 1985 the UFW commissioned a video entitled *The Wrath of Grapes* (directed by Lorena Parlee and Lenny Bourin), where graphic footage showed the birth defects and high rates of cancer that pesticide poisoning produced among farm workers and consumers. The UFW distributed 250,000 free copies of the film worldwide. In 1987 and again in 1988, César traveled to the midwestern and eastern cities, where grape consumption was viewed as a luxury item, and where union support had always been the strongest.

Finally, César decided to protest against pesticide usage by beginning a fast on midnight July 16, 1988. The fast went largely unnoticed by the public until the children of Robert Kennedy visited César in La Paz to lend their support. Finally on Sunday August 22, César gave up his water-only fast. As an expression of support, Jesse Jackson, a presidential candidate, and actors Martin Sheen and Robert Blake vowed to continue the fast for three days to keep alive the "chain of suffering." Thereafter for several months individuals joined three-day mini-fasts to demonstrate their support for the union.

During the thirty-six-day fast, César issued a statement that summarized his commitment to the union and the boycott:

> As I look back at this past year, I can see many events that precipitated the fast, including the terrible suffering of farm workers and their children, the crushing of farm worker rights, the denial of fair and free elections and the death of good-faith bargaining in California agriculture. All of these events are connected with the great cause of justice for farm worker families."[7]

Alambrista graphically shows us the ways in which farm workers are exposed to pesticides. In the film, Roberto gets a job as a flagman in the spraying of a field by a crop duster. He is entirely unaware of the health risks he is being exposed to. This is also true for hundreds of thousands of farm workers who are forced by poverty to endure pesticide exposure.

In the 1990s Chávez had the same qualities of character that had brought about victories in the earlier boycotts. Most of all he was tenacious in his leadership, despite an apparent change in the activist mood of the country. He believed that the modern boycott could be won with an alliance among Latinos, Blacks, and other minorities, plus allies in labor and the church. He also had faith that for the generation of activists from the sixties and seventies the boycott would become a social habit. By 1991 statistics of grape consumption seemed to bear out his optimism. During the crucial period May to August 1990 grapes delivered for sale declined in twelve major cities. In New York City grape consumption was down 74 percent; in Los Angeles it declined by 37 percent and by

36 percent in San Francisco. The UFW could cite official statistics showing that the growers were selling grapes at a loss.

Chávez was confident about the ultimate success of the UFW struggle and remained so until his unexpected death in Yuma, Arizona, on April 23, 1993. He had been coordinating the boycott and fighting legal battles against the growers, traveling to raise money and fasting for spiritual enlightenment. The tremendous outpouring of condolences and support that followed his death was a testimony to his importance as a leader who touched the conscience of America. César Chávez's crusade had been part of a worldwide commitment to human and civil rights, inspired by ideas and issues arising from the age in which he lived. He was correctly identified as a civil rights leader as much as a labor leader. More than thirty thousand people followed his casket for three miles from downtown Delano to the union's old headquarters at the Forty Acres. Expressions of regret for his passing came from around the world, from international political, labor, and spiritual leaders as well as from thousands of the poor migrant farm workers to whom he had dedicated his life.

César Chávez's most lasting significance as a leader of the farm worker's movement is that he made millions aware of the plight of Mexican Americans and enlarged the nation's conscience. In that respect, although he thought of himself as a labor leader, he was part of the U.S. civil rights movement of the 1960s. Indeed he knew and communicated with many of the leaders of the civil rights movement, including Dr. Martin Luther King. The emphasis on nonviolence within the farm-workers movement was reinforced by the civil rights struggle in the South. In fighting for labor rights he always was aware that he was expanding the rights of all working men and women.

Chávez's strength were the moral principles he believed in: self-sacrifice for others, courageous struggle despite overwhelming odds, respect for races and religions, nonviolence, belief in a divine soul and moral order, a rejection of materialism, and a faith in the moral superiority of the poor, as well as a central belief in justice. He embodied the struggles of a people, *la raza,* to achieve a better life in America. He will always be remembered for his humility and total dedication to the cause of social and economic justice.

■

Discussion Questions

1. As you watch the film *Alambrista*, note the working conditions that Roberto experiences as a farm worker. Analyze what César Chávez did as a farm labor leader to improve these conditions.

2. The film is about the lives of the poorest and most powerless workers in our society and their struggle to survive in America. After reading the chapter on César Chávez, discuss what tactics the farm-worker movement used to empower the working poor.

3. As you watch the film *Alambrista*, note the segments of the film that remind you of César Chávez's life. For example, Roberto having to leave home to support his family as a farm worker was similar to César's family having to leave Yuma to follow the crops. Find at least four similarities.

Notes

1. Jacques E. Levy, *César Chávez: Autobiography of La Causa* (New York: W. W. Norton, 1975), 99, 102.

2. Ronald Taylor, *Chávez and the Farm Workers* (Boston: Beacon Press, 1975), 136.

3. Levy, *César Chávez*, 196.

4. Ibid., 273.

5. Ibid., 285.

6. Ibid., 286.

7. *Los Angeles Times*, August 23, 1988.

Bibliography

Day, Mark. *Forty Acres: César Chávez and the Farm Workers.* New York: Praeger Publishers, 1971.

Dunne, John. *Delano, Story of the California Grape Strike.* New York: Farrar, Straus and Giroux, 1967.

Fusco, Paul and George D. Horowitz. *La Causa! The California Grape Strike.* New York: Collier Books, 1970.

Kushner, Sam. *The Long Road to Delano: A Century of Farmworker Struggle.* New York: International Publishers, 1975.

Levy, Jacques E. *César Chávez: Autobiography of La Causa.* New York: W. W. Norton, 1975.

London, Joan and Henry Anderson. *So Shall Ye Reap: The Story of César Chávez and the Farm Worker's Movement.* New York: Thomas Crowell, 1970.

Matthissen, Peter. *Sal Si Puedes: César Chávez and the New American Revolution.* New York: Random House, 1969.

Meister, Dick and Anne Loftis. *A Long Time Coming: The Struggle to Unionize America's Farm Workers.* New York: Macmillan, 1977.

Nelson, Eugene. *Huelga: The First Hundred Days of the Great Delano Grape Strike.* Delano, Calif.: Farm Workers Press, 1966.

Taylor, Ronald. *Chávez and the Farm Workers.* Boston: Beacon Press, 1975.

The Drama of Immigration and the Cry of the Poor

The Voices of *Alambrista* Yesterday and Today

Daniel Groody

Introduction

Immigration is a worldwide phenomenon that affects every nation and every neighborhood in the world. Nowhere is this truer than in the United States, which is a country of immigrants. In recent years, one of the greatest waves of immigrants to land in the United States is the Mexican. The movie *Alambrista* helps us look more closely at the trials and tribulations associated with Mexican immigration by entering into the particular life of one immigrant, named Roberto. Throughout the movie, various characters bring to light the complex drama of the movement from one country to another. Some of these characters are placed at center stage, some enter briefly and then recede into the background, and still others play a minor role in the movie but a major role in shaping the conditions of immigrants in America today. Each character plays an important role in the movie because each one prototypes an element of the narrative of millions of Mexican immigrants who live this story each day.

In this article I would like to examine the characters of *Alambrista* in light of the stories of undocumented Mexican immigration today. Each person in the film has something important to say, and he or she brings out the cries of the poor who are struggling to be heard in contemporary American society.

My purpose is to identify these voices more clearly, to listen to their struggles and to reflect on the implications of their voices. The voices in this article do not come from Hollywood actors or fictional characters but actual human beings who have gone through the immigration experience from Mexico to the United States.[1] They bring out more clearly what is happening on the "inside" of the immigrant, that is, what they hope for, dream about, and struggle with as they break from Mexico, cross the border, and enter the United States. By listening to their voices today, we can better grasp the cost of immigration and the challenges their voices pose for us today.[2]

La Familia: The Voice of the Poor

Mexicans have a saying that goes, "*un texto fuera del contexto es un pretexto*" (a text out of its context is a pretext). In a similar way, if we look at immigrants' lives outside of the economic, political, and social conditions that shape them, we will never be able to hear what they are saying. In order to understand any voice, we have to understand the context from which a person speaks. The story of *Alambrista* begins in a small remote village of Michoacán, Mexico.[3] Located in central Mexico, Michoacán is a state that is rich in natural resources but, like many places in Mexico, poor in economic development. One of its greatest exports today is its young people, who, like Roberto, come to the United States looking for a living wage.[4] In many parts of Mexico, people make their living by working the land for simple crops like corn, onions, mangos, and other fruits and vegetables. The work is hard, the machinery is often primitive, and the pay is minimal. Even today, many villages of Michoacán and other states in Mexico look like they do in the movie, far removed from the technologically sophisticated world of the United States. Like Roberto, many people in these towns live in simple houses. Often they do not have electricity, and few can afford the luxuries of appliances, if any, except for a natural-gas stove and perhaps at most a television. Only a few would have telephones, and computers would be as rare as a two-dollar bill. While Mexico is geographically close to the United States, it is economically in another hemisphere.

At the beginning of the movie, Roberto and his wife have a baby. The child is born in the home, not in a hospital, as it would be too far away, and his parents lack both immediate transportation and funds to pay medical expenses or insurance. When we are first introduced to Roberto, we are present at the But not even economic poverty can rob Roberto and his wife of the priceless gift of a new child: the smile between a son and his mother and the tenderness of the father in the loving embrace with his child. The opening scene tells only part of the story. Behind the joy of a new family is the harsh reality of what many people have to endure: many families like Roberto's struggle simply to survive.

Ironically, the birth of Roberto's child actually breaks up the family. In virtually no time, impending economic responsibilities quickly eclipse the beauty of their life together. The joy of birth is overshadowed by another kind of labor pain: providing for a child in such an economically destitute place. In the movie, Roberto jokes about living only on potatoes, but many families like him are limited to a subsistence diet in Mexico. Raul Jimenez from Jalisco said he too faced a similar situation. He said, "My family got to the point where we could only afford sugar, eggs and tortillas, and when we could not afford even these, I had to immigrate."[5] Roberto represents the face of thousands of Mexican immigrants each day who painfully leave their families every day for work in the United States in order to provide for their families.

Mexican immigrants come to the United States primarily for economic reasons.[6] Over forty million Mexicans live in poverty and dream of making more than the national wages of 35 cents an hour or 200 pesos (about $20) every two weeks.[7] Amid such scarcity, buying a Coke and a simple hamburger is a luxury. Mexico's 40-percent unemployment rate and low-paying jobs, when contrasted with the high demand for labor and comparatively high wages in the United States, draw Mexicans into the United States like a magnet.[8]

Mexican immigrants often come to the United States not because they want to get rich but, like Roberto, because they lack a steady job and a decent wage in Mexico.[9] Saul Gutierrez from Michoacán, shortly after being apprehended by immigration officials at the U.S.-Mexican border, said,

> I left Mexico because many of us are desperate and poor. There are few jobs, and those that are available pay almost nothing. In my region of Michoacán, I only make about forty dollars a week, which is very little to live on for a family. If I pay the rent, I end up with little left over to buy food. After food

and rent, I have nothing left over for the kids. But if I buy something for them, how can I pay the rent? I feel so caught. I crossed the border last night because I want to provide for my family. As it is, we're barely making it.[10]

Many are forced to choose between poverty at home and the perils of immigration. Such decisions render the soul and divide families.

While the demands of poverty are difficult, the emotional pains are sometimes even greater. The family that the immigrant leaves behind often suffers one of the greatest costs, as it means that the fathers and sons leave for six to eight months out of the year or longer. Of all the trials the immigrant faces, leaving home is one of the most difficult. As Xavier Mendoza said,

When I came to the United States, I felt awful about leaving my family behind. I'm afraid at times, and I am constantly aware of the dangers. But it doesn't matter, and I try not to think about it because it is too painful. My family's need is even greater than my fears, and I just have to keep going; they need me if we are going to live a more dignified life.[11]

Another immigrant expressed similar sentiments. "The worst is leaving the family behind, and especially the kids...it is what hurts the most...but I do it so that we can have something in México."[12]

La Esposa y La Madre: The Voice of the Women Left Behind

Some of the voices in the film that are hardest to hear are those of Roberto's mother and Roberto's wife. While Roberto treks up north in search of a job, they are left at home in Mexico. In the movie, we do not even know their names. Like many other women in similar situations, they are often known only in terms of their functional roles as wives and mothers, but we never hear what they have to say. They rarely speak, and, in relationship to the men of this world, their words have little to no effect. "I don't want you to go," said Roberto's wife, "but if you have to, whatever you think is right." They are left alone to cry in tears that no one will hear.

In many parts of Mexico today, women are often compelled to accept the decisions of their husbands without much recourse to their own points of view. They are some of the most powerless in the whole process, as they have the fewest choices. They often accept their difficulties and simply suffer in silence, burying their own needs and frustrations. Because they are often bound to the home as mothers, they have the least freedom of movement. After Roberto leaves in the movie, his wife will have even fewer options. When the husband immigrates, the mother becomes a dual provider. Like many wives of immigrants, she functions as both mother and father to the children, but she cannot work anywhere but in the house because the pressing needs of the family will absorb all her attention and energy. She loses the physical support of her husband, but she must now become parent, educator, and farm hand. Now she lives with loneliness and the fear of not being able to provide for her family while her husband looks for work up north.

Only rarely do families immigrate together. Most often, the man leaves home and his wife and children stay behind. Crossing together as a family is complex and dangerous. As Miguel Ortiz said,

> When my wife and I tried to cross the border together, the immigration officials apprehended her and not me, and we were separate from each other. I spent weeks worrying about her. I did not even know where she was. Because she could not read, she could not even understand the numbers on a phone to dial me and tell me where she was. I felt so helpless and so did she.

Some who try to immigrate together end up regretting it, as seventeen-year-old Jesus Jimenez knows. After working in the fields of Fresno, California, he returned to Mexico to marry his girlfriend from his hometown in Mexico. After they married, he and his wife tried to cross the border by traversing the Otay mountains, near where Roberto crossed over the border in the movie. In the process, he and his wife hit a snowstorm, and the *coyote* who was guiding them abandoned them to die in the cold. Within a few hours, his wife of two weeks, Osveia Tepec Jimenez, age twenty, died in his arms amid the freezing temperatures of the mountains. While recuperating in the hospital, Jimenez said, "I've loved her all my life. We had so many plans. We were going to make a new life here, so much better than the one we had. We had so many dreams, but we will never live them now. It's all my fault for bringing her."[13] Many immigrants like Jimenez have to choose between the guilt of leaving their families behind and the guilt of putting them through the dangerous trek and its consequences.

Many women whose husbands leave for months at a time speak about the impact of their husband's absence on their children.[14] Maria Orozco from Aguas Calientes, who is the mother of twelve children, said,

> When my husband goes up north to work, he can be gone for anywhere from six months to a year and a half at a time. The kids miss him at first but eventually they simply began to resent him because he isn't there for them. On one level they know he has to leave to provide for us, but in the end they never feel he becomes a father to them because he is not there when they need him.[15]

Such is the case of many women in Mexico. They find some comfort in sharing their pain with other women who are going through similar ordeals, but they often feel powerless to change their situation. As a result, it is common for husbands and wives simply to shut down emotionally on both sides of the border. We see this in the movie when Roberto's mother pleads with him to stay and he ridicules her and walks away. When he leaves his wife, he does not even hug her. It is too painful to dwell too long on the choices. We are left with a picture of a mother holding a child while the husband rides away in a bus, a poignant, painful moment of the immigrant's perilous journey ahead and the women left behind.

El Coyote: The Voice of the Hired Smuggler

In the movie, little time is devoted to the actual experience of crossing the border. While Roberto has some challenges with the border patrol, he does not face any life-threatening dangers. Roberto simply finds his way to the border, crawls through a hole in the fence, and works his way northward. *Alambrista*'s opening scenes do little to portray the disorientation many immigrants feel when they come to major cities like Tijuana (especially those immigrants who come from rural areas) and the challenges they face as they try to navigate their way to the other side.

The politics of border control have changed much since the movie was first shot in the 1970s. Now, immigration is even more difficult than it was for Roberto. Major urban areas like San Diego, El Paso, Laredo, and others are virtually sealed off with physical barriers like walls, pushing immigrants into even more dangerous territory in remote mountains and snake-infested deserts. Increased border patrol agents, better technology, and bigger migration streams have also forced immigrants to move into more dangerous territory. Whereas previously an immigrant like Roberto could cross on his own, those who do so today inevitably need the assistance of hired guides or *coyotes*. Now it is more difficult than ever to cross over into the United States, making *coyotes* indispensable; immigrants cannot cross without them anymore.

Coyotes are often expensive and risky, and place in the immigration drama speaks of the demands and dangers of the journey ahead. Although many Mexican nationals barely make $1,000 in a year, the cost of a *coyote* is currently almost $2,000. Immigrants make up the financial difference with the help of relatives and friends who are already in the United States. The trek into the United States is also costly physically. "When I smuggle someone across," said one *coyote*, "I usually only bring along a can of beans, some tortillas, a can of tuna fish and two gallons of water. I have to ration it pretty carefully, as it can take us from three to four days to cross. But sometimes we get so tired and the food is so bad that we don't want to eat anything."[16]

Immigration now means enduring a long journey across a barren desert where temperatures reach up to 120 degrees in the summer. In contrast to Roberto's overnight crossing, it takes as long as three days today. "It's a difficult trek," commented another *coyote*, "because the wind blows sand in your face, and very often people's legs get swollen and blistered from the heat and the difficultly of walking for three or four days in a row, day and night."[17] Immigrants often have to wear high-heeled leather boots to protect them from snakebites in the desert, where rattlesnakes thrive and flourish. The *coyotes* and immigrants have only the clothes on their backs and the food they can carry, often without sufficient water to make it through the whole journey. The scenery, especially through California, can be breath-taking, but it is not a camping trip for the immigrant. In the words of photojournalist John Annerino:

> [Immigrants] will be wearing cheap rubber shower sandals and ill-fitting base-ball cleats to protect their feet from rocks, thorns, hot sand, and lava, not form-fitting one hundred dollar hiking boots; they will carry their meager rations of tortillas, beans, sardines, and chilis in flimsy white plastic bags, not freeze-dried gourmet meals cooked over shiny white gas stoves carried in expensive gortex backpacks. And they will sleep on the scorched bare earth in thin cot-ton t-shirts, not in cozy two hundred dollar, down sleeping bags. They will follow vague routes, passed down from one desperate generation to the next, across a horizonless no-man's land, not well-manicured trails. Their signposts will be sun-bleached bones, empty plastic water jugs, a distant mountain, not hand-painted fluorescent signs with arrows pointing the trail every quarter mile. They will cross a merciless desert for jobs, not for scenic vistas. And they will try crossing it during the deadly summer months when harvest work is most plentiful, not during the clear, brisk days of a glorious Sonoran Desert winter when bird watchers delight in counting colorful migrating birds that flirt from one cactus blossom to another. And nothing will stop these honest people in their quest for a better life, not the killing desert, and not the trans-formation of the "tortilla curtain" into the Iron Curtain.[18]

Women are particularly vulnerable, as *coyotes* sometimes demand sex as payment or they take it by force. Pablo Sanchez noted one experience with immigrants soon after they crossed over:

> A few weeks ago when I was down by the Salton Sea [in Southern Califor-nia], I saw this group of people sitting by the side of the road. They looked lost, so I went up to them and asked if they needed any help. They told me they had just crossed the border, and the *coyote* grabbed one of the young women in the group, took her behind one of the mountains and raped her. They said the girl was screaming and yelling, but there was little we could do; it was like the *coyote* had taken all of us hostage, and we were fighting to get out alive.[19]

Immigrants need the *coyotes* but fear them; they trust them with their lives but they are sometimes robbed, exploited, and raped by them; they look to *coyotes* to help them but the *coyotes* often take advantage of their vulnerability; they cry out for help but often no one hears them.

La Migra: The Voice of the Border Patrol

In various scenes throughout the movie, Roberto comes face to face with the border patrol. Sometimes they keep Roberto from coming across while at other times they deport him after he has come into the United States. The immigrant is constantly on the alert for government agents who guard against their entry into the United States. Immigrants refer to them as *la migra,* a major branch of the Immigration and Naturalization Service (INS). The role and function of the INS also has changed much since the 1970s and continues to undergo major restructuring since the September 11th terrorist attacks, but generally speaking, for the immigrant, the border patrol symbolizes all that stands in the way of the immigrants' search for a better life.

Like Roberto, the immigrant faces the constant threat of la migra. The immigrant always must face the threat of deportation, and like Roberto, cannot evade this risk even in the workplace, in the restaurant, or the nightclub. Such deportations ruptured the little relational gains Roberto made on the other side of the border, and, when he was deported, he had to go through the painful process of making a living and making new relationships all over again. Immigration and deportation become a way of life for many immigrants as they find themselves trapped in a vicious cycle of hope, loneliness, and desperation.

For many immigrants, however, the INS has a Jekyll-and-Hyde persona. On the one hand, its agents represent the cruel face of the American government that is hardened to their economic plight. Yet on the other hand, immigration officials have many dedicated men and women who actually save the lives of the immigrants. Many agents rescue immigrants who are stranded and in distress amid the difficult, daunting, and dangerous terrain of the Southwest. Shortly after the border patrol apprehended him, Mario Velasquez said,

Last night was incredibly difficult. We were walking all through the night in the cold of the desert. And after awhile, everything in my body was in pain, my legs, my whole system was exhausted, because we didn't sleep either. We had to sleep in the mountains, but it was freezing there. And then we ran out of water. We were lost in the desert, and it was dangerous. And so eventually we had to turn ourselves into immigration officials just to survive, or we would have dehydrated out there.[20]

While there are documented cases of abuse of immigrants by border patrol agents, many immigrants speak about how the border patrol has rescued them in the midst of life-threatening conditions, even in snowstorms.[21] When faced with freak snowstorms in the mountains just north of San Diego, border patrol agent Johnny Williams said, "It's not an issue of how many apprehensions you make, it's how you rescue stranded immigrants. It pulls at the heartstrings of every agent out there to see a young lady or anyone jeopardized by these conditions. When you find someone that didn't make it, it's an experience you never forget."[22] Some immigration officials admit to feeling caught between the rock of government policy and the hard place of human suffering.

Others are more critical of the border safety initiatives, for they argue that they are token initiatives that mask a fundamentally unjust border strategy that violates human rights. As lawyer Claudia Smith says, "There is no way you can protect immigrants when you have a political policy that pushes them into vast expanses of hell."[23] With temperatures soaring into the 120-degree range in the summer, Smith believes that the current government policies do not protect but they endanger the lives of the immigrant.[24] They endanger them because the U.S. "prevention through deterrence" policy has not diminished immigration but simply pushed immigrants like Roberto into more dangerous and life-threatening routes.

Los Muertos: The Voice of the Dead

Many people each year lose their lives in the process of crossing the border. Yet we rarely hear anything about these deaths. They die swimming the canals, dehydrating in the deserts, or suffering through snakebites or even neo-nazi and vigilante groups. Many die in the deserts, without anyone even knowing they are there. "When I brought people across last week," said Jesus Garcia, "I passed someone who died on the way. Birds were picking at its flesh, and animals had eaten away at its arms and legs."[25] If they are discovered at all, they are often unidentifiable, leaving the families in the dark about their whereabouts. Such bodies are often buried in cemeteries like the one in Holtville, California, where they are put in the back of a burial ground, next to a garbage dump, without a marker, with just a brick that says, "John Doe," or "Jane Doe." It is sobering to think that after all they have gone through, this is how many come to the end of their lives—and at such young ages. Many of these young immigrants who die are in their teens and twenties.

Some newspapers have begun to chronicle these immigrant deaths, which in some regions have risen over 1000 percent in the last couple of years: "At least seven Mexican Immigrants died and more than 50 others were rescued in rural San Diego County canyons Friday after a freak spring storm dropped a foot of snow on mountains that are a favorite route of illegal border crossers;"[26] "Six illegal immigrants sleeping on railroad tracks in south Texas, possibly to avoid snakebites, were killed when a Union Pacific freight train ran over them;"[27] "A stolen pickup truck filled with suspected illegal immigrants careened off a winding mountain road in rural Riverside County on Saturday as it attempted to evade border patrol agents, killing seven men and injuring 18 others...;"[28] "Six suspected illegal immigrants trying to escape border patrol agents plunged 120 feet into a ravine near San Diego on Saturday night, leaving one dead;"[29] "Abandoned by smugglers in driving snow, overcome by freezing temperatures or hit by cars as they crossed isolated roadways, eight illegal immigrants have died...as they tried to make their way across the treacherous terrain...."[30] The dynamics of Mexican immigration are full of stories like these. The most common cause of death is the canals, and others die from dehydration from desert heat, hypothermia from the cold temperatures in the mountains, or suffocating in confined spaces like box cars on trains or trucks. Some die from train or vehicle accidents. Others die from snakebites in the desert.

When people get bitten by a snake, and they are tens of miles from any help, in the middle of a desert-nowhere, their bodies often swell up and they are sometimes left behind to die by the group they are traveling with.

I'll never forget the time a mother came to me in Mexico and said, please, take my son with you when you go across the border. He is fifteen now and talented, and he has no future here in Mexico. At least he would have a chance up there. So I took him with me. And in the middle of the night, while we were sleeping on the ground, a rattlesnake came up and bit him. He started going into convulsions and there was nothing we could do. By morning he was dead. I felt so bad. And I just didn't have the heart to tell his mother. So I even wrote her for years in his name, so she would think he was still alive. Not a day goes by when I don't think about it. And, you know, sometimes I ask, why did this have to happen? And all I keep coming up with is that we were hungry.[31]

Some find passage through stowing away on trains or aboard any vehicle that can help them get across to the other side:

I've come across the border in a number of ways. Sometimes I've hid myself in a box-car full of flour. Other times I've stowed away on the inside tire-wall of a truck. And other times I've buried myself in a truckload of carrots. I find if I position myself in the right way, the carrots give me the most breathing space, because in between the carrots, I can still breathe pretty well.[32]

Others, like Joe in the movie, are not so lucky and are wounded or die from falling off or jumping from trains. Diego Aceves was barely nineteen when he was forced to immigrate because his mother had abandoned him; he had to make a living shining shoes and selling candies on the street. Seeking a better life, he came to the United States, crossed the border, and stowed away on a train. While the train was still moving, one of his companions shouted that immigration was near, and each jumped off the train. Never having jumped trains before, he got as close as he could to the tracks before jumping, but the undercarriage of the train caught his legs and the wheels of the train cut off his legs from just below the hip.

Yet even amid such tragedies, many immigrants do not have the luxury to mourn. When Joe died in the movie, Roberto did not have time to deal with his loneliness or his pain at the loss of his only companion in the United States. He needed to survive, and, as is brought out at the end of the movie in the junkyard, many are pressed to the breaking point. The immigrants have an economic gun at their backs, but as they face the prospect of immigration across the border, they often look down the nozzle of a tank. Since 1996, the border has become more and more militarized. As a result, more than 2,300 people have died making the dangerous trek from Mexico to the United States; more than a planeload of people die each year.[33] Because many deaths go unreported and undiscovered, the number of those who die trying to cross the border is presumably even more.[34] Until the United States dedicates resources to addressing the human costs of migration comparable to what it dedicates to the economic costs, many immigrants will continue to die in the process of crossing the Mexican-U.S. border. It is scandalous to think that an immigrant like Roberto dies each day since new and more restrictive border controls were implemented in 1994.

Joe: The Voice of American Culture

Those who are fortunate enough to make it across the border face further challenges, especially as they try to find work and integrate into society and the American culture. Joe is a complex character in *Alambrista* who functions as a composite character. Joe shepherds Roberto through the first stages of the socialization process into American life. He represents the many facets of the process of entering a new culture. On the one hand, he welcomes him. On the other hand, he teaches him how to leave his past behind. He teaches him the mannerisms of how to walk in the world as a "gringo," how to order food in a restaurant, and how to speak like an "American." One of the greatest costs of the process of immigration is not just Roberto's leaving his family behind but leaving his culture and history behind. Not afforded the benefit of a language school, he learns the English he needs to survive. The physical, psychological, emotional, and physical challenges are enormous. Gustavo Magala said, "Sometimes it can take you thirty days or longer to recover from the trauma of immigrating, but you don't really have any time to rest because you have to start work right away."

Not surprisingly, as Roberto goes through similar trials in the movie, he spends a large part of the first days in a complete daze, wandering around in a hungry stupor, drunk with the promise of a better life yet burdened by the painful realities of being an alien in a foreign land. He leaves Mexico because he cares for his family, but he arrives in the United States where people only care about the work he can do. He speaks words but is not understood. He hears them but does not understand. Like many immigrants, he does not even understand himself and how to put into words what he is experiencing. As Roberto struggles to find his way in the United States, we see the immigrant's experience of alienation, and alienation means feeling disconnected from major political, social, and even religious institutions. It also means being a stranger to others and even oneself.

El Contratista: The Voice of Corporate America

Another unnamed voice in the movie is the "person" behind the multinational corporation and the *contratistas* or supervisors who help make the capital machine function. Some of these hired overseers and their bosses often view immigrants as just arms and limbs without heart or soul, unrecognized bodies viewed in terms of their profit potential rather than their human potential. We can see the dynamics of corporate exploitation of the poor when Roberto acquires is in one of the fields. When the immigration patrols came on the scene, it was not because they were making daily rounds through the area. They came because the *contratistas* called them. After having exploited them for their labor, they had them deported so they would not have to pay them their wages. It is not uncommon for growers to use immigrants for their labor and then call immigration. Ironically, Roberto's own Mexican/Mexican American "brothers" are the ones that take advantage of him. This kind of exploitation still happens today. The immigrant is oppressed because he cannot speak, and if he speaks, others will take his place. "What about my pay?" protests Roberto. His pleas for justice fall on deaf ears as the *contratistas* drive away.

Throughout the movie, there are various scenes dealing with difficulties of labor, fieldwork, and exploitation of the vulnerable. Even today, California continues to be one of the major producers of fruit and vegetables in the country, and most of the work of tending and harvesting the crops is done by immigrant workers. One third of all agriculture in the United States comes from California. Eighty-five percent of all agricultural workers in California are Mexican workers, and 66 percent of these workers are undocumented. Imagine what would happen to the U.S. economy if suddenly people like Roberto did not show up for work?

Agriculture depends on Mexican labor, as we see in the end of the movie when Roberto tries to come back to the United States and he gets recruited by the *contratistas* and other corporate agents who benefit from their labor but often deny them living wages and human dignity.

As an illegal alien, he has no rights, and his cries for justice fall on deaf ears. For those who exploit, Roberto is a good business deal: He's cheap labor, and, if he complains, he can be manipulated through the threat of deportation. As in the initial work scene where he hides himself inside a water-trough pipe, he literally is hanging on for his life. "Things haven't really changed that much for our people," said José Ramirez, "We're really in a new epoch of the *hacienda*. While technically we are not enslaved, we still find ourselves oppressed by the multi-national corporations who abuse us because of our economic need."[35] Like in the movie, when workers strike, they are either dismissed or others are brought in to take their place. "For every field worker in this valley," said one man from the Coachella Valley in California, "there are ten who can take their place. The corporations have the upper hand, but when we have a problem, what can we do?"[36]

The low price of labor and difficulty of work makes fieldwork attractive to no one except the most desperate. Immigrants like Roberto do stoop labor in the burning sun and work amid poisonous pesticides for long, backbreaking hours under the burning rays of the sun so that people might have good fruit and vegetables at low prices. Even despite their difficulties of entering the country, immigrants go through extreme measures to cross the border in order to find jobs that no one wants or is willing to do regardless of the pay. What seems like a promotion for Roberto is a recipe for cancer. Exposed to chemicals that cause cancer, birth defects, and early death, many die early deaths. "Sometimes I come home at night," said Mario Rodriguez, who works in the fields, "and I have these painful coughing spells. I get these tremendous headaches from breathing in these chemicals all day. I mentioned it to my boss, but she doesn't do anything about it."[37] While there have been some changes in legislation since César Chávez fought for more just conditions for migrant workers, growers still find ways around these laws, and immigrants are still the ones who pay the greatest cost. Nonetheless, the immigrant's fingerprint is part of every vegetable that is eaten and every piece of fruit that is consumed each day.

Conclusion

The movie *Alambrista* is a prototype of the immigration drama that happens every day. Fathers leave their children, women are left behind, immigrants come looking for work, *coyotes* take advantage of their need and vulnerability, the border patrol chases them into the desert and mountains, many die along the way, and those who do make it are forced to work in low-paying, exploitative, high-risk jobs that no one wants except the desperate. The story of Roberto is not a new story. While many of the particular aspects of immigration have changed since the movie was made in the 1970s, many of the essential dimensions remain the same or have become even worse. Immigrants still break from home seeking a better life, and jobs on the horizon lure them to promises of a more dignified future. They are often aware of the costs of leaving home but staying home leaves them no options either. This is the story of Mexican immigrants today, but their voices are not unique. They echo the voices of almost every family in the United States, whose ancestors immigrated to the United States at one point or another and faced pains, insults, vulnerabilities and difficulties, and even death for the sake of a better life. Beneath the voices of the immigration drama, we hear the voice of the poor seeking to become full human beings. The tragedy of the immigrant, to paraphrase the words of the director Bob Young, is that while they often spend much of their time cultivating the soil, they are left with little to develop their human potential.

■

Discussion Questions

1. Which voice in the immigration drama is new to you? Which one most challenges you?

2. What is your own immigration heritage? What are some of the stories of your ancestors' journeys to the United States? In what ways are they similar or different from that of Roberto and his family and other immigrants today?

3. If you faced an economic situation similar to Roberto's (or other immigrants today), would you be willing to take similar risks for the sake of your family? Why or why not?

4. Is illegal immigration to the United States justified, even if one does not have proper documentation? Why or why not?

5. One of the chief causes of immigration is economic need. Is it justifiable for companies to pay immigrants below the minimum wage for the sake of better profits? Why or why not?

6. Do you agree with this statement: While much energy has gone into analyzing the economic costs of migration, little has gone into analyzing the human costs of migration. What do you see as the human costs of migration?

7. Discuss the following statement: "It is not possible to eat breakfast in the morning, or any meal of the day without eating food that has been brought there by immigrant labor." In what ways does your lifestyle depend on immigrant labor?

■

Notes

1. The voices in this article are based on actual conversations with immigrants but the names have been changed.

2. For more on voices of the immigrant, particularly as related to their spiritual lives, see Daniel Groody, *Border of Death, Valley of Life: An Immigrant Journey of Heart and Spirit* (Lanham, Md.: Rowman & Littlefield Press, 2002).

3. Mexicans who immigrate to the United States generally come from Mexican states where there is high unemployment, particularly Jalisco, Michoacán, Guanajuato, Durango, Zacatecas, and San Luis Potosí.

4. For more on Mexican migration streams and social and economic dimensions of the topic, see Jorge A. Bustamante, *Cruzar la línea: la migración de México a los Estados Unidos*, 1. ed. (México: Fondo de Cultura Económica, 1997).

5. Mexican immigrant, interview by author, 12 January 2000, tape recording, El Centro Detention Center, El Centro, California.

6. Even a cursory look at the global economy illustrates why migrants come to the United States. According to the United Nations, if the population of the world were proportioned out to one hundred people, 59 percent of the world's resources would be in the hands of six people, and *all six of these* would live in the United States. Of these one hundred, only one would have a computer and only one would have a college education.

   Other immigrants like Central Americans also have come to the United States because of political instability in their country. For more on this subject, see Leo R. Chavez, Estévan T. Flores, and Marta López Garza, "Migrants and Settlers: A Comparison of Undocumented Mexicans and Central Americans in the United States," *Frontera Norte* 1, no. 1 (1989): 49–75.

7. For a descriptive account of the beauty and poverty of Mexico, see John Annerino, *Dead in Their Tracks: Crossing America's Desert Borderlands* (New York: Four Walls Eight Windows, 1999).

8. Mexicans, on the whole, earn about one-fifth to one-fourth of the wages earned by inhabitants of the United States. See John H. Coatsworth, "Commentary on Enrique Dussel Peters' 'Recent Structural Changes in Mexico's Economy: A Preliminary Analysis of Some Sources,'" in *Crossings: Mexican Immigration in Interdisciplinary Perspectives,* edited by Marcelo M. Suárez-Orozco (Cambridge, Mass.: Harvard University, David Rockefeller Center for Latin American Studies, 1998), 75–78.

9. CONAPO (Consejo Nacional de Población), COLEF (El Colegio de la Frontera Norte), and STPS (Secretaría del Trabajo y Previsión Social), *Encuesta sobre Migración en la Frontera Norte* (Tijuana: El Colegio de la Frontera Norte, 1994).

10. Mexican immigrant, interview by author, 12 January 2000, tape recording, El Centro Detention Center, El Centro, California.

11. Mexican immigrant, interview by author, 19 January 2000, tape recording, El Centro Detention Center, El Centro, California.

12. Mexican immigrant, interview by author, 12 January 2000, tape recording, El Centro Detention Center, El Centro, California.

13. Anne-Marie O'Connor, "Conditions Turn More Perilous For Border Crossers," *Los Angeles Times,* 16 January 1999.

14. While both men and women immigrate to Mexico, over 85 percent of Mexican immigrants apprehended by U.S. immigration officials are male. U.S. Immigration officers Henry Rolon and Manuel Figueroa, interview by author, 18 January 2000, tape recording, U.S. Immigration offices, El Centro, California, 19 January 2000.

15. Mexican immigrant, interview by author, 12 January 2002, tape recording, Northern Indiana.

16. Mexican immigrant, interview by author, 18 January 2000, tape recording, Coachella, California.

17. Mexican immigrant, interview by author, 18 January 2000, tape recording, Coachella, California.

18. John Annerino, *Dead in Their Tracks: Crossing America's Desert Borderlands* (New York: Four Walls Eight Windows, 1999), 40–42.

19. Mexican immigrant, interview by author, 18 January 2000, tape recording, Coachella, California.

20. Mexican immigrant, interview by author, 19 January 2000, tape recording, El Centro Detention Center, El Centro, California.

21. Associated Press, "Border Patrol Agent Who Sank Raft Carrying People to Resign," *Los Angeles Times,* 12 December 1999, Sec. A, p. 14.

22. O'Connor, "Conditions Turn More Perilous For Border Crossers."

23. Interview by author, 21 April 2002, tape recording, Casa de Migrante, Tijuana, Mexico.

24. For a descriptive account of desert rescues of immigrants by the border patrol, see Annerino, *Dead in Their Tracks,* 82–101, 173–75.

25. Mexican immigrant, interview by author, 18 January 2000, tape recording, Coachella, California.

26. Ken Ellingwood, H. G. Reza, and James Rainey, "At Least 7 Migrants Perish in Cold," *Los Angeles Times,* 3 April 1999, Sec. A, p. 1.

27. Times Wire Reports, "Asleep on Tracks, 6 Immigrants Die," *Los Angeles Times,* 13 October 1998, Sec. A, p. 10.

28. Tony Perry, Josh Meyer, and Henry Weinstein, "7 Die as Truck Evading Border Agents Crashes," *Los Angeles Times,* 7 April 1996, Sec. A, p. 1.

29. Greg Miller, "6 Fleeing Border Patrol Fall Into Ravine; 1 Killed," *Los Angeles Times,* 22 January 1996, Sec. A, p. 3.

30. O'Connor, "Conditions Turn More Perilous For Border Crossers," Sec. A, p. 1.

31. Mexican immigrant, date unknown, San Antonio, Texas.

32. Mexican immigrant, interview by author, 23 January 2000, tape recording, Los Angeles, California.

33. Eschbach, "Death at the Border," 430–54.

34. While more than 1,600 people died between 1993 and 1997, these figures are arguably very conservative. These are the documented deaths, and the actual figures are much higher, given the fact that these estimates do not include those who die in the deserts and are buried in the sands, those who drown in the canals or rivers and float into the Gulf of Mexico, and those who die on the Mexican side of the border. See Eschbach, "Death at the Border," 430–54.

35. Mexican immigrant, interview by author, 23 January 2000, tape recording, Los Angeles, California.

36. Mexican immigrant, interview by author, 23 January 2000, tape recording, Los Angeles, California.

37. Mexican immigrant, interview by author, 18 January 2000, tape recording, Coachella, California.

Operation Gatekeeper

The War against the *Alambristas* of the 1990s

Bill Ong Hing

Introduction

Since the institution of the U.S. border patrol's Operation Gatekeeper along the Mexico-California border in 1994, more than 750 migrants have died trying to cross this segment of the border,[1] mostly from environmental causes such as hypothermia, heat stoke, and drowning.[2] These deaths are the direct result of the philosophy of "control through deterrence" embodied in Operation Gatekeeper, which has closed off traditional corridors of entrance used by undocumented migrants that were far less treacherous.[3]

In this essay, I review the development and background of Operation Gatekeeper and its related programs and its effects. The hope is to understand where Operation Gatekeeper fits into the scheme of the movement of Mexican migrants to the United States and to question whether Gatekeeper is really the best way to go about doing business on the Southwest border.

The Development of Operation Gatekeeper

The San Diego Sector of the Immigration and Naturalization Service Border Patrol covers the section of the U.S.-Mexican border that historically has been the preferred site of entry for those entering the United States without inspection.[4]

The sector contains sixty-six miles of international border.[5] Tijuana, Mexico's third largest city, lies directly south of San Diego, California, the sixth largest city in the United States.[6] A smaller Mexican city, Tecate, is situated in the eastern end of the sector.[7]

In 1994, over 450,000 apprehensions of illicit border crossers were made in the San Diego sector.[8] This number far surpassed the sectors with the next-highest apprehensions: Tucson (139,473) and McAllen, Texas (124,251).[9] In the period prior to the end of 1994, undocumented border crossers in the San Diego sector commonly entered in the western part of the sector near the city of San Diego. Often many of these individuals traveled through private property, and some were even seen darting across busy freeways near the international border inspection station. Clearly, most of the illicit crossers entered along the fourteen-mile area from Imperial Beach (at the Pacific Ocean) to the base of the Otay Mountains.[10] Most of that stretch involves "easy terrain and gentle climbs," where the crossing lasts only ten or fifteen minutes to a pick-up point.[11] Even individuals who were apprehended and turned back across the border were just as likely to attempt reentry in the westernmost part of the sector at that time.[12]

These highly visible border crossings resulted in tremendous public pressure on the Immigration and Naturalization Service (INS) to act. Residents of San Diego complained.[13] Anti-immigrant groups demanded action. Politicians decried the lack of border control. Thus, in his State of the Union speech on January 24, 1995, Clinton signaled a renewed get-tough policy against undocumenteds, including "mov[ing] aggressively to secure our borders more by hiring a record number of border guards," and "cracking down on illegal hiring."[14] Facing reelection in 1996, administration officials hoped that a renewed enforcement effort against undocumented aliens would help shore up the president's support among voters in California, who overwhelmingly passed the anti-immigrant Proposition 187 in 1994.[15]

Operation Gatekeeper was one of several operations that resulted from the Clinton administration's commitment to a new aggressive enforcement strategy for the border patrol.[16] In August 1994, INS Commissioner Doris Meissner approved a new national strategy for the border patrol.[17] The heart of the plan relied on a vision of "prevention through deterrence," in which a "decisive number of enforcement resources [would be brought] to bear in each major entry corridor" and the border patrol would "increase the number of agents on the line and make effective use of technology, raising the risk of apprehension high enough to be an effective deterrent."[18] The specific regional enforcement operations that resulted include (1) Operation Blockade (later renamed Hold the Line), which commenced in September 1993 in the Greater El Paso, Texas, areas;[19] (2) Operation Gatekeeper, which commenced in October 1994 south of San Diego, California; (3) Operation Safeguard, which also commenced in October 1994 in Arizona; and (4) Operation Rio Grande, which commenced in August 1997 in Brownsville, Texas.[20] The idea was to block traditional entry and smuggling routes with border enforcement personnel and physical barriers.[21] By cutting off traditional crossing routes, the strategy sought to deter migrants or at least to channel them into terrain less suited for crossing and more conducive to apprehensions.[22] To carry out the strategy, the border patrol was to concentrate personnel and resources in the areas of highest undocumented alien crossing, increase the time agents spent on border-control activities, increase use of physical barriers, and carefully consider the mix of technology and personnel needed to control the border.[23]

In the San Diego Sector, efforts would be concentrated on the popular fourteen-mile section of the border beginning from the Pacific Ocean (Imperial Beach) stretching eastward.[24] That stretch had been the focus of some resources before Gatekeeper. Steel fencing and bright lighting was already in place in sections of this corridor, erected in part with the assistance of the U.S. military.[25] Yet because of the persistent traffic of undocumented entrants along this corridor, phase I of Gatekeeper continued to concentrate on increased staffing and resources along the fourteen-mile area.[26]

As INS implemented its national border strategy, Congress supported these efforts; between 1993 and 1997, the INS budget for enforcement efforts along the southwest border doubled from $400 million to $800 million.[27] The number of border patrol agents along the southwest border increased from 3,389 in October 1993 to 7,357 by September 1998—an increase of 117 percent.[28] State-of-the-art technology, including new surveillance systems using electronic sensors linked with low-light video cameras, infrared night-vision devices, and forward-looking infrared systems for border patrol aircraft were installed.[29]

Given these additional resources, Operation Gatekeeper build-up has been impressive. Before Gatekeeper, the San Diego sector had nineteen miles of fencing. By the end of 1999, fifty-two miles were fenced. Half of this fencing runs from the Pacific Ocean to the base of the Otay Mountains. Fourteen miles contain primary fencing (a ten-foot wall of corrugated steel landing mats left-over from the Vietnam War). Two back-up fences—each of them fifteen feet tall—have been constructed. The first back-up fence is made of concrete pillars. The second back-up fence is made of wire mesh, with support beams. Both are topped with wire. Almost twelve miles of this stretch are illuminated with stadium lights. Some fencing has been erected on sections of the Otay Mountains, as well as around various East San Diego County communities along the border.[30] The Department of Defense's Center for Low Intensity Conflicts as well as the Army Corps of Engineers have provided guidance to INS on the development of Gatekeeper features.[31]

In contrast, in areas other than San Diego, the construction has not been as significant. The El Centro sector covers 72 miles of the border, is sparsely populated on the U.S. side, and has only 7 miles of fence—all of it between the contiguous border cities of Calexico and Mexicali. Arizona has 17 miles of fencing—6 in the Yuma sector and 9 in the Tucson sector. That fencing was erected exclusively in the towns and cities. Texas has the Rio Grande river and 7 miles of fencing in the El Paso/Ciudad Juarez area—2 miles of primary and 5 of secondary. Thus, 73 miles of fencing has been erected on the 2,000-mile border, and the 66-mile San Diego sector has 72 percent of it, as well as 54 percent of the illumination.[32] The 144-mile-long San Diego and El Centro sectors have almost a third of the border patrol agents stationed on the 2,000-mile Southwest border.[33]

The Results of Operation Gatekeeper

In implementing its national strategy beginning in 1994, INS made a key assumption about its "prevention through deterrence" approach: "[a]lien apprehensions will decrease as [the] border patrol increases control of the border."[34] In other words, INS anticipated that as the show of force escalated by increasing agents, lighting, and fencing, people would be discouraged from entering without inspection so the number of apprehensions naturally would decline. In fact, the border patrol predicted that within five years, a substantial drop in apprehension rates border-wide would result.[35] The deterrence would be so great that "many will consider it futile to continue to attempt illegal entry."[36] These assumptions and predictions have not been borne out.

Apprehension levels have not declined. The national enforcement strategies began with Operation Gatekeeper in San Diego and Operation Blockade in El Paso in 1994. True, the apprehension levels for those two sectors were considerably lower in 1998 than in 1993 (e.g., 531,689 apprehended in San Diego in 1993 compared to 248,092 in 1998).[37] However, the apprehension levels surged in El Centro, Yuma, and Tucson during the same period (e.g., from 92,639 to 387,406 in Tucson; 30,058 to 226,695 in El Centro; and 23,548 to 76,195 in Yuma).[38] In 1999, apprehensions at the California border fell by more than 65,000 from the previous year, but increased by more than 100,000 at the Arizona border.[39] The January 2000 apprehension figures along the Arizona border were 30,000 more than the previous January—a jump of 72 percent and 56 percent in the Yuma and Tucson sectors, respectively.[40] From 1994 to 1999, total apprehension statistics along the southwest border actually increased by 57 percent![41] The increase continues. In Arizona, 563,000 crossers were apprehended in 1999, but in 2000 the figure rose to 724,000.[42] For the first three quarters of 2000, the number of apprehensions is 10 percent higher than for the same period in 1999.[43] In 1994, the apprehensions in the San Diego sector totaled 450,152, but dropped to 151,678 in fiscal year 2000. Meanwhile, as migrants were being pushed east, the apprehension figure for the El Centro sector skyrocketed from 27,654 in 1994 to 238,127 in 2000.[44] But a clearer picture developed even farther eastward. From October 1994 to September 2000, there were 88,001 fewer apprehensions at the California border, but 564,409 more at the Arizona border and 1,888,170 more at the Texas border.[45]

In short, the apprehension data confirm that what Operation Gatekeeper has actually achieved is to move the undocumented foot traffic relatively out of the public eye. Empirical research demonstrates that undocumented Mexicans keep trying to enter until they are successful. In sending communities restudied since Gatekeeper began, most prospective migrants "said that they would only consider changing their destination within the United States (avoiding California, for example) rather than foregoing migration altogether."

Migrants have learned quickly to avoid the heavily fortified areas and now cross "in places where their probability of apprehension is no higher than it used to be."[46] It's safe to say that border enforcement strategies begun in 1994 are "affecting migration patterns, but not preventing unauthorized entry."[47]

The "prevention through deterrence" strategy has also bolstered the smuggling industry. As operations were stepped up, most migrants turned to smugglers. This helps explain why most migrants attempting unauthorized entry succeed despite significantly more agents and technology on the border.[48] The INS did not foresee the extent of this effect. Commissioner Meissner said that architects of a nationwide border crackdown, launched in California in 1994, expected that hostile terrain and deadly weather conditions in remote mountains and deserts along the 2,000-mile U.S.-Mexico frontier would act as a greater deterrent to illegal crossings than has been the case.[49] Yet, in its 1995 report, the U.S. Commission on Immigration Reform noted that given the difficult terrain crossers faced after Gatekeeper, undocumented aliens "would need guides to cross such terrain, jacking up the cost of illegal entry."[50] In fact, get-tough campaigns like Operation Gatekeeper are creating new opportunities for sophisticated immigrant smuggling rings with ties to organized crime and drug traffickers. Smugglers have increased their fees and have turned to more sophisticated smuggling tactics.[51] Before Operation Gatekeeper, smugglers charged about $300 in the San Diego sector for help in crossing and transportation to Los Angeles; now the charge is $800 to $1,200.[52]

Given increased apprehension rates and greater reliance on smugglers, one could hardly say that the INS has done much to attain its primary goal of controlling the border. Yet these results may say more about the will and desire of undocumented aliens to enter the United States than about any particular agency's inability to control the border.

Entering the Dark Side

The ineffectiveness of INS to "control the border" after six years of a new strategy would be easy enough to dismiss in a "so what else is new" attitude were it not for a dark side of border enforcement that has resulted from Operation Gatekeeper. Certainly, southwest border control has always had an evil, racist dark side, with its targeting of Mexican migration during a thirty-year period when Mexicans make up far less than half the undocumented population in the United States.[53] However, the tragedy of Gatekeeper is the direct link of its "prevention through deterrence" strategy to an absolutely horrendous rise in the number of deaths among border crossers, who have been forced to attempt entry over terrain that even INS knows to present "mortal danger," due to extreme weather conditions and rugged terrain.[54]

As Operation Gatekeeper was implemented, closing the Imperial Beach corridor, the border-crossing traffic moved east. Frustrated crossers moved first to Brown Field and Chula Vista, and subsequently to the eastern sections of the San Diego sector.[55] Before Gatekeeper began in 1994, crossers were just as likely to make their second try in the westernmost part of the sector; but that changed very quickly. By January 1995, only 14 percent were making their second try near Imperial Beach. The illicit border traffic had moved "into unfamiliar and unattractive territory."[56] Clearly, the increasing number of deaths by dehydration and exposure was the result of concentrated efforts to block the normal, easier crossing points, forcing migrants "to take greater risks in less populated areas," as migration was redirected rather than deterred by Gatekeeper.[57]

The death statistics are revealing. In 1994, 23 migrants died along the California-Mexico border. Of the 23, 2 died of hypothermia or heat stroke and 9 from drowning. By 1998, the annual total was 145 deaths—68 from hypothermia or heat stoke and 52 from drowning. Figures for 1999 followed this unfortunate trend, and in 2000, 84 were heat stroke or hypothermia caualties.[58] In 1994, only 1 border crosser died of heat stroke; within five years 140 were heat-stroke casualties.[59] The count for the year 2000 continues. INS estimated that 369 immigrants died crossing the U.S.-Mexico border during the year; of those, 100 died crossing the desert along the Sonora-Arizona border.[60]

Why the radical surge in deaths? The new routes are death traps. The correlation between increasing deaths and Gatekeeper's closure of the westernmost corridors is clear. The border patrol chief has stressed that although the distances migrants must traverse in places like Texas are enormous, California has the "more difficult terrain." In fact, the San Diego and El Centro sectors encompass three of the four places considered by the border patrol as "the most hazardous areas," i.e., East San Diego County, the Imperial Desert, and the All-American Canal. The fourth is Kennedy County in Texas.[61] The INS recognizes the challenges of the new routes: rugged canyons and high desert, remote, desolate stretches, and risks of dehydration and exposure.[62] On the other hand, the fourteen-mile area from Imperial Beach to the base of the Otay Mountains, the less-rigorous original route, is "easy terrain and gentle climbs." A typical crossing there lasted only ten to fifteen minutes from point of crossing to pick-up point. The eastern mountain-route crossings can last anywhere from twelve hours to four days.[63] The Otay Mountains are "extremely rugged, and include steep, often precipitous, canyon walls and hills reaching 4,000 feet." Extreme temperatures ranging from freezing cold in the winter to searing heat in the summer can kill the unprepared traveler.[64] The Tecate Mountains are full of steep-walled canyons and rocky peaks. Nighttime temperatures can drop into the twenties and snow can fall to altitudes as low as eight hundred feet. From mid-October to mid-April, there is a greater than 50-percent probability of below-freezing temperatures.[65] The All-American Canal parallels the border for forty-four of its eighty-five Imperial County miles. It is unfenced and unlighted, twenty-one feet deep, and nearly as wide as a football field. It has strong currents, and is one of the most polluted rivers in the United States.[66]

Border patrol agents acknowledge that the number of bodies recovered may only be indications of a much larger death toll; many bodies simply have not been discovered in the rugged territory.[67]

An even more troubling aspect of the deaths that have resulted from Operation Gatekeeper is that INS officials knew or should have known that increased environmental deaths would result. Furthermore, now that the evidence is clear that such deaths have increased as a result of Gatekeeper, INS continues to implement its strategy, knowing that additional deaths under the same circumstances will continue.

As the INS developed its plan to cut off the westernmost corridor—the foundation for Operation Gatekeeper—knowing that foot traffic would be pushed toward the east, its "Strategic Plan for 1994 and Beyond" described the heat it anticipated that migrants would encounter as "searing." Overwhelming evidence reveals that INS officials were aware that border crossers would continue their attempts to enter while and even after Gatekeeper developed, and officials also knew about the life-threatening circumstances that border crossers would face.

The Immorality of Operation Gatekeeper

Assigning Blame

Whose fault is it that hundreds of migrants have died of environmental causes along the California-Mexico border since the implementation of Operation Gatekeeper? Certainly, the fact that INS officials are aware of the fact that their policies have resulted in these deaths is troubling.[68]

Smugglers ■ The chief INS response to the question of "Who's to blame?" is "the smugglers." INS officials and even Mexican authorities have pointed fingers at smugglers when it comes to migrant deaths. The border patrol says smugglers paid by the migrants fail to warn their customers adequately of the harsh conditions and the long journey through the desert;[69] the coyotes falsely tell people the trips will be short and that little water will be needed.[70] But are the smugglers really to blame here? True, Operation Gatekeeper has bolstered smuggling fees and has made smugglers indispensable to many who want to enter.[71] Gatekeeper has led to the environment that breeds expanded use and reliance upon smugglers.[72] Without Gatekeeper, the use of smugglers would decline. So blaming the smugglers begs the question and smacks of scape-goating. Isn't Gatekeeper more of the problem than are the smugglers? Smugglers are all too often merchants of death, but that does not absolve Operation Gatekeeper from its proximate role in these deaths.[73]

Employer Sanctions ■ Blame for continued migration that leads to deaths is also assigned to the failure to enforce employer sanctions laws. Some critics and supporters of Gatekeeper, alike, point to the failure to prosecute employ-ers for hiring undocumented workers as part of the problem. The conventional wisdom goes like this: if the country seriously enforces the laws that make it illegal for employers to knowingly hire undocumented workers, employers will stop hiring undocumented workers, undocumented migrants will get the mes-sage and stop migrating, and environmental deaths at the border will disap-pear. Thus, INS Commissioner Meissner argued that border enforcement should be coupled with workplace disincentives.[74] Yet, between 1992 and 1997,

INS fines levied against employers decreased from 2,000 to 888, and fines levied decreased from $17 million to $8 million.[75] And the Department of Labor had only nine hundred investigators to enforce workplace requirements such as minimum-wage laws, in 7 million U.S. workplaces in 1995.[76] Even representatives of California Rural Legal Assistance Foundation—ardent critics of Operation Gatekeeper—while not supporting employer sanctions, note the inconsistencies of U.S. policies: "During the last five years the INS has done virtually nothing to counteract the employer magnet that pulls migrants here—the undeniable hypocrisy of its immigration policy. For example, since the start of Gatekeeper, only a half-dozen employers of undocumented laborers have been prosecuted in either of California's border counties."[77] In short, given the fact that government officials are aware of the dangers they have created, failing to enforce labor laws is dishonest and immoral.

The logic of the "enforce employer sanctions to reduce unlawful entries" argument is appealing at first blush. However, the complexities of the underground economy in which undocumented aliens work suggest that the conventional wisdom is too simplistic. Could the employment of undocumented workers really be stopped? What would it take? Why is a healthy bit of skepticism in order at the suggestion that the employment of undocumented workers could be stopped? And what of the fortitude, drive, and unbelievable desire to migrate north among border crossers given the economic disparities that all parties have recognized? Can that really be nullified? In other words, would the enforcement of employer sanctions really deter the employment of undocumented workers and deter their continued migration? Doubtful. Assuming that employer sanctions will discourage further migration is unrealistic. Employer-sanctions enforcement—even with greater resources—amounts to little in the face of the overwhelming push-pull factors related to family reunification,[78] historical patterns of migration,[79] and particularly economic disparities.

The Mexican Economy ■ Before blaming or assigning fault, examining the reason for the continued flow of Mexican migrants is helpful. The primary cause of the continued flow of undocumented migration from Mexico is economic. This is not a new observation,[80] but the timing of Operation Gatekeeper could not have been worse. On December 20, 1994—about two months after the institution of Gatekeeper—the Mexican peso was devalued, immediately plummeting 40 percent.[81] The devaluation, which came on the heels of an ill-fated privatization of eighteen state-owned banks in 1992, threw Mexico into its worst economic crisis since the Great Depression; a million people lost their jobs and thousands of borrowers stopped paying their loans as annual interest rates neared 100 percent![82] Within six months, Mexico's annual inflation rate jumped 90 percent, and 17 percent of the nation's 34 million workers could not find work for even fifteen hours a week.[83] Unemployment doubled and wages sank.[84]

The attraction of the United States is obvious. The strong economy in the United States pays Mexican workers eight to nine times more than what can be earned in Mexico. As the Mexican Consul in Douglas, Arizona observes, "These are people trying to get a better job so they can provide for their families, so they can improve their lot."[85] Specific aspects of the Mexican economy—loss in value of the peso, the cut in federal spending, increased taxes, and slowed job growth—have increased the pressure to migrate north.[86] In 1993, 31 percent of Mexicans were considered extremely poor; by 1996 the figure was 50 percent.[87]

Migrant traffic will not be stopped with the installation of more fences. Human rights advocates who have interviewed the migrants sense that they are desperate to cross. "If we mined the border, people would be blown to pieces trying to avoid the land mines as they continued to come."[88] Given the economic realities, even though the risks have increased, the potential gain from successfully crossing the border will always be greater than having nearly nothing back home. In a sense, the only choice for many crossers is to attempt the journey. The domestic economic crisis has forced Mexico's poorest citizens to leave their homes because they cannot earn enough—even when they have jobs—to feed their families. And more of the same can be expected in the near future.

Changes afoot in Mexico are important to keep in mind. Experts on Mexico and the border note that within the next fifteen years, demographic and economic factors within Mexico are likely to reduce emigration pressures. The birthrate is declining and fewer new job seekers will be entering the labor force. By 2015, the supply-push emigration pressures from the areas with some of the best network connection to the United States will diminish.[89] Until then, the United States should recognize that its economy and the lower strata of

Mexico's have become completely interdependent.[90] The forces that cause legal and illegal migration are powerful. Without positive, long-term changes in the root causes that prompt undocumented migration, such as improvements in the Mexican economy, the "push" and "pull" factors will remain strong.

The North American Free Trade Agreement (NAFTA) certainly has not been the short-term solution to the economic crisis in Mexico nor has it stemmed the flow of migrants north. In fact, NAFTA may have contributed by creating economic displacement in Mexico.[91] Apparently, jobs created in Mexico by NAFTA are not as numerous as the jobs eliminated thus far.[92] NAFTA has had to contend with the long-established precept that the U.S. demand for immigrant labor is structurally imbedded in our economy.[93] One agricultural economist observes that the process of integrating economies tends to stimulate migration in the short and medium term, generating a migration hump that lasts five to fifteen years—there is a temporary increase in migration.[94]

Other Motivations ■ The economic imbalance between Mexico and the United States may be only one important reason for the flow of migrants. When migrants who cross near El Paso are contrasted with those near San Diego, the difference lies much deeper than the more difficult terrain facing the San Diego crossers; somehow those crossing in the San Diego sector have higher motivation. According to Commissioner Meissner, unlike El Paso,

> only 1% of the people that have crossed in San Diego habitually will have been daily crossers. Ninety-nine percent are crossers destined for the interior of the country, many for Los Angeles but many for other places in the United States, and they are by and large from deep within Mexico, so they have expended extraordinary resources in relative terms to get to the border, and they will try again and again. So what you have is a situation that is not only one of terrain and tactics, but also one of the motivation of the people that are trying to cross. In San Diego, we think that . . . we have four kinds of crossers. We have people who are . . . trying for the first time, possibly as a result of devaluation [or] other push factors within Mexico. . . . The second group is [composed] of regular crossers who cross

several times every year for periodic jobs in California. Those are somewhat harder to stop.... The third and fourth groups are very difficult. This third group [is composed] of seasonal workers who have for decades.... come to the U.S. to work seasonal jobs. They are sophisticated in that they are able to cross many times. If they can't do it one way, they will do it another way.... Those are people who have families in the United States, people who although they may be from another country ... identify their residence as a U.S. residence. They live here illegally, and they have very, very high motivation. So you have a much more complex situation where it takes a more sustained effort in order to achieve deterrence.[95]

Others simply split undocumented Mexicans into two groups: those who are entering as temporary agricultural workers, and those who intend to remain in the United States. Whichever categorization one chooses, the economics, history, and sociology of the border strongly suggest that the United States is responsible for a pattern of dependency that has developed—a pattern that is not only economic.[96] The pattern of Mexican migration that has been witnessed in spite of Operation Gatekeeper's hurdles is one that was established long, long ago.[97] While attributing the current flow to economics and uneven wages makes sense,[98] the flow is part of a historical pattern attributable to a complex mixture of political, economic, social, and cultural factors developed generations ago.[99]

Gatekeeper is a misguided response to the situation. We have a problem and a sociocultural phenomenon. The problem is the economic situation in Mexico. The phenomenon is the long, historical travel patterns between Mexico and the United States, coupled with the interdependency of the two regions. Migration from Mexico is the manifestation of the economic problem and social phenomenon. The use of force (and violence) represented by Gatekeeper does nothing to address the economic problem.[100] It truly is a blind, unthinking response to human difficulties. It does nothing to get rid of the social/economic problem; instead it kills individuals who are caught up in the problem. Gatekeeper represents a false *practical* solution to moral questions raised by the flow of migrants pushed and pulled by economic and social phenomena. The migrants have become objectified, or problematized and demonized,[101] allowing proponents to skirt the moral questions. Thus, Gatekeeper has moral implications in an abstract way (as in "what kind of people are we to permit such things to happen to?") and in a concrete way (the death toll and the hardship for Gatekeeper's victims, and the attitude of those who enforce it, and live with it).

The Racism of Gatekeeper and Police Power

Conflicts that are at bottom about race often get masked by language about "problems." The "problem" in this case is one of people coming across the border. Problematizing undocumented migrants allows us to demonize them,[102] and, in turn, the racism involved can be ignored. But in fact, the migrants involved are human beings—Mexican human beings. With Gatekeeper, the stories of human existence (and struggle, and difficulty) are solved by police power, and when we ask, "How is this possible?" the question feels naïve because that lost human existence is viewed through a very particular racist lens and does not have a powerful meaning or resonance. Thus, in the popular image, the border patrol is eliminating a problem. But in a humanized image, the border patrol is eliminating—killing—people.

Reverting to Pre-Gatekeeper Days

Is the country willing to revert back to pre-Gatekeeper strategies? Given the results of Gatekeeper—its ineffectiveness in stemming the flow, while causing danger to crossers—one way to defuse the situation might be to back away from today's enforcement strategy. Gatekeeper has caused an untenable situation, while the value to border control is not clear. Under earlier models, in which some illicit immigration was allowed, there were more opportunities for Mexican workers to enter legally. The obvious question is "why not revert to the old strategy?" It was no less effective than Gatekeeper and relatively few deaths occurred at the California border before October 1, 1994. The only reason for not reverting to the old strategy is the political advantage that has been realized from moving the migrant foot traffic out of the public eye.

Migrant border deaths raise important ethical questions. The persons who die are the citizens of Mexico, other countries in Latin America, and elsewhere. The policies that lead to those deaths are set by another country, the United States. The United States claims sovereign authority to control its own borders. Yet to do so creates conditions leading to a relatively high volume of death among migrants. If these were U.S. citizens who were dying, mortality bills this high would doubtless raise considerable controversy. As it is, migrant deaths have received relatively little attention. Gatekeeper has not ameliorated the fundamental problem of impoverished immigrants flocking to this country surreptitiously to take low-wage jobs that are readily available to them. Is it time to acknowledge that physical measures alone never will succeed in securing the border? These types of operations do not solve the problem, yet they produce the obvious consequence of placing human beings in mortal danger. Does moral responsibility for the creation of hazardous conditions that increase the probability of death extend across international boundaries?

Given the immediate intractability of the economic imbalance, the resulting deaths, and the billions of dollars invested in border-control measures, does the continuation of Operation Gatekeeper really make sense? The resulting deaths, without signs of impact on apprehension rates, should tell us to slow down, back up, and figure out what Gatekeeper is. Gatekeeper has been a tragic, destructive undertaking. It should be viewed as a moral undertaking rather than as an instrument for producing useful effects. In that light, we soon realize that the focus of energy has been at the wrong place. In fact the concentration should be on the mainstream activities in Mexico related to its economy, banks, and job markets, as well as on U.S. immigration laws that would facilitate the travel of individuals seeking family unity. Tellingly, a former INS General Counsel now concedes that Operation Gatekeeper does not "deter the way we thought it would. Operation Gatekeeper has become our Vietnam, mistakenly thinking that if we added just a little more, then a little more, that we would get results."[103] To paraphrase one socio-legal commentator, the things that Gatekeeper has done well, such as "scapegoating, venting frustration, hardening social divisions, and offering popular, repressive responses to social problems—are in the long term destructive" of the long-term goal of assisting Mexico out of its poor economic times and working with the tradition of migrant Mexican workers who benefit from the movement, but who also benefit U.S. society.[104]

Reverting to pre-Gatekeeper enforcement strategies would be no less effective, in terms of apprehensions and deterrence, but with so many fewer deaths—deaths resulting from the knowing participation of INS officials. The less dangerous routes to entry would be reopened and the need for high-priced smugglers reduced. Does this amount to "throwing in the towel" on border enforcement? No, this amounts to at least a more humane policy that would be just as effective in terms of limiting the number of illicit border crossers as the Operation Gatekeeper strategy.

Conclusion

The issue presented by Operation Gatekeeper is not whether the United States has a right to control its border. Rather, the issue is whether the United States has abused that right with a strategy designed to maximize the physical risks, thereby ensuring that hundreds of migrants would die. The dark side of Operation Gatekeeper reveals "knowledge" of the high probability of deaths on the part of the U.S. government officials. The INS has knowingly created a death trap to control the Southwest border. The push-pull factors that continue to drive undocumented migration do not appear to be subsiding. The safest routes to cross the border surreptitiously have been foreclosed. INS officials recognize that the terrain over which crossers are now forced to enter creates mortal danger. Yet instead of retreating from its life-threatening strategy, INS forges on, creating even greater physical challenges for crossers. The picture is reprehensible. Operation Gatekeeper is not simply a law-enforcement operation that has created a harsh result. Gatekeeper is a law enforcement operation that imposes a death sentence on individuals—principally Mexicans—who simply are seeking a better life by violating an international border.

■

Questions for the Reader/Viewer

1 How does Roberto's entry into the United States in the film differ from what he might face if he tried to enter today?

2 Has the role of smugglers changed since the time period in the film and after the implementation of Operation Gatekeeper?

3 Who is to blame for the deaths that have occurred along the U.S.-Mexico border since the implementation of Operation Gatekeeper?

■

Notes

1. California Rural Legal Assistance Foundation Border Project, "Operation Gatekeeper Fact Sheet," at http://www.stopgatekeeper.org/English/index.html.

2. Ibid.

3. "Petition to the Inter-American Commission on Human Rights of the Organizations of American States, Alleging Violations of Human Rights of Persons in Danger at the United States-Mexico Border by Actions and Inaction of the United States of America Pursuant to its 'Operation Gatekeeper,'" submitted on behalf of petitioners, American Civil Liberties Union of San Diego and Imperial Counties and California Rural Legal Assistance Foundation against the United States of America, February 9, 1999 (hereinafter "OAS Petition"), 40-48.

4. Gustavo De La Vina, U.S. Border Patrol San Diego Sector Strategic Planning Document, April 29, 1994, 1.

5. Ibid., 3.

6. Ibid.

7. Ibid.

8. See California Rural Legal Assistance Foundation (CRLAF) Border Project, "Apprehension Statistics for the Southwest Border," (chart prepared by California Rural Legal Assistance Foundation), at http://www.stopgatekeeper.org/English/index.html.

9. Ibid.

10. Border Patrol report, "Operation Gatekeeper: 3 Years of Results in a Glance" (1997).

11. Ibid.

12. "Frustrating Illegal Crossers at Imperial Beach and Moving the Traffic Eastward," INS Fact Sheet, October 17, 1997.

13. "State's Great Debate: Some Border Residents Simply Accept the Unlawful Journeys of Undocumented Immigrants as a Way of Life; Others Want Preventive Measures Taken," *Press Enterprise,* November 6, 1994, A1. Many wanted the El Paso project Operation Blockade duplicated in San Diego.

14. "Clinton Vows More Immigration Enforcement," 72 *Interpreter Releases* 72 (January 30, 1995): 169.

15. "Clinton Will Seek Spending to Curb Aliens, Aides Say: Political Balancing Act," *New York Times,* January 22, 1995, A1. Matthew Jardine, "Operation Gatekeeper," *Peace Review* 10 (1998): 329, 333.

16. Early in 1993, the Clinton Administration's Office of National Drug Control Policy commissioned a study of new methods to increase border security from the Sandia National Laboratories, which is a federal government-supported facility devoted to research for the military. The study recommended that the border patrol focus on preventing illegal entries by deterring them rather than trying to apprehend undocumenteds once they have entered the country. The Sandia report recommended various measures to increase the difficulty of illegal entry, including the installation of multiple physical barriers, the use of advanced electronic surveillance equipment, and so forth. Wayne A. Cornelius, *Death at the Border: The Efficacy and "Unintended" Consequences of U.S. Immigration Control Policy, 1993-2000* (Stanford: Stanford University Press), 3.

17. U.S. Border Patrol, "Border Patrol Strategic Plan: 1994 and Beyond—National Strategy," July 1994.

18. Ibid., 6.

19. Operation Blockade was initiated by the head of the local border patrol in El Paso on his own initiative in 1993. Initially, his ideas of deterrence were opposed by the INS central officials in Washington. In El Paso, Texas, the regional border patrol supervisor, Sylvestre Reyes, had his own ideas about what to do. His idea was to station his agents in closely spaced vehicles, right along the Rio Grande, and keep them there continuously, thereby intimidating would-be illegal entrants from even trying to cross. With only half-hearted approvals from his superiors in Washington, Reyes implemented his strategy, and it had dramatic short-term results, causing apprehensions to plummet within the El Paso sector. This outcome was noticed by the media and Congress; and the INS soon

found itself under great pressure to replicate what was immediately dubbed as the "successful" El Paso experiment along other segments of the border, beginning with San Diego County. This set off a chain of policy decisions, leading to the establishment of concentrated enforcement operations.

20. "OAS Petition," 16, n. 4.

21. U.S. Border Patrol, "Border Patrol Strategic Plan: 1994," 6–9.

22. Ibid., 7; U.S. General Accounting Office, report, "Illegal Immigration: Status of Southwest Border Strategy Implementation," May 1999, p. 3.

23. Ibid.

24. Ibid., 1, 4, 8.

25. Ibid.

26. Ibid., 8.

27. "Operation Gatekeeper: New Resources, Enhanced Results," INS Fact Sheet, July 14, 1998.

28. GAO, "Illegal Immigration: Status of Southwest Border Strategy Implementation," 7.

29. INS Fact Sheet, February 2, 1998.

30. Letter from Claudia E. Smith to Mary Robinson, UN High Commissioner for Refugees, November 19, 1999.

31. GAO, "Illegal Immigration: Status of Southwest Border Strategy Implementation," 12.

32. Letter, Smith to Robinson, November 19, 1999.

33. Claudia E. Smith, Operation Gatekeeper Report, May 10, 2000, pp. 17-18.

34. De La Vina, "Border Patrol Strategic Plan," 4.

35. Letter from Claudia E. Smith to Mary Robinson, UN High Commissioner for Refugees, September 30, 2000.

36. De La Vina, "Border Patrol Strategic Plan," 4-5.

37. GAO, "Illegal Immigration: Status of Southwest Border Strategy Implementation," 17–18, 20.

38. Ibid., 18–20.

39. Letter, Smith to Robinson, November 19, 1999.

40. Letter, Smith to Robinson, September 30, 2000.

41. CRLAF, "Apprehension Statistics for the Southwest Border," October 7, 1999, at http://www.stopgatekeeper.org/English/index.html.

42. Rosenberg Foundation, report, "Changing Environment," Nov. 22, 2000, 11.

43. Letter, Smith to Robinson, September 30, 2000.

44. CRLAF, "Apprehension Statistics for the Southwest Border."

45. Ibid.

46. Smith, "Operation Gatekeeper Report," 21–22.

47. Ibid., 7.

48. Ibid.

49. Ken Ellingwood, "INS Chief Targets Risky Rural Crossings," *Los Angeles Times,* September 7, 2000.

50. U.S. Commission on Immigration Reform, report, "Border Law Enforcement and Removal Initiatives in San Diego California," 1995, 3.

51. GAO, "Illegal Immigration: Status of Southwest Border Strategy Implementation," 16.

52. Cornelius, *Death at the Border.*

53. Kevin Johnson, "Race Matters: Immigration Law and Policy Scholarship, Law in the Ivory Tower, and the Legal Indifference of the Race Critque," *University of Illinois Law Review* (2000): 525.

54. Immigration and Naturalization Service, report, "Border Management Overview," September 20, 1999.

55. INS Fact Sheet, February 2, 1998.

56. Ibid.

57. Tom Zeller, "Migrants Take Their Chances on a Harsh Path of Hope," *New York Times,* March 18, 2001, 4-14.

58. CRLAF, "Operation Gatekeeper Fact Sheet."

59. Ibid.

60. Rosenberg Foundation, *Changing Environment.*

61. Letter, Smith to Robinson, November 19, 1999.

62. Border Patrol, "3 Years of Results in a Glance."

63. Ibid.

64. Ibid.

65. Smith, Operation Gatekeeper Report, 23-24.

66. Ibid., 25. One migrant had to have his foot amputated because an injury became infected while crossing the river.

67. Letter from Claudia E. Smith to Jorge Taiana, of the Organization of American States, July 22, 1999.

68. Are the migrants themselves at fault for attempting to cross in spite of harrowing circumstances? Perhaps they should know the risks, or perhaps they do know them and accept them. Faced with few choices economically, the domestic crisis has forced Mexico's poorest citizens to leave their homes because they cannot earn enough, even when they have jobs, to feed their families. Family motives and historical patterns impel others. Migrants have no choice: the potential benefits of crossing outweigh the risks given what little benefit there is in staying home. These are victims we should be hard-pressed to blame.

69. Gregory Alan Gross, "U.S.-Mexican Border Agents Train for Immigrant Rescues," *San Diego Union-Tribune,* November 17, 2000, B1.

70. Ibid.

71. Letter from Claudia E. Smith to Gabriela Rodriguez Pizarro, UN Special Rappateur, September 23, 1999.

72. Ibid.

73. Ibid.

74. Smith, Operation Gatekeeper Report, 42.

75. Ibid., 41.

76. Ibid., 43.

77. Letter, Smith to Rodriguez Pizarro, September 23, 1999.

78. Numerical visa limitations for family immigration categories are severely back-logged for Mexican nationals.

79. See generally, Gerald P. López, "Undocumented Mexican Migration: In Search of a Just Immigration Law and Policy," *UCLA Law Review* 28 (1981): 615.

80. Ibid.

81. Susan Ferriss, "Mexico's Troubles Are Felt up North," *San Francisco Examiner,* January 1, 1995, C1.

82. Brendan M. Case, "A Sale Gone Sour; Much of Mexico's Economic Crisis Traced to the Privatization of 18 Banks," *Dallas Morning News,* December 18, 1998, F1.

83. Tracey Eaton, "Zedillo Predicts Strong Growth by 2000; Mexican President Details 5-Year Plan," *Dallas Morning News,* June 1, 1995.

84. "U.S. Says Mexico Recovering," United Press International, May 31, 1995.

85. Jacques Billeaud, "Border Deaths Double in Arizona," The Associated Press, October 9, 2000 (citing Miguel Escobar, Mexican Consul in Douglas, Arizona).

86. Smith, Operation Gatekeeper Report, 13.

87. Ibid., 12.

88. Ignacio Ibarra, "Migrants Will Die in Arizona Desert until U.S. Strategy Shifts, Expert Says," *Arizona Daily Star,* June 9, 2000.

89. Smith, Operation Gatekeeper Report, 7–8.

90. See generally López, "Undocumented Mexican Migration."

91. Robert Collier, "NAFTA Gives Mexicans New Reasons to Leave Home," *S.F. Chronicle,* October 15, 1998, A11.

92. Smith, Operation Gatekeeper Report, 12.

93. Ibid., 39.

94. Ibid., 12.

95. Ibid., 16.

96. López, "Undocumented Mexican Migration."

97. Ibid.

98. This is the perspective that those without a sense of the U.S.–Mexico border history may take.

99. López, "Undocumented Mexican Migration."

100. Similarly, employer sanctions do nothing to address the economic problem in Mexico.

101. See generally Bill Ong Hing, "The Immigrant as Criminal: Punishing Dreamers," *Hastings Women's Law Journal* 9 (1998): 79.

102. Ibid.

103. Statement of Alex Aleinikoff, former INS General Counsel, January 6, 2001, American Association of Law Schools, Immigration Law Section, San Francisco, California.

104. *Cf.* David Garland, *Punishment and Modern Society: A Study in Social Theory* (Chicago: University of Chicago Press, 1990).

Watching Over Greater Mexico

Recent Mexican Initiatives on Migration and the

Alambristas of the New Millennium

Teresa Carrillo

The United States and Mexico are American neighbors tightly bound in an interdependent yet asymmetrical relationship. Nowhere in the world are two more unequal countries pushing against each other with such intensity and over such a great geographical expanse. The two-thousand-mile Mexico-U.S. border is one of the most fluid international boundaries in the world, with an unprecedented volume of goods, services, and people crossing on a daily basis. The free-trade movement of the 1990s added to the porous nature of this international border by lifting tariffs and barriers to trade on goods and services, but the free movement of labor was pointedly excluded from the North American Free Trade Agreement (NAFTA). Instead, as barriers are lifted on goods and services, movement of workers north across the U.S.-Mexico border has become more restrictive, costly, and dangerous. We are now faced with the growing contradiction of a "borderless economy with a barricaded border" (Andreas 1999:14).

Hardworking immigrants like Roberto, the main character in *Alambrista,* bear the brunt of this contradiction. Every day new obstacles spring up in the well-worn paths going north, making the journey to jobs in the United States more precarious. Being a "sending" country, Mexico has a viewpoint on migration that is in many ways diametrically opposed to U.S. views. Yet the age-old practice of employing Mexican labor in certain sectors of the U.S. economy remains unchanged. While nativist sentiments surge and recede, and states such as California mount attacks on immigrant workers and their access to public services, key industries such as agriculture, tourism, restaurants, construction, and services continue to maintain a heavy reliance on low-cost immigrant labor. Middle-class families have also become dependent on immigrant labor in their households for low-cost domestic services that facilitate family life in two-income households, including childcare, house cleaning, cooking, elder care, and gardening. Outside of their homes, U.S. families rely on immigrant labor for affordable services such as fast foods, restaurants, auto repair, building contracting, janitorial services, and child and elder care outside the home. Mexican workers, unable to find adequate work and adequate pay in Mexico, respond to the strong push and pull factors of migration and make the difficult and costly decision to look for work in the United States. As we see clearly in the plight of workers in *Alambrista,* Mexican nationals pay a high price when they leave their homes and families to cross the border, find and maintain employment, and create a place for themselves in a society that shuns them, labeling them "illegal alien" or worse. In exchange, they manage to support themselves and send money home to their families in Mexico at a rate that makes remissions from Mexican nationals working in the United States the third largest source of foreign exchange for Mexico, behind only oil and tourism (Ortiz 1999, Millman 1998).

In *Alambrista,* we witness a painful scene between Roberto and both his wife and mother as he leaves his home in Mexico. The need to migrate is a commonly lamented misfortune among Mexicans. Contrary to mainstream assumptions in the United States about the desirability of going "north," Mexicans often describe the phenomenon as a costly burden. In Mexico, migration is being portrayed with increasing frequency as a terrible drain on Mexico's human resources, taking the younger, more educated, and more efficient workers out of the Mexican labor force and lending their enormous capacity for productivity to their closest competitors. Mexicans admit that they rely on remittances from family members working in the United States and acknowledge migration as a necessary evil. Mexico continues to lose a significant proportion of her labor force to Greater Mexico—the extraterritorial Mexican spaces that lie outside of the national boundaries of Mexico where millions of Mexicans reside and work.

As the Mexican presence in the United States continues to grow, Mexican interest in Greater Mexico increases. New initiatives on the part of Mexican governmental officials, non-governmental organizations, community groups, and village or family networks attempt to reach across the U.S.-Mexican border and shape the transnational interactions connecting Mexican nationals in the United States to their homeland. Some government initiatives are protective of Mexican nationals, but others are protective of governmental authority and control over Mexicans and the fruits of their labor. In the film *Alambrista,* the Mexican government was absent as Roberto and his *paisanos* faced dehumanizing challenges to their labor rights, civil rights, and human rights in the United States. In the contemporary setting, little has changed in terms of the actions of the Mexican government on U.S. soil, but within Mexico there is a growing sense of importance and interest in the Mexican work force in the United States, and a greater acknowledgment of its significance for Mexico.

This chapter outlines four Mexican initiatives on migration: the enactment of the 1998 Law of Dual Nationality, a proposal for absentee balloting in Mexican elections, the transfer of funds and support from the United States to Mexico through individual remittances and hometown clubs, and efforts on various levels to mediate transnational family life. Each example represents a Mexican endeavor to negotiate transnational citizenship across geographical space and at least one national boundary. In the case of governmental initiatives, there is also an element of adapting outmoded, cooptive mechanisms of political control to an emerging transnational reality. With such a large proportion of Mexicans residing outside of Mexico's national boundaries, the government is challenged to extend its reach into the political and economic lives of its nonresident citizens. Adding to this challenge is the fact that the once hegemonic Party of the Institutional Revolution (PRI) lost the presidency to the Party of National Action (PAN) in 2000. The parties are now vying for power among three major political parties: the PAN on the right, the PRI in the very wide center, and the Party of the Democratic Revolution (PRD) on the left. None of the three parties can afford to ignore the large and potentially influential bloc of Mexican nationals living in Greater Mexico. Neither can government, political organizations, the civil service, or non-governmental organizations. At the same time, those watching over Greater Mexico are treading lightly on foreign soil, acutely aware of the anti-immigrant climate in the United States, and the constraints under which they operate. What has Mexico been willing or unwilling to do for its nationals living in the United States? What are Mexican immigrants in the United States doing for themselves?

The Law of Dual Nationality

The issue of dual nationality was raised in the 1995–2000 National Development Plan, a document designed to chart the course of political change through each six-year administration in Mexico. By March 1998, the Mexican Congress had instituted reforms to Articles 30, 32, and 37 of the Mexican Constitution, establishing that Mexicans who are citizens by birth can maintain their Mexican nationality independent of other nationalities they may have adopted. This benefit is limited to those who are Mexican by birth, meaning that they were either born in Mexico or born to parents or one parent who is Mexican by birth. The only Mexican nationals who do not benefit from this new legislation are naturalized Mexican citizens.

Those who have dual nationality take on the rights and responsibilities of a Mexican national if they enter or leave Mexican territory as a Mexican national. These include such rights as legal equality with other Mexican nationals under the Mexican Constitution, access to Mexican educational institutions, membership in *ejidos,* access to state-sponsored credit, and the right to work in Mexico under the protections extended by the labor law. Economic rights include the right to invest in enterprises reserved for Mexicans by birth, such as certain areas of the communications, petroleum, banking, and transportation industries. There is a difference between Mexican nationality and Mexican citizenship, which boils down to the right to vote in popular elections. Mexican nationals must establish residence in Mexico and register in order to practice active citizenship by voting. They also must vote in Mexican territory. Mexican nationals with dual nationality can be exempted from the Mexican military-service requirement by filing a form with the government.[1] In practice, many of these observances existed before 1998; the new law merely confirms that the rights of a Mexican national by birth or by parent's birth cannot be taken away—even if the dual national has taken on a second or third nationality.

Even though de facto dual nationality has long been accepted by Mexico, the constitutional change that officially confirmed its legality in 1998 may prompt millions of Mexican nationals living in the United States to become naturalized U.S. citizens, since they can now do so without concern for losing rights in Mexico. This prompt has come at a time of (and perhaps in part in response to) rising anti-immigrant sentiment in the United States. Two U.S. anti-immigrant initiatives along with major reforms to the Welfare and Immigration Acts preceded the new Mexican law of dual nationality: California's Proposition 187 in 1994 (the "Save Our State" Initiative to deny access to public services to immigrants); the 1996 reform to the Immigration Act, the major overhaul to the welfare system that "ended welfare as we know it" in 1996; and California's Proposition 227 in 1997 (the California initiative to do away with bilingual education). As these major U.S. reforms and legislative changes place a premium on citizenship status in the United States, Mexican legal residents in the United States are applying for naturalization at an unprecedented rate.

In a climate of nativist aggression, Mexican immigrants are both pushed and pulled toward dual nationality. No one has put their finger on an exact number of Mexicans eligible for U.S. citizenship who could maintain their Mexican nationality after naturalization, but even the lowest estimate is well over a million, with other well-founded estimates ranging from 1.5 million to over 5 million (Spiro 1997). Even if just a fraction of those eligible were to apply for dual nationality, the numbers would be significant for both Mexican Americans and Mexicans, psychologically and legally freeing immigrants to pursue U.S. citizenship through naturalization while maintaining their identity as Mexican nationals.

Mexican leaders encourage dual nationality and have given high priority to developing relationships with Mexicans in the United States, and with U.S. Latino leaders and business people. There is growing recognition of the influence and importance of Mexicans in Greater Mexico, not only for the individual and collective remissions they send, but also as intermediaries that bring information, knowledge, experience, training, contacts, expertise, investment possibilities, and prosperity to families and hometowns in Mexico. One indicator of the importance that President Vicente Fox places on the Mexican community in the United States is the fact that on the first weekend of his presidency, Fox met with Mexican residents of the United States and U.S. Latino representatives in a highly publicized meeting at Los Pinos, the Mexican White House. The Fox administration has taken other actions demonstrating the administration's emphasis on the important role of migrants during the first year of his presidency. One of Fox's first organizational changes was to move the Office for Migrant Affairs from the Secretary of Foreign Relations into the Office of the President. He then expanded the budget and functions of the office and focused continuous attention on his administration's goal of negotiating a bilateral guest-worker program. Fox also created a new office for free consultations for Mexican nationals regarding U.S. immigration law in the Mexican consulate in El Paso, Texas.[2] During the Christmas season when an estimated 195,000 émigré Mexicans temporarily return to their homes in Mexico, President Fox kicked off a "zero tolerance" policy against corruption by the Mexican border patrol and federal police on the border. He visited Nogales and Sonora, and personally greeted Mexican nationals re-entering Mexico while publicly reiterating the "zero corruption, zero dirty dealings" policy with members of the Mexican border patrol and border politicos.

In 2001, Fox took his migration agenda to Washington, D.C. Just after he was elected in July 2000 (and before the U.S. November 2000 elections) Fox met with both major candidates for the U.S. presidency and challenged them to begin a process of reinventing U.S.-Mexico relations, utilizing the European Union as a model for regional economic integration with open borders. In his first month in office, Fox met with Republican Congressmen Phil Gramm of Texas and Pete Domenici of New Mexico to begin discussing a proposal for a new guest-worker and legalization program for undocumented Mexican immigrants in the United States. In response, George W. Bush chose Mexico as the destination for his first trip abroad as President of the United States in February 2001. In preparation for President Bush's trip to Mexico, Colin Powell, the U.S. Secretary of State, and Jorge Castañeda, the Mexican Secretary of Foreign Relations at that time, scheduled a meeting to discuss, among other things, the condition of Mexicans in the United States. These plans indicate a heightened sense of U.S. interest in Mexico, yet there were few indications in Washington, D.C., of any political will to back up this interest and concretely address problems of Mexican nationals in the United States or to loosen restrictions on Mexican immigration that plague Mexican workers.

In early September 2001, after weeks of preparation and anticipatory political debate over guest-worker program proposals, Presidents Bush and Fox met in Washington, D.C. The U.S. media reported detailed accounts of this much-touted visit, right down to the guest list of the huge state dinner and the differences between the proposals being set forth by the Mexican leadership, the Democrats, and the Republicans. On September 9, 2001, President Fox returned to Mexico convinced that major reform of U.S.-Mexican migration policies was eminent. Two days later the twin towers were attacked and the issue of U.S.-Mexican migration policy reform was completely overshadowed by the war on terrorism. Months later when members of Congress hastily passed the U.S. Patriot Act, laws governing immigration and due process for immigrants and asylum seekers became even more restrictive, further constraining migrant Mexican workers. During the post-9/11 period, President Fox and the Mexican government have taken a "wait and see" approach with U.S.-Mexican migration policy reform but have persisted in their efforts to negotiate a bilateral guest-worker program with the United States.

In the first days of 2004, President Bush raised the hopes of all immigrant-rights advocates with a bold new proposal for a temporary-workers program that would extend temporary legal status for three-year periods to selected immigrant workers. Although the Bush proposal was met with immediate opposition from those supporting a restrictionist position on immigration, there was also measured support among varied sectors, ranging from Latinos to employers and worker-rights advocates. While generally supportive of the idea of a work visa as a start to immigration reform, immigrant-rights advocates were critical of some of the details of the Bush plan, including the fact that there is no real provision for earned permanent residence, that a work visa tied to a particular employer would ramp up the level of worker exploitation, and that the proposal includes a 10-percent *fianza*, or deposit of wages, that would theoretically be returned to the worker upon his or her return to the country of origin. Immigrants and advocates alike have every reason to question whether such a deposit would be returned, given the history of the Bracero Program, with a similar deposit built in, the bulk of which were never returned to the workers. Immigration reform was thus thrust into public debate in the United States just in time for the 2004 election campaigns.

On the Mexican side, frequent pronouncements of the importance of the Mexican population abroad translated mainly into an effort to pursue two limited policy proposals: absentee balloting to allow nonresident Mexican nationals to vote in Mexican elections, and government fund-sharing schemes with hometown clubs that support development projects in Mexican hometowns by matching funds sent by Mexican nationals in the United States.

Absentee Ballots for Mexican Nationals Abroad

Fox campaigned on a promise to pursue absentee balloting for Mexican nationals residing abroad. In a 1998 report commissioned by the Mexican Federal Electoral Institute, electoral experts estimate that up to 7 million Mexicans living in the United States could be eligible to vote via absentee balloting if the Mexican Congress decides to implement such a plan. Citizens of forty-three countries in the world, including Argentina, Nicaragua, the United States, and South Africa, already have the right to vote while residing abroad. Mexican nationals in the United States have begun to lobby for the absentee ballot, and if won, absentee voting could prove to be decisive, given that an estimated 14 percent of the Mexican electorate resides in the United States (Ortiz 1999). Estimates of the number of Mexicans who could be affected by absentee balloting vary widely according to population data and balloting proposals, with the most restrictive proposal affecting 1 million voters, and the least restrictive estimated at 7 million additional voters (Smith 1998). The proposal would not extend the absentee vote to dual-national Mexicans who have become U.S. citizens.

Absentee balloting is controversial largely because of the widespread perception that absentee votes would favor some parties over others in Mexico. Immigrant-rights advocates, along with both the PAN and the PRD, pushed for absentee balloting in time for the 2000 election, but the only compromise reached was to provide a limited number of extra ballots for voters in transit along the northern border of Mexico (Ross 1998; Ortiz 1999). The PAN and the PRD actively campaigned in the United States and made plans to sponsor bus caravans of eligible voters to the border, but many of the plans were not realized. Some voters who did make the journey were unable to vote when they encountered a shortage of out-of-district ballots, long lines, and confusion at the sixty-four special balloting booths set up across the six states of Mexico's northern border. Each special voting site had only 7,500 ballots for voters in transit, for a total of 48,000 extra ballots distributed across the entire northern border. Early polling of Mexican voters in the United States suggested that a large majority would vote for opposition parties rather than for the PRI (Smith 1998). Mexican nationals abroad argue that they deserve to have a say in Mexican politics in part because they have sent billions of dollars in remittances back to their families and home towns in Mexico.

Remittances and Hometown Clubs

In the film *Alambrista*, we see how driven Roberto is in his struggle to send money home to his wife. There is one telling scene in the post office when Roberto is aided by both Sharon, his Anglo friend and lover, and a helpful bilingual woman who happens by, in filling out the forms for the wire transfer of a modest amount of money. Roberto's dedication to his family in Mexico plays against his obligations in the United States to support himself and ideally contribute to the support of his new "family" in California. Despite the fact that he has earned very little money, the portion he sends home is a source of great pride for Roberto, a vital form of support for his wife and mother in Mexico, and a potential source of tension for Sharon.

Remittances sent to Mexico from the United States have grown at an astounding rate from an estimated 1 billion dollars in 1984 to just under 5 billion dollars in 1998, reaching an estimated $10 billion in 2002 (Lowell and de la Garza 2000). Every category of migrant sends money home: legal/illegal; permanent/temporary; upper-class/lower-class; middle-age/young; married/single; and male/female. Certain categories of Latino migrants in the United States tend to remit more funds as compared to others, but migrants generally send between 6 and 16 percent of their earned income back to their countries of origin (De la

Garza, et al. 1997). Remittances, however, have tended to decrease after the first or second generation, creating need for new migrants for a continuous and growing flow of funds to Latin American countries (Lozano-Ascencio 1993). There are different ways of tracking remittances and each method results in a different total, but all findings attest to the fact that remittances are one of Mexico's principle sources of foreign exchange. Governments and banking institutions track international money flows using sophisticated measures of transfers through banks, transmitter companies such as Western Union or MoneyGram, the U.S. postal service via the Dinero Seguro (safe money) program, or credit unions such as IRNet (Orozco, 2000). Figures vary widely but lead to an undeniable conclusion that there is rapid growth in remittances. The International Bank for Reconstruction and Development reported that in 1998, remittances to Mexico alone totaled 4.9 billion dollars. The *Wall Street Journal* reported remittances to Mexico of $5.5 billion for the same year. As recently as 2001, an Inter-American Development Bank study reported that remittances to Mexico exceeded $9.2 billion, almost doubling the 1998 figures (U.S. Agency for International Development [USAID] 2002). According to these sources, "remittances are more than twice the value of agricultural exports, and over 50 percent of oil exports" (USAID 2002:1). The funds are used largely for local consumption in the home communities, a use that creates a significant multiplier effect, especially in the rural setting where consumers are more likely to buy locally produced goods and local services. According to the Mexican Migration Project (MMP), remittances yield a strong multiplier effect, adding $6.5 billion in production annually to the Mexican economy.[3] Mexican nationals in the United States have shown a headstrong determination to send remittances home, even though their average income is very low. The MMP reports that even with an average annual income of $7,455, Mexican immigrants managed an average monthly remittance of $240 (annualized, this is $2,880) (Lowell and de la Garza 2000). Adding to this figure are transfers that take place irregularly and not on a month-to-month basis, such as through accumulated savings personally delivered by returning migrants, grants made through hometown clubs, and gifts or contributions such as cars, merchandise, electronics, or clothes.

An estimated two million Mexican nationals living and working in the United States are organized in what have been called "Hometown Clubs," which reportedly funnel billions of dollars into their Mexican hometowns (Cleeland, 2000; Kraul 2000). The Mexican government has encouraged hometown club funding to public works in Mexico by offering matching government funds, as in the case of a health clinic in Talpa de Allende, Jalisco, where hometown funds will be matched three to one by federal, state, and local funds. Hometown clubs are growing by leaps and bounds; in 1998, one researcher counted 400 clubs throughout the United States, with concentrations in Los Angeles, Chicago, and Dallas (Orozco 2000). In 2000, the *LA Times* reported that there are about 1,500 clubs in the United States—most set up as nonprofit organizations (Kraul 2000). The Mexican government has jumped at the chance to work with these groups by offering matching funds for projects that might create jobs and development in migrant-sending regions of Mexico. President Vicente Fox has talked about job-creating projects as a way of reversing the social costs of emigration.

What is certain is that Mexican government officials on all levels are paying attention to the hometown clubs and are making concerted efforts to work with them in order to encourage remittances to both families and hometown development projects. The Mexican government has channeled their outreach to Mexicans abroad mainly through hometown clubs. In the early 1990s, President Salinas de Gortari set up two outreach programs, the Paisano Program under the authority of the National Institute of Migration as part of the Secretary of State (Gobernación), and the Program for Mexican Communities Living Abroad (PMCLA), under the authority of the Secretary of Foreign Relations (SRE). During the first half of President Fox's administration, he greatly expanded the Paisano Program and completely restructured the PMCLA. After having moved the PMCLA from the SRE to the Office of the President when he first took office, in 2003 he terminated the program and established its predecessor, the Institute of Mexicans Abroad (Instituto de los Mexicanos en el Exterior, IME) under the authority once again of the SRE. The Paisano Program was designed to address the problems of corruption and abuse at points of entry as migrants return to Mexico, and is implemented by thousands of Mexican citizens who volunteer their time to observe and offer assistance at the border. Volunteers wear white t-shirts and jackets with the Paisano logo to identify themselves to migrants. The PMCLA, which became the IME, on the other hand, is staffed by government employees and operates through a network of consulates and Mexican cultural centers in the United States, offering services and promoting fundraising for development through hometown clubs as well as formal interaction with the Mexican government (Orozco 2000; González and Schumacher 1998).

At the state level, governors of Jalisco, Michoacán, and Veracruz have traveled to hometown clubs in Los Angeles, Milwaukee, and Washington to encourage contributions (Cleeland, 2000). Fox, as governor of Guanajuato, developed Casa Guanajuato, a state outreach program to formalize ties with the two million people from Guanajuato who live in the United States. Casa Guanajuato organized job-creation programs in Guanajuato with hometown club funds matched by state government funds (Goldring 1999). Many of the hometown clubs grew out of informal networks of immigrants to the United States who originally came together around a specific project, such as building a school or upgrading a water system in their hometown. The hometown clubs provided services and information to migrants, and eventually grew in their level of organization and range of function. These groups now pool remissions and pursue collective investment plans and public improvement projects in hometowns across Mexico.

Up until very recently, hometown clubs have limited their activities to raising funds for projects in Mexico, often through events such as dances or raffles. Hometown clubs have evolved in size, levels of sophistication, and scope of activity. In early 2000, a coalition of hometown clubs in Los Angeles joined the county Labor Federation to support immigration policy reform, including a new amnesty program for immigrant workers and aggressive enforcement of worker-protection laws for undocumented workers. Club presidents from Zacatecas, Jalisco, Guanajuato, Oaxaca, and Sinaloa demonstrated their support for the proposal in a public meeting in conjunction with the County Federation of Labor. This action marks a turn toward political activism for the hometown clubs, which have up until recently shied away from domestic policy issues. Lately, however, the clubs have increasingly turned their focus inward to address the needs of immigrants in the United States. The clubs provide scholarships to children of immigrants, hold citizenship classes and voter-registration drives, and spearhead education and information campaigns to inform migrants of the dangers involved in undocumented migration, especially for women and children. Hometown clubs have joined together with immigrant-rights advocacy groups and other NGOs to call upon the Mexican government and Mexican consulates to step up their efforts to ensure labor and human-rights guarantees to Mexican migrants (Cleeland 2000; Ramírez 2000). Hometown clubs have placed a great emphasis on conditions in their Mexican hometowns as well, and have used collective remittances to guide development and create jobs in those towns in an effort to allow more people to remain home. They acknowledge that the high cost of widespread migration and dependence on remittances is felt in all aspects of Mexican life—especially in family life.

Transnational Family Life

In *Alambrista*, we saw Roberto's family broken apart in the process of migration. His father left Mexico to work in the United States and he and his mother waited, anticipating his return. When Roberto made the decision to migrate, both his wife and his mother knew that they would be facing a long and painful separation. He left a child at home, just as he had been left behind by his father. Later, Roberto finds his father at the moment of his death, and in going through his meager possessions, discovers that his father had a second family in the United States. Roberto himself begins to form a relationship with Sharon, his Anglo lover, who offers him shelter and friendship during his first days of work in Stockton, California. Roberto's story is typical of the complex knot of relationships that result from transnational family life.

Anywhere you go in Mexico, you'll meet people with family members in the United States. In some "sending" regions such as the state of Guanajuato, the proportion of migrants to non-migrants is as high as two to three; for every three adult residents at home there are two migrants in the United States. The high rate of migration has fundamentally altered Mexican society, creating changes in the ways that communities support themselves, constitute their families, and carry out their day-to-day lives. Families enjoy the benefits of remittances often at the expense of family separation—not just between husbands and wives, but often between parents and children as well.

A separation that is becoming more common is between mother and child. More and more Mexican women are finding work in the United States in the informal sector as nannies, elder caregivers, and housekeepers. As White women "win their independence" by moving into the professional workforce, they often turn to women of color to fill the gap their employment has left in their family's domestic work. In the early 1990s, as the newly elected President Clinton was attempting to appoint female cabinet members, the scandal dubbed "nannygate" arose around the issue of who was performing the domestic duties in the household of Clinton's first nominee for attorney general, Zoe Baird, and then in the households of a succession of female appointees that followed. At issue was the immigration status of the domestic services workers in these households and whether their employers had paid social security taxes and other payroll taxes in the course of their employment. It is curious that among male nominees, the question of who was performing household duties in their homes was never made an issue, yet for female nominees, this question was fair game. In many cases, Latinas had been employed as domestic service workers, often caring for children or elderly parents and keeping house.

Caring for the families of others makes it difficult to care for your own. In Pierrette Hondagneu-Sotelo's excellent analysis of domestic service workers, *Doméstica: Immigrant Workers Cleaning and Caring in the Shadows of Affluence,* she found that almost half of the workers with children had at least one of their children "back home" in their country of origin. Among the live-in domestic workers, the percentage was highest at 82 percent; among domestic workers who did not live-in it was 42 percent, and for hourly-wage house cleaners, in was 24 percent (Hondagneu-Sotelo, 2001:50).

It is common for immigrant women to be separated from their children for long periods of time and over great distances. Their role as mother is reduced to letters, costly telephone calls, financial support, and short periods of time with their children in between work commitments. The irony of the situation is that in caring for and nurturing the families of others, Mexican women are often denied the opportunity to actively raise and nurture their own children. It is the grandmothers who are often left to raise the children while the mothers are caring for children other than their own.

This is the paradox of transnational motherhood. Hondagneu-Sotelo and Avila point out that this is not an entirely new phenomenon—that there is "a long historical legacy of people of color being incorporated into the US through coercive systems of labor that do not recognize family rights" (Hondagneu-Sotelo and Avila, 1997:568). In attacking immigrant access to social services and public education, California's Proposition 187 and other anti-immigrant initiatives challenge the right of immigrants to live with their families and to provide for their dependents. By creating an environment hostile to children, recent policy reforms reinforce the message to leave the dependents at home. This impedes Mexican parents from parenting while forcing Mexico to pay the costs of raising and educating the next generation of migrant labor. Extended families are made up of old as well as young dependents. By cutting off access to services for older migrants, new U.S. policies also externalize costs associated with elderly dependents while infringing on the Mexican tradition of extended, multigenerational familism. The new formulation of "family" for purposes of family reunification in the Immigration Reform Act of 1996 further curtails immigrant family rights by redefining "family" as the nuclear family, creating new exclusions for extended family members such as adult siblings, adult offspring, and aging parents (Fix and Zimmerman 1995).

There is a keen awareness in Mexico of the costs of widespread migration for Mexican families. On a trip to Mexico, a headline that caught my eye read, "The Church Laments the Fact that Mexico's Young People are Going North" (Torres 2000:3). The article reported on a national speech delivered by Luis Morales Reyes, the Archbishop of San Luis Potosí and the President of the Conference of Religious Leaders of Mexico. He opened his speech by calling upon the Mexican government to create more job opportunities so that young people would not have to migrate to the United States. He said, "It is the most able, the bravest, and the most skilled that go" and that "what hurts the most are the repercussions for the family; the disintegration of the family that comes with migration" (Torres 2000:3).

Negotiating Transnational Citizenship

Immigration issues look very different from the vantage point of the sending or receiving country. In the United States, political debates focus on controlling the flow of undocumented immigration, limiting the rights and access to public services of immigrants in the United States, and in the post-9/11 setting, security issues related to immigration. For Mexico, one of the most problematic aspects of migration is the brain drain and the cost of educating and providing social-welfare benefits to a past or future working class in their dependent years, as elders who have devoted or as children who will devote their most productive working years to the development of the U.S. economy as a migrant workforce. Mexico also struggles with a more general question of governance of the growing proportion of the Mexican population that lives and works in Greater Mexico. At this historic juncture, Mexico's President Fox is calling upon U.S. leaders to reformulate U.S.-Mexico relations and the practices involved in the widespread use of Mexican labor. Perhaps the moment is right to revisit Mexican proposals to defend migrant rights as an important component of binational relations. Mexican NGOs together with immigrant-rights advocate groups on both sides of the border are calling for an integrated strategy for change, including a bilateral migration accord to ensure protections for migrants under INS authority; a strengthening of consular protections; implementation of employment programs in Mexico to deter migration; and permanent campaigns to inform and educate migrants of the risks of crossing into the United States without documents.

Mexicans both within Mexico and in Greater Mexico are encountering new transnational situations and responding with innovative solutions. In the face of U.S. INS authority, migrants are demanding special protections for women and children, access to detention sites and deportation schedules, and humane standards for treatment during arrest, transport, and deportation. Migrants are beginning to voice expectations for a much fuller role for consular protection, including increased, trained personnel in consulates in the United States, a greater role for consular intervention in INS enforcement practices, and an emergency 800 number for information regarding family members who may have been detained, injured, or lost. Mexican citizens and NGOs have announced expectations for the Mexican government to step up efforts to create employment on Mexico's northern border, assist in the voluntary return of migrants in crisis situations, provide assistance to migrants who have been injured, and enact effective sanctions against public servants who violate migrants' rights (Ramírez 2000). Some groups have even called for the establishment of a permanent office of the Mexican Human Rights Commission for the border region. In some very visible cases, such as the demand for the recovery of the Bracero-workers pension fund for forty thousand ex-Braceros, or the request for legal confirmation of dual nationality, the Mexican government has been responsive. But in many other cases, Mexican governmental action has lagged far behind expectations. Mexicans in Greater Mexico regularly send remissions to their families and hometowns at tremendous personal sacrifice. They maintain their political gaze on Mexico even while engaging the Latino community in the United States in a constant negotiation of ethnic politics. Most impressive of all, Greater Mexico projects a forward-looking transnational vision that is an odd contrast to a stale backdrop of nationalist notions and closed borders. Greater Mexico can juggle citizenship, jump borders, and parent across transnational space. To anyone complacently lost in a nationalist past, Greater Mexico presents a challenge and a road map.

■

Discussion Questions

1. What are some of the measures that the Mexican government is taking in their attempt to govern over their citizens abroad?

2. How does the possibility of dual nationality for Mexican citizens in the United States affect the willingness of Mexican immigrants to become naturalized U.S. citizens? What kind of impact could this new possibility have on Latino politics in the United States?

3. Do you think that Mexican immigrants in the United States should have the right to vote in abstentia in Mexican elections while residing in the United States?

4. How does the determination to send remissions back to Mexico impact the lives of immigrants while they are in the United States?

5. What is the Mexican government doing to promote or facilitate the practice of sending money home?

6. What is the care deficit? What role do Mexican immigrants play in the care deficit? What are the gender dynamics involved in the care deficit?

■

Notes

1. The Law of Double Nationality and its provisions are delineated in the following government document: *Dirección General de Asuntos Jurídicos de la Secretaría de Relaciones Exteriores.* La Ley de Nacionalidad (México D.F.: The Secretary of Foreign Relations [SRE], 1998).

2. Notimex (2001), "Asesorará Gobierno Mexicano a Migrantes Sobre Ley Estadunidense," January 28, 2001. Posted on the internet at: http://www.presidencia.gob.mx/.

3. For up-to-date changes in the Fox administration's migration policies, see the following websites: The Mexican Migration Project (MMP) is an ongoing binational research effort that aims to study and document the process of Mexican migration to the United States. It is codirected by Professors Jorge Durand of the University of Guadalajara, and Douglas S. Massey of the University of Pennsylvania. They sponsor a website that provides public access to a comprehensive database of social and economic information on Mexican-U.S. migration at http://www.pop.upenn.edu/mexmig/. The second site, http://www.americaspolicy.org, is sponsored by the Interhemispheric Resource Center (IRC) and contains excellent up-to-the-minute information and analysis on Mexican migration issues.

■

Sources

Andreas, Peter. 1999. "Borderless Economy, Barricaded Border." *NACLA Report on the Americas* 33, no. 3 (November/December): 14–21.

Cleeland, Nancy. 2000. "Mexican 'Hometown Clubs' Turn Activist." *Los Angles Times,* June 8, 2000, p. A-1.

De la Garza, Rodolfo, Manuel Orozco, and Miguel Baraona. 1997. "Binational Impact of Latino Remittances." Policy Brief of the Tomás Rivera Policy Institute (March). available at www.trpi.org/publications.html.

DeSipio, Louis. 2000. "Sending Money Home . . . For Now: Remittances and Immigrant Adoption in the US." Tomás Rivera Policy Institute and Inter-American Dialogue Working Paper Series. Los Angeles, Calif.: Tomás Rivera Policy Institute.

DeSipio, Louis and Rodolfo O. de la Garza. 1998. *Making Americans, Remaking America: Immigration and Immigrant Policy.* Boulder, Colo.: Westview Press.

Durand, Jorge, Emilio A. Parrado, and Douglas S. Massey. 1996. "Migradollars and Development: A Reconsideration of the Mexican Case." *International Migration Review* 30(2): 423–44.

Fix, Michael and Jeffrey Passel. 1994. *Immigration and Immigrants: Setting the Record Straight.* Washington, D.C.: The Urban Institute.

Fix, Michael and Wendy Zimmerman. 1995. "Immigrant Families and Public Policy." Research Paper from the Urban Institute. Washington, D.C.: The Urban Institute.

García, Cristóbal, et al. 2000. "Demandarán ex-braceros a México y EU." *La Jornada,* December 4, 2000.

Goldring, Luin. 1999. "From Market Membership to Transnational Citizenship? The Changing Politicization of Transnational Social Spaces." Chicano/Latino Research Center Working Paper. Santa Cruz: University of California, Santa Cruz, Center for Chicano/Latino Studies.

González Gutiérrez, Carlos. 1997. "Decentralized Diplomacy: The Role of the Consular Offices in Mexico's Relations with its Diaspora." In *Bridging the Border: Transforming Mexico-U.S. Relations.* Edited by Rodolfo O. de la Garza and Jesús Velasco. Lanham, Md.: Rowman and Littlefield.

González Gutiérrez, Carlos and Ma. Esther Schumacher. 1998. "La Cooperación Internacional de México con los Mexicano-Americanos en Estados Unidos: El Caso del PCME." In *México y Estados Unidos: las rutas de la cooperación.* Edited by Olga Pellicer and Rafael Fernández de Castro. México D.F.: Instituto Matías Romero.

Gutierrez, David, ed. 1996. *Between Two Worlds: Mexican Immigrants in the United States.* Wilmington, Del.: Scholarly Resources Press.

Hondagneu-Sotelo, Pierrette. 2001. *Doméstica: Immigrant Workers Cleaning and Caring in the Shadows of Affluence.* Berkeley: University of California Press.

Hondagneu-Sotelo, Pierrette and Ernestine Avila. 1997. "'I'm Here But I'm There': The Meanings of Latina Transnational Motherhood." *Gender and Society* 11(5): 548–71.

Kraul, Chris. 2000. "Tapping Generosity of Emigrants." *Los Angles Times,* June 8, 2000, p. A-1.

Lizarraga Chavez, Pablo. 1997. "Creating A United States-Mexico Political Double Helix: The Mexican Government's Proposed Dual Nationality Amendment." *Stanford Journal of International Law* (33): 119.

Lozano-Ascencio, Fernando. 1993. *Bringing It Back Home: Remittances to Mexico from Migrant Workers in the United States.* San Diego: Center for U.S.-Mexican Studies.

Meade, Everard. 1999. *Mexico-US Advocates Network News,* no. 2. (March 16, 1999).

Meyers, Deborah Waller. 1998. "Migrant Remittances to Latin America: Reviewing the Literature." Tomás Rivera Policy Institute Working Paper Series, May.

Millman, Joel. 1998. "Mexicans Are Home for the Holidays Bearing Gifts for a Rural Economy." *The Wall Street Journal,* December 30, 1998.

North American Congress on Latin America (NACLA). 1995. "The Immigration Backlash." *Report on the Americas* 29, no. 3. (November/December).

Orozco, Manuel. 2000. "Remittances and Markets: New Players and Practices." Paper prepared for the Tomás Rivera Policy Institute. Los Angeles, Calif.: Tomás Rivera Policy Institute.

Ortiz, Michelle Ray. 1999. "Absentee vote pushed for next election, seen as risk to ruling Party." *The Detroit News,* June 2, 1999.

Ramírez, Raul. 2000. "Mexican Proposals to Defend Migrants' Rights." Excerpts from La Nueva Política Norte Americana de Migración: Antecedentes y Consequencias. Tijuana, BC: Casa del Migrante. Excerpts posted to: http://www.igc.org/nnirr/Fact_sheets/1997/spring 97/mexican-proposals.html.

Ross, Raul. 1998. "El voto incómodo: Mexicanos en Estados Unidos." *Masiosare, Supplement of La Jornada,* September 13, 1998.

Sassen Koob, Saskia. 1996. "U.S. Immigration Policy Toward Mexico in a Global Economy." In *Between Two Worlds: Mexican Immigrants in the United States.* Edited by David Gutierrez, pp. 213–28. Wilmington, Del.: Scholarly Resources Press.

Smith, James F. 1998. "Expatriate Mexican Voting Is Feasible, Panel Reports." Mexico City: *The Times,* Friday, November 13, 1998.

Spiro, Peter J. 1997. "Dual Nationality and the Meaning of Citizenship." *Emory Law Journal* 46, no. 4 (fall): 1411–86.

Torres, Sergio. 2000. "Lamenta la iglesia que la sangre joven de México se vaya al vecino pais del norte." *Cambio de Michoacan,* December 31, 2000, p. 3.

USAID. 2002. "USAID Announces Innovative Program to Facilitate the Flow of Remittances to Mexico." Press Release from the U.S. Agency for International Development, September 27, 2002. Washington, D.C.: USAID Press Office.

Vargas, Jorge A. 1996. "Dual Nationality for Mexicans? A Comparative Legal Analysis of the Dual Nationality Proposal and Its Eventual Political and Socio-Economic Implications." *Chicano-Latino Law Review* 18.

Figure 1: Isolation: Mexican migrant Roberto (Domingo Ambriz) experiences the alien sights and sounds of a diner in the United States.

All photographs by Andrew Young ©Bobwin Associates, 2003.

Figure 2: Home and Faith: Roberto (Domingo Ambriz) and his mother pray at a family shrine before he, like his father before him, leaves his home in Mexico to seek work in the United States.

Figure 3: (top right) Fellowship: After crossing the United States-Mexican border fellow migrants share food with Roberto in the desert.

Figure 4: (bottom right) Adaptation: In the farm workers quarters Joe and Berto (pictured, Paul Berrones)teach Roberto how to order breakfast in a diner.

Figure 5: Culture Shock: Roberto (Domingo Ambriz) experiences an American revivalist meeting with new friend Sharon (Linda Gillen).

Figure 6: (top right) Work: Roberto joins in the backbreaking labor to supply the American table.

Figure 7: (bottom right) Harvest of Shame: Roberto works gathering grapes—an activity which exposed migrant workers to both exploitative pay and harmful pesticides.

Figure 8: Agony: Roberto (Domingo Ambriz) is captured by the United States authorities.

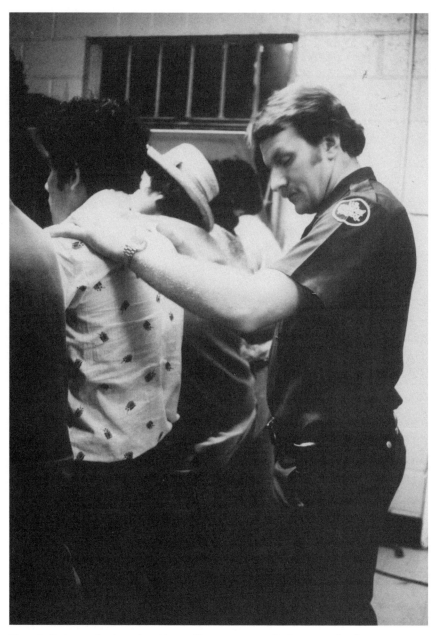

Figure 9: Return: An immigration officer prepares Roberto and other undocumented migrants for their return to Mexico.

Figure 10: The cinema of Robert M. Young: *Nothing But a Man* (made with Michael Roemer in 1964) tells the story of a Black railway worker Duff Anderson (Ivan Dixon, left) and his struggle to make his way in the world. Like *Alambrista* it uses a documentary style and deals with an ignored group.

Figure 11: (top right) On the set of *The Ballad of Gregorio Cortez* (1982) Robert M. Young (left)and Edward James Olmos (right). The film returned to the subject of the border, telling the story of a Mexican-American folk hero.

Figure 12: (bottom right) Greek-Jewish boxer Salamo Arouch (Willem Dafoe) faces his Nazi persecutors led by Major Rauscher (Harmut Becker) in Robert M. Young's true story of surviving the Holocaust, *Triumph of the Spirit* (1989).

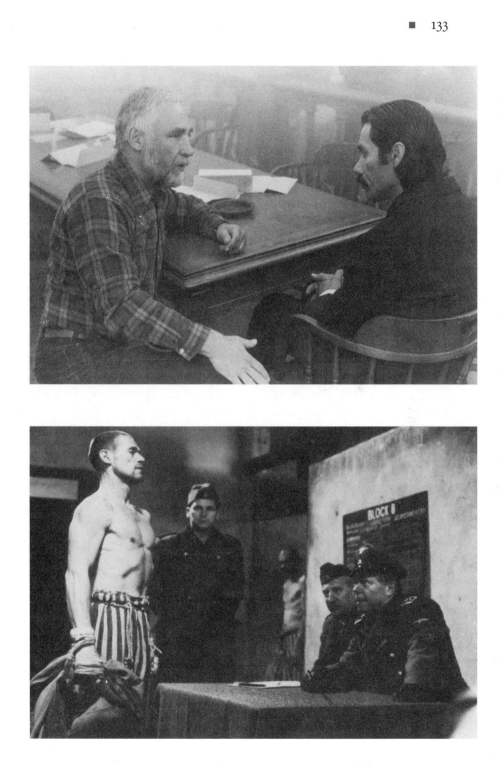

Figure 13: On the set of *Dominic and Eugene* (1988) Young directs Ray Liotta (left) and Tom Hulce (center) in a story of the brothers coming to terms with the memory of abuse. Like *Alambrista* and many other films by Young it reflects the director's interest in the father-son relationship.

PART TWO

Alambrista
Sights and Sounds

Film Criticism and Analysis

Tightrope Walking the Border

Alambrista and the Acrobatics of Mestizo Representation

Cordelia Candelaria

Alambrista occupies a unique position in American movie history as a product of the late Chicano Renaissance[1] era contributed by a respected Anglo filmmaker. Written and directed by Robert M. Young, whose credits include *Nothing but a Man* (1964), *Short Eyes* (1977), and many other independent films, *Alambrista!*—without the initial exclamation point (¡) required by standard Spanish spelling—was first released in 1976 to favorable reception, particularly among Mexican American intellectuals and other progressives in the United States (Keller 1985; Candelaria 1981). Shown at the 1980 Denver International Film Festival (DIFF), the movie received accolades for its "authenticity and aesthetic grace" (Moshowitz 1981) in capturing the abject experience of undocumented Mexican workers whose hard and life-threatening labor plants, harvests, and processes the food Americans eat.

Contributing to the film's uniqueness is its re-release in 2002 with the addition of a superb musical score composed by anthropologist and ethnomusician José B. Cuellar, a saxophonist and bandleader professionally known as Dr. Loco, in collaboration with Francisco Herrera, Greg Landau, and Tomás Montoya. The added musical soundtrack is stunningly performed in the director's-cut version available for this review by Dr. Loco's Los Tiburones del Norte. For the 2002 version Director Young also re-edited the film to add selected scenes from outtake archives to strengthen the plot and characterization of his protagonist, Roberto Ramirez, the *alambrista* or "illegal" of the movie's subtitle translation.

Like many solid films of progressive critique, the original *Alambrista!* languished commercially in its first circulation despite its successful screening at the 1980 DIFF (Cardenas and Schneider 1981) and also despite Young's award-winning respectability as an indie filmmaker.[2] Like the classic *Salt of the Earth* made by left-leaning Hollywood professionals blacklisted during the McCarthy era of persecution,[3] *Alambrista!* faded into the obscurity of mostly radical-left cult interest (Williams 1980; Wilson and Rosenfeldt 1978). Thus, despite its reputation, it never enjoyed the wide circulation experienced on college campuses by such cult classics in Chicana and Chicano Studies, labor history, and border studies as, for example, *Salt of the Earth* and *The Ballad of Gregorio Cortez.* Not surprisingly, when I first tried to locate the original *Alambrista!* in the mid-1990s for use in the newly established Department of Chicana and Chicano Studies (CCS) at Arizona State University, neither the ASU libraries nor local commercial vendors listed it in their inventories. It was usually replaced on my syllabi by *El Norte, The Border, Lone Star,* and similar films of the border-crossing genre.

My search for *Alambrista!* intensified when I proposed to then Department Chair Vicki Ruiz the teaching of "The Reel Aztlán: Framing Mexican America," the first Chicana/o studies *film* class offered at ASU and one of the first such courses to span the representations of Mexicans and Mexican Americans from the silent-movie era through *Luminarias* (1999). The search for a copy was intense because without *Alambrista!* I felt that the required filmography for "Reel Aztlán" would contain a major gap in substance. For example, unlike other Hollywood-style movie representations of Mexicans and Chicanas and Chicanos, Robert M. Young captures a basic respect for his subject matter that is shown in the dignity of his characterizations and his interest in visualizing the lived texture of their actual lives, a texture that is usually absent, stereotyped, or overly sanitized in Hollywood renditions. Another gap that would be missed without *Alambrista!* would be Young's distinctive filmmaking style, which strives for a documentary *cinema verité* effect for his fictional dramas. For these reasons, then, I appealed to ASU's Film and Media Library to conduct an exhaustive search for a copy of the film for screening in my "Reel Aztlán" class. Unfortunately, it didn't surface in time for the class and, coincidentally (in relation to this book project's editor), the closest we came to locating it was a reference to a showing at Harvard University in spring 2000 by Dr. Davíd Carrasco. This personal context is intended to help situate the work's historic importance in the actuality of classroom teaching; that is, to show how curriculum development, course preparation, and basic scholarly research often collide and elide in the literal *doing.*

Further *pre*text to this review of the re-scored 2002 release relates to the material sociohistorical reality that provides the source and subject of *Alambrista*—the daily flow of immigration across the U.S.-México border. Young's movie puts a personal, individual face on a human experience that in the public discourse is frequently perceived and understood solely as a socio-logical, demographic, and political policy issue. Immigration, particularly Mexican immigration, to the United States occurs for many compelling rea-sons existing in the countries of origin, including poverty, lack of employment, political turmoil and torture, repression, unsafe living conditions, and a desire to reunite families (Gutiérrez 1995; DeSipio and de la Garza 1998; Magaña 2003). It also results from employer demands for cheap labor in the United States as well as from economic expansion policies instituted by the United States and México to stimulate both economies, notably the labor-exchange policy officially named the Mexican Farm Labor Supply Program, known today by its informal nickname, the Bracero Program (DeSipio and de la Garza 1998; *Bracero* means worker, from the Spanish *brazo,* or arm, as in a field hand).

Initiated in 1942 by the United States, the Bracero Program was a response to corporate business requests for federal help to compensate for the absent workers who had been drafted for military service in World War II. Set up in conjunction with the Mexican government, the contracted-worker system granted legal temporary worker status to Mexican laborers on a season-by-sea-son basis to meet American industry's demands for labor, particularly in the food industry. Thus the Bracero Program originally was lauded as one way that México contributed significantly to the Allied war effort (Craig 1971). However, even though it was extremely effective in meeting corporate demands for labor, the program was eventually criticized because of employer abuses committed against the Mexican workers due to the lenient terms of the policy. These terms gave the employer unregulated power over pay, working conditions, and food and living arrangements—all realities that Young's *Alambrista* chronicles through the experience of one immigrant bracero.

The end of World War II did not bring an immediate end to the Bracero Program, for an expanded labor force was still needed for the postwar boom, and the number of immigrant workers actually increased after the war, especially in the farm and food-processing industries (DeSipio and de la Garza 1998). As a result, the number of undocumented Mexican workers and their families grew and eventually created an anti-immigrant backlash. Special interests on both sides of the border pushed to keep the contract-worker system in place, arguing that Mexican labor boosted the economies of both nations (Magaña 2003). Thus, the U.S. politics of three decades favored an open border and the continuous, fluid two-way traffic and cultural interchanges that had defined the north-south frontier since before the 1848 Treaty of Guadalupe Hidalgo, which ended the U.S. war with México. Officially extended by the U.S. government in 1947 and again in 1951, the Bracero Program finally was terminated unilaterally by President Lyndon B. Johnson in 1964 (Craig 1971). These material facts of sociopolitical history are part of the reality that gave birth to *Alambrista* Young's achievement is to put an individual face on the vast, interrelated social issues of immigration, corporate business, foreign policy, and labor.

This essay's title, "Tightrope Walking the Border: *Alambrista* and the Acrobatics of Mestizo Representation," offers a logical beginning for the substantive *text* of this review. Young's poetic decision to give his film about undocumented workers the one-word Spanish title holds symbolic significance in that it simultaneously can refer to an *undocumented immigrant* and to a high-wire stunt *acrobat,* because the word's stem derives directly from the etymon *alambre,* meaning *wire.* Thus *"alambrista"* immediately packs plural meanings for the bilingual viewer, who can equate the complex and often terrifying reality of undocumented border crossers, pejoratively called "illegals" and "wetbacks" or *mojados,* with that of tightrope acrobats, a term also equivalent in Spanish to *equilibristas.* Specifically linking the idea of *tightrope walking* and life-balancing *acrobatics* with the daily experience of the undocumented immigrants provides a metaphor of interlocking, exponential significations. First, for the film's protagonist, Roberto Ramirez, portrayed appealingly by novice actor Domingo Ambriz, the title underscores his harrowing tightrope walking to survive throughout the story as a husband, as a father and provider, as a farmer and worker, and fundamentally as a man. The beautiful opening scene of Roberto plowing the field in México and hastily running and jumping across the barbed wire when he is called to his wife's bedside at the birth of their first child establishes early in the movie a code of mutual aid—i.e., *un lazo de amistad*—that functions as a figurative rope or lifeline to hold them up in the face of hardship. When coupled with other scenes—like the first "bed" he is offered in the chicken coop by fellow *alambrista* and farm worker Joe (strikingly played by experienced actor Trinidad Silva)—the *lazo* image of mutual support offers the only respite to Roberto's repeated encounters with hunger, fear, longing for home, and exploitative employers who cheat them when payment of their earned wages are due by calling *la migra*, the agents of the Immigration and Naturalization Service (INS), to deport the undocumented braceros back to México. The scenes of mutual aid among the immigrants as they support and balance each other, like high-wire acrobats working together to maintain equilibrium on the tight*rope*, implicitly deepen the title symbol of the film by adding the *lazo* and *enlacer* ("rope" and "roping") metaphors.

By extension, the tightrope also represents the social and cultural cartwheels and contortions performed every day by millions of undocumented immigrants who are forced by governmental failures in their countries of origin to emigrate for survival and the eternal human quest for better lives. The tragedy and suffering of these contortions have been brought into stark public awareness at the threshold of the twenty-first century by the increase of hundreds of border-crossing deaths in the desert. In the film several scenes present graphic tableaux of these acrobatics of torture and also of the catastrophic results that occur when the alambrista(s) fall(s) off the wire of shoestring survival as an "illegal." The scene of Roberto and his mother praying at the altar before he leaves México offers a subtle foreshadowing of what is to come. With the camera catching the interlacings of flickering candlelight as a backdrop for the mother and son's silhouetted shadows, just as it caught Roberto's wife and newborn son, his mother sadly but matter-of-factly voices her fear that like his father he too will never return.

Another graphic sequence that underscores these acrobatics of suffering is the scene when Joe shows Roberto how to ride the dangerous underbelly of the train to escape INS capture and move farther north to the tomato-picking harvest in Stockton, California. Featured as it is alongside the friendly, funny optimism of Joe's lessons on how to survive in the United States with a little English and a confident smile, the striking contrast of the speeding train and intermittent shots of soaring telephone wires underscores the constant vulnerability and teetering danger of the alambrista's moment-to-moment fate. When Roberto tumbles off his makeshift pallet underneath the train and discovers that Joe didn't make it, his dazed agony captures the viewer's feelings: first surprise, then disbelief and unspeakable sadness. What also flashes back to mind after Joe is killed is the subtle visual image of the dangling rope in the earlier, brighter, and upbeat chicken-coop scene, which at first sight reminded me of a hangman's noose. From here to the end, the tone of the movie shifts to a palpably darker, heavier atmosphere to match the devastating consequences of falling off the shoestring tightrope of an illegal's subsistence survival in the north.

A second thread of the exponential alambrista tightrope metaphor concerns the soundtrack added to the 2002 version of *Alambrista,* which strengthens the film's multifold aesthetic, cinematic, and sociopolitical qualities. The music brilliantly enhances the original film's excessively slow pace and unfolding of narrative by providing both a sense of greater action and also a stunning melodic and rhythmic continuity. Although the 110-minute-long story still drags several scenes and sequences longer than film or thematic integrity requires (e.g., the car ride atop the train and the tempo of the final field scene), the added musical soundtrack to the 2002 edit produces a more natural and evocative cinematic flow. The haunting three-note phrase that underlies the score's melody provides a basic tonal simplicity, like a simple high wire, that lends itself to versatile repetition in different rhythms, speeds, and instrumentations. Composed by Cuellar, Herrera, Landau, and Montoya, and performed by Los Tiburones del Norte, the score varies effectively from the soft and lyrical notes of the opening pastoral scenes of Roberto with his family, to the aptly up-tempo chase-scene music when the workers are dodging la migra, to the chaotic discordance of the urban night scenes when Roberto is sick, surrounded by predatory drunken vagrants before he loses his balance and falls off the tightrope of his alambrista life. One of the most moving examples of this convergence of music and title metaphor is the use of the bluesy guitar and jazz saxophone for "Dog-tired Stockton Blues" in the cafe scene when Roberto collapses from exhaustion and illness, presumably caused by overwork and pesticide exposure. The sax's tradition in jazz and rhythm and blues as an instrument for expressing the emotional language of struggling through pain and solitude helps rescue the scene from sentimentality. Also artistically effective was the funereal improvisation of the "Star Spangled Banner" woven into the score's three-note base melody near the film's conclusion at the border. Accompanying the Mexican woman who forces herself to give birth on the U.S. side to ensure citizenship for her child, the improvisation emphasizes an irony that can be missed in the unscored version, which, by presenting the birthing woman in close-up, allows the visual focus solely on her unrelieved public suffering but misses the underlying politics of immigration. The score is also punctuated by country western, folk, and *corrido* music that connect Roberto and the viewer to the broader social context and thereby improve the film's overall cinematic quality.

A third deepening of this essay's argument that the title offers an exponential metaphor of tightrope acrobatics relates to the crafting of the film itself. When Young and his cinematic collaborators chose their subject matter in the 1970s, their progress from seed of idea to canned movie reel required the usual equilibristic balancing act of conceptualization, research, scripting, casting, direction, and coproduction that typifies filmmaking. Young's characteristic desire as a filmmaker to capture documentary authenticity presented particular challenges as he approached his choice of subject, a day-in-the-life representation of an undocumented border crosser. The director's approach led him to cast American and Mexican actors unfamiliar to most U.S. audiences, as well as to include local people as background extras. He also elected to use extensive Spanish-language dialogue with English subtitles to convey the remote, underground-railroad qualities of the undocumented worker labor stream north. When first released the movie was praised in part for its success in representing the consciousness and gaze of a mestizo worker with a freshness and integrity that combined the medium's tendency to reduce characterization to simple types, i.e., Everyman, with a documentary approach that added complexity and depth. In my first viewing I recall being especially moved by the movie's use of untranslated Spanish, a technique I interpreted as treating me and the millions of bilinguals like me (whose ancestry in the Southwest antedates by over one hundred years that of the 1621 European landing on Plymouth Rock) as part of the mainstream American audience we actually are, instead of marginalized as outside "others." Young's creative choices in casting and language contribute to the final product's psychological tension and add to the visual appeal of Roberto individually and as a representative of millions of other alambristas and their fate.

The 2002 re-release of an adapted *Alambrista* offers a third facet of the metaphor by underscoring the importance of a Chicano and Chicana intellectual consciousness for preserving this amazing work. It is this intelligentsia of advocates alone who recuperated the movie from anonymity by seeking sponsorship for its preservation and for promoting its addition to the dynamic canon of Latina- and Latino-themed subjects. This intellectual and political commitment by critical culture studies specialists and other researchers continues from the last two decades of the twentieth century into the present. Building a collaborative team (Carrasco, Camarillo, Cuellar, et al.) and attending to copyrights, funding, re-editings, and, importantly, composing an integrated score and soundtrack, suggest only a hint of the tightrope balancing of this essay's conceptual metaphor. Part of the balancing includes the interanimating significations of debate, research, writing, editing, and, importantly, also the *enlace* of academic collaboration (Candelaria, ed. 2004).

The title of this essay is also intended to draw attention to the U.S.-México border as a powerful symbol of the *mestizaje*[4] of the Americas, north and south, east and west, central and Caribbean. The Spanish word for racial mixture, *mestizaje* refers specifically to the hybrid mixture of Spanish, Native American, and African heritage that has constituted Latina and Latino cultural and anthropological identity in the Americas since the colonial period (Bost 2004). Although often overlooked, interracial mixture is fundamental to the human species because of the (trans)migration, trade networks, and exogamy required for human survival. By its very hybrid nature of interlocking characteristics, *mestizaje* complicates the drawing of strict racial boundaries. The term *mestizo* is still used to describe Latin Americans and Latinos throughout the Americas and refers to a broad range of genetic, cultural, historical, and physical identities.

Though their colonial histories differ significantly, Latin American nations share with North America a foundation of racial and cultural mixture. In recognizing the reality of human interaction as a constant flow of interanimating exchanges and as a fundamental *necessity,* the peoples of the Americas—and the world—can come to accept that *mestizaje* is one of humankind's greatest inheritances. Part of what accounts for the 1977 film *Alambrista's* vanguard politics is its recognition of this fact and its concomitant representation of the border in its fluid dynamism of interlocking cultures.

The film illustrates that the Mexican worker with a green card or without; the Mexican American by birth or naturalized; the border patrol whether Anglo, Chicano, or another ethnicity; and the U.S. American worker share the same immigrant and hybrid story of transmigration. This is effectively illustrated in the movie's subplot love story of Roberto and the waitress Sharon (poignantly portrayed by Linda Gillin), who are united by their abject need for love, protection, and mutual friendship. Although complicated by Roberto's guilt about his wife and family back home, the subplot exposes the shared reality of the lovers as downtrodden workers trapped in similar circumstances with identical needs regardless of ethnicity. The psychology of a mestizo hybridity that is not only denied by official policy but actually punished is also dramatically apparent in the disturbing ending when Roberto goes berserk: a worker driven to madness by the unrelieved desperation of his circumstances. Like similar trapped characters in American literature (e.g., Bigger Thomas in Richard Wright's *Native Son,* Edna Pontellier in Kate Chopin's *The Awakening,* and Cayo in Leslie Marmon Silko's *Ceremony*—to name but three of many martyred anti-heroes of American fiction), Roberto's repressed rage explodes when he is confronted with the death and abandonment of his father. His eyes suddenly open to the realization that he himself has replicated his father's life without any appreciable gain. Thus, his rage and insane violence reflect a mestizo microcosm of the insanity of a macrocosmic system and the political and economic structures that produce them. The film makes it clear that the culpable macrocosm is both U.S. American *and* Mexican, both political *and* economic.

The heart of that truth returns me to the title metaphor, the tightrope-walking acrobatics of the border and the multiplicity of its mestizo consciousness. The simultaneous tumbling and juggling of multiple racial and cultural elements and contorting north-south histories that border crossers like Roberto and the Chicano and Anglo coyotes represent offer insight into how mestizos must constantly negotiate difference. Evolved *mestizaje* requires a constant balancing of contradictions and defying of binary oppositions while simultaneously embracing the very alienation produced by colonized marginality—embracing it as a fuel and/or tactic for subversion just as the *equilibrista* dares to defy the tightrope with amazing feats of courage, creativity, and respect. The musical score added to the revised *Alambrista* provides an appealing dimension that bridges ethnicity, race, nation, and transnationality outside singular or binary frameworks. In the end, it is each viewer who ultimately makes the tightrope metaphor exponential. Each must come to terms with the unignorable facts of the border as a site of current social, political, and cultural tumult, and also of multiple historical and artistic (re)constructions. Every American(o) north *and* south of the U.S.-México border walks the tightrope, and it is one's knowledge, viewpoint, and experience that determines whether the perspective one possesses is that of a multiply victimized alambrista, a high-wire equilibrista, and/or an aware and politically conscientized amalgam of both.

■

Discussion Questions

1. With reference to the chapter "Tightrope Walking the Border," explain the aptness of the movie's title both as a description of Roberto's individual situation and also as a symbol of the larger diaspora of Mexican workers.

2. Define *mestizaje* and discuss the arguments made in this chapter supporting it as an important unifying motif for the film and its subject. How does the romance between Roberto and the waitress support or refute the chapter's thesis?

3. Identify at least two scenes in the movie that you found especially moving to you personally (i.e., funny, sad, pathetic, scary, etc.). What visual cinematic elements help make the scene work for you? What role does the background music play in contributing to the scene's impact? Be specific.

Notes

1. The Chicano Renaissance refers to the period of flourishing Mexican American literary and other artistic production in the United States, which is variably dated 1967–1983. These dates mark the start of the first Chicano-identified bilingual journal, *El Grito*, at Berkeley, and the publication of *This Bridge Called my Back*, the influential anthology that in hindsight appears to have moved early Chicana feminism to another wave of decolonized, post-colonialist consciousness. See *Decolonial Voices: Chicana and Chicano Cultural Studies in the 21st Century*, edited by Arturo Aldama and Naomi Quiñonez (Bloomington: Indiana University Press, 2002), and *Women Poets of the Americas: Toward a Pan-American Gathering*, edited by Jacqueline V. Brogan and Cordelia Candelaria (Notre Dame: University of Notre Dame Press, 1999).

2. Young's online biography lists a Cannes Camera d'Or, an Emmy, a Peabody, and two George Polk Heroism in Journalism prizes among his filmmaking honors.

3. Senator Joseph McCarthy, Republican from Wisconsin, actively publicized his spurious hunt for communist subversives through many means, including the House Un-American Activities Committee. He was eventually exposed and censured by the U.S. Senate in 1954 for his baseless attacks.

4. For these and other reasons associated with differences between genetic inheritance, recessive genes, and physical appearance, many anthropologists reject the very concept of *race* as an accurate trait for human grouping. The makeup of *mestizaje* varies throughout Latin American nations and regions based on their different racial histories, economies, and patterns of development and slavery: more Europeanized in Argentina, more predominantly indigenous in Guatemala, more Africanist in Cuba and Brazil (often described as "afro-*mestizaje*"). Moreover, in an effort to solidify national unity, *mestizaje* has historically been embraced as a defining characteristic in Latin American nationalist movements. Both the Cuban and the Mexican revolutions of the twentieth century were represented as movements of racially mixed peoples. Both Martí and Vasconcelos turned to *mestizaje* as a source of commonality within racially and culturally diverse nations, and their emphasis on unity overshadowed the existing material reality of racial prejudice and Caucasian-based hierarchies. (Taken from Suzanne Bost's entry on *Mestizaje* in the *Encyclopedia of Latina and Latino Popular Culture(s) in the United States*, Cordelia Candelaria, et al., eds. Forthcoming 2004.)

Works Consulted

Anzaldúa, Gloria. *Borderlands/La Frontera: The New Mestiza.* San Francisco: Spinsters/Aunt Lute, 1987.

Bhabha, Homi K. *The Location of Culture.* London and New York: Routledge, 1994.

Bost, Suzanne. "Mestizaje" in *Encyclopedia of Latina and Latino Popular Culture(s) in the United States.* Cordelia Candelaria, General Editor, with Co-Specialist Editors Arturo J. Aldama and Peter J. Garcia. Westport, Conn.: Greenwood Publishing Group, forthcoming 2004.

Candelaria, Cordelia. *Cursing Fujimori and Other Andean Reflections.* Madison, Wisc.: Hilltop Press, 2004.

———. "*Différance* and the Discourse of 'Community' in Writings by and about the Ethnic Other(s)." In *An Other Tongue: Nation and Ethnicity in the Linguistic Borderlands.* Edited by Alfred Artéaga. Durham, N.C.: Duke University Press, 1994, 185–202.

———. "Perspectives on Social Equity in Film Criticism." In *Chicano Images in Film,* edited by Don Cardenas and Suzanne Schneider. Denver: Bilingual Communication Center, 1981.

———. "Social Equity and Film Portrayals of *La mujer hispana.*" In *Chicano Cinema: Research, Reviews, and Resources.* Edited by Gary Keller, pp. 64–70. Binghamton, N.Y.: Bilingual Review/Press, 1984.

Candelaria, Cordelia, ed. with Arturo J. Aldama and Peter J. Garcia. *Encyclopedia of Latina and Latino Popular Culture(s) in the United States.* Westport, Conn.: Greenwood Publishing Group, in press, 2004.

Cardenas, Don and Susanne Schneider. *Chicano Images in Film.* Denver: Bilingual Communication Center, 1981.

Craig, Richard B. *The Bracero Program: Interest Groups and Foreign Policy.* Austin: University of Texas Press, 1971.

De la Peña, Guillermo. "Nationals and Foreigners in the History of Mexican Anthropology." In *The Conditions of Reciprocal Understanding: A Centennial Conference at International House, the University of Chicago,* September 12–17, 1992. Edited by James W. Fernandez and Milton B. Singer. Chicago: The Center for International Studies, the University of Chicago, 1995.

DeSipio, Louis and Rodolfo O. de la Garza. *Making Americans, Remaking America: Immigration and Immigrant Policy.* Boulder, Colo.: Westview Press, 1998.

Gutiérrez, David. *Walls and Mirrors: Mexican Americans, Mexican Immigrants, and the Politics of Ethnicity.* Berkeley: University of California Press, 1995.

Keller, Gary D. "The Image of the Chicano in Mexican, United States, and Chicano Cinema: An Overview." In *Chicano Cinema: Research, Reviews, and Resources,* edited by Gary D. Keller. Binghamton, N.Y.: Bilingual Review/Press, 1985.

Magaña, Lisa. *Straddling the Border: Immigration Policy and the INS.* Austin: University of Texas Press, 2003.

Movshovitz, Howie. "Review of *Alambrista!*" In *Chicano Images in Film.* Edited by Don Cardenas and Suzanne Schneider. Denver: Bilingual Communication Center, 1982.

Samora, Julian and Patricia Vandel Simon. *A History of the Mexican-American People.* Notre Dame, Ind.: University of Notre Dame Press, 1993.

Sedillo López, Antoinette, ed. *Historical Themes and Identity: Mestizaje and Labels.* New York: Garland Publishing, 1995.

Williams, Linda. "Type and Stereotype: Chicano Images in Film." *Frontiers: A Journal of Women Studies* 5(2) (1980): 14–17.

Wilson, Michael and Deborah S. Rosenfelt, eds. *Salt of the Earth: Screenplay.* Old Westbury, N.Y.: Feminist Press, 1978.

Border Crossings

Alambrista and the Cinema of Robert M. Young

Nicholas J. Cull

Robert M. Young's *Alambrista* is doubly worthy of scholarly attention. It is an innovative but neglected work by one of the most innovative but neglected filmmakers working in U.S. independent film. The theme of border crossing, which is so prominent in the content (and technique) of *Alambrista,* permeates Young's career. He has negotiated borders in more than one way. In terms of content, he has frequently transcended borders of identity, addressing issues of race, class, gender, and handicap that mainstream American film has preferred to avoid. He has called his films "drama of the commonplace."[1] As he explained to an interviewer in 1982: "All my stories are the same. They're about people to whom life gave a raw deal. But they're not losers. They have dignity."[2] In terms of technique, Young has mixed the cinema in which he came of age—documentary film—with traditional narrative film.

Film scholars are used to finding alternatives to the dominant U.S. cinema in the work of filmmakers like Ken Loach or Mike Leigh in Britain, but in Young we have someone who was doing much the same thing on Hollywood's doorstep. But one border that Young has been unable to cross is the border of the Hollywood mainstream. His commercial work has been limited, and none of his radical films have been "picked up" for wholehearted distribution or broken through into commercial success.

The historical significance of this body of work is to show how one career links a number of initiatives from the pioneering days of TV documentary through to contemporary independent film; and to point to a milestone in the representation of the fastest-growing, and arguably most underrepresented American minority group: American Latinos.

Background to Robert M. Young

Robert M. Young was born on Long Island, New York, in 1924 into a secular Jewish migrant family. His uncle, songwriter Joe Young ("I'm sitting on top of the world"), had changed the family name from Youdavich. Uncle Joe claimed that he liked the first three letters but as the rest was 'no good' in America he substituted 'NG'. Although relatively privileged, Young's background was different enough to provide firsthand experience of life as an outsider. Young's father, Al, founded New York's DuArt film laboratory, and hence film was always part of Young's world. At just fifteen Young attended MIT to study chemical engineering. He dropped out to serve in the U.S. Navy during World War Two as a reconnaissance photographer in the Pacific Theater, and then read literature at Harvard, where he was a founder member of the film society. Young graduated in 1949.

His early film work was in nature documentary film. His mentors included documentary pioneer Merian C. Cooper. Young formed a partnership with two Harvard friends, Murray Lerner and Lloyd Ritter, and the three began making education films, eventually signing for a series of shorts for Marineland Aquarium in St. Augustine, Florida. In 1957 these shorts, together with new footage became the pioneering underwater documentary feature *Secrets of the Reef.* In 1960, after a spell in India working with Willard Van Dyke, Young began to make films for the influential NBC White Paper series.

The early NBC White Paper films took TV news into new and uncomfortable places. Young's first film was an account of the front line of the Civil Rights Movement in Nashville, *Sit In* (1960). The film became the second White Paper transmitted. It won a George Polk prize. Young's footage brought the struggle in Nashville into American living rooms—it has more recently been seen as the core archive film source of episode three of the early '90s TV series *Eyes on the Prize.*

Next came *Angola, Journey to a War* (1961), which also won a George Polk Award for foreign correspondence, and *Anatomy of a Hospital* (1962). For the Angola film Young hiked four hundred miles through the jungle to hook up with rebel troops. His film included some scenes cut from the broadcast version of the film by NBC because they showed American-made napalm bombs ready for use by the Portuguese against the Africans. It proved an ominous precedent. In 1961, inspired by reading about the work of the Italian campaigner against poverty and the mafia, Danielo Dulce, Young and Harvard classmate Michael Roemer traveled to the slums of Palermo, Sicily, to film a searing exposé of the poverty there, called *Cortile Cascino*. The scenes included both poverty and shots of cynical scenes of Italian political parties handing out food at election times. NBC declined to screen the film, allegedly for fear of playing into the hands of the radical left in Italy. The tussle over screening became very unpleasant, with NBC executives alleging that Roemer and Young had faked key scenes with hired prostitutes. Their careers at NBC were over. NBC reportedly destroyed the negative, but a colleague, Robert Rubin, smuggled a print out of the NBC vaults for Young. In 1993, Young's son updated the film, showing the later lives of the family he had followed. The film, released as *Children of Fate,* was nominated for an academy award in the documentary feature category, and won the grand-jury prize at the Sun Dance Film Festival.

Although wounded by the response to *Cortile Cascino,* the experience of working on *Sit In* encouraged Young to return to the South, this time with Roemer to research a feature film. Their project owed much to the approach of the Italian neo-realists: finding drama in ordinary lives. Roemer as director and Young as cowriter and cinematographer set out to tell a story of African American life. Their title, *Nothing But a Man,* came from the lyrics of the traditional ballad *John Henry* (in which an African American railroad worker competes against a steam drill). *Nothing But a Man* follows a section hand— Duff—in the 1960s and his struggles against racism of the White world and class prejudice of Black Alabama. In the course of the film Duff (Ivan Dixon) falls in love with the daughter of a preacher (Abbey Lincoln). After meeting his estranged father, Duff decides to go against his example. He leaves the railway to start a new life in a small town. He gets a reputation as a troublemaker and finds it hard to get work. His frustration mounts until he finally leaves home. He revisits his dissolute father in Birmingham and is present as the old man dies. He then returns to his wife, bringing his own estranged infant son from a previous relationship, and starts married life again.

Filming took place in the momentous summer of 1963. The cast took a day off to attend the March on Washington. Cape May, New Jersey, doubled for the Deep South in the film and Atlantic City for Birmingham, Alabama, but plenty of critics failed to detect the difference. *Nothing But a Man* broke new ground in its realist style and unsentimental approach to its subject matter. *Nothing But a Man* also broke Hollywood taboos by showing Black faces in close-up, center screen, and even kissing. The film did not shrink from depicting the internal problems of the Black community, including class prejudice, single parenthood and absent fathers, and Black compromise with White racism. But unlike the heavy-message films of Stanley Kramer, Roemer and Young allowed their audience to draw their own conclusions.

Young's free camera style went wherever the "story" took it. He refused to use a zoom, but preferred to physically move his hand-held camera into the midst of the action. The film was a critical success and became something of a legend in African American circles for having been much praised by Malcolm X. Other critics have seen it as a document of the liberal Jewish commitment to African American civil rights.[3] Arguably it was a Black-Jewish coproduction, as Roemer and Young depended on improvisational input from their cast. In time African Americans would film themselves. *Nothing But a Man* is now seen as a pioneering transitional project. Commercially it sank without trace.

While Roemer settled into a new career as professor of film at Yale, Young (who was coincidentally going through a divorce) returned to his documentary roots, with films including *In the World of Sharks* (1966). The two reunited to make the comedy *The Plot Against Harry* (1969) (Roemer wrote and directed; Young produced/photographed). The subject matter, the alienation of a Jewish criminal released to find his old neighborhood is now dominated by Blacks and Hispanics, seemed unpromising to the distributors. It did not appear for twenty years. Young's most successful piece in these years was a 1969 TV film in the CBS Children's Hour series called *JT* about a boy in Harlem who secretly adopted a cat, which won a Peabody Award.

In his choice of documentary subjects Young deliberately sought out the stories that others ignored. In the late 1960s he became interested in the American Indian movement and lived on an Indian reservation in Montana. In 1970 Young lived in the arctic filming the Emmy-winning *Eskimo: The Fight For Life*. Although still exploring an anthropological track with films like *Man of the Serengeti* (1971) and *Bushman of the Kalahari* (1973) for National Geographic, during this period he became interested in addressing the conditions of Mexican migrant labor in the United States, and began the creative pathway that would lead to *Alambrista*.

The Making of *Alambrista*

In 1954 a group of blacklisted filmmakers had produced *Salt of the Earth*, an account of a strike in New Mexico. The film broke new ground in its representation of both Mexican Americans and women (who are shown as a mainstay of the community's resistance). The film was famously banned at the time. The intervening twenty years had seen little else to match this in the representation of Mexican Americans. Ed Murrow's celebrated CBS "See It Now" documentary *Harvest of Shame* (1960) had at least placed the issue of farm labor on the agenda. Young's idea for a feature film about Mexican American workers was breaking fresh ground. Young's interest in the subject led first to the Xerox organization for a short children's film in their "Come Over to My House" series. He began work on what would become the short *Children of the Fields* (1973). He began research in Arizona knowing very little about Mexican American life or culture. Indeed, Young later recalled that at this point in his life he didn't actually "know" any Latinos.

At an early stage of research Young attended a vigil just outside of Phoenix, Arizona, led by the Latino civil and labor rights activist César Chávez. Chávez had come to national prominence in 1965 when he began a nonviolent strike against the California grape growers for fair wages and the right to unionize. In 1966 he led a march on Sacramento; he led a hunger strike in 1968 and in 1969 a pilgrimage through California's Coachella Valley. Although he won substantial concessions from the grape growers in 1970, he was still engaged in the battle for extended unionization through the United Farm Workers. Like

Martin Luther King in the 1960s he worked closely with the church. By 1970 the struggle in the fields had changed to include the issue of undocumented migrant labor. A crisis in the Mexican economy prompted a surge of migration not seen since the aftermath of the Mexican Revolution in the early years of the century.

The experience of watching Chávez in action transported Young back to formative experiences filming *Sit In*. Over the course of ten days Young took part in activities, including handing out leaflets. During this time he met the Galindo family, farm workers who agreed to be the core of his documentary. The father of the family, Paolo Galindo, was not a union member himself, and took care that Young's film not portray him as a radical out of worry that it might affect his ability to get work. Young agreed—he wanted to make a "human statement" rather than a "political statement." Over the course of six weeks Young followed the Galindos from Phoenix, Arizona, onion fields to Stockdale, California. On the road with the Galindo family Young heard about the parallel lives of the undocumented Mexican workers who worked in even worse conditions than legal workers like the Galindos, working without papers, living underground lives, picking by day and even by lantern light at night. Young also heard a story of a Mexican woman who had crossed illegally into the United States when pregnant and who, although set for return, gave birth clinging to a pole at a border crossing to ensure that her baby was born in the United States and wouldn't need papers to find work. Clearly the experience of the illegal migrants lay outside the remit of *Children of the Fields*. Young felt compelled to recreate the scene on film, and indeed this became the final scene of *Alambrista*.

Before any film about the undocumented Mexican laborers could develop further Young went to Borneo to make a film about orangutans for National Geographic: *Search for the Great Apes*. He fell seriously ill on the way home, and spent some nine months unable to work. At the prompting of fellow documentarist James Blue (and others), Young applied for a Guggenheim Fellowship to make a film about undocumented migrant workers. He submitted *Cortile Cascino* and his Eskimo film as samples of his work. In 1975 $12,500 arrived to get the film started. Young began research by rejoining Paolo Galindo in the Southwest. With Galindo as his translator Young traveled around the region and down into Mexico, interviewing as they went. Here they became familiar with the slang of the border, including the ironic nickname given to illegal immigrants at that time: *Alambrista!* The nearest English term would be 'high-wire artist' or 'tightrope walker', equating the feat of jumping the border wire with a circus trick.[4] The term is not explained in the body of the film, and released versions have been variously subtitled "the wire-jumper" and more problematically, "The Illegal."

Young developed a story around the experience of a single Mexican farmer who crossed the border and experienced conditions in the United States. He is deported and then, in keeping with experience on the border, crossed over once more. He suffers further exploitation and returns home. Young's idea was to humanize the Immigration Service statistics by giving a face and feelings to one of the undocumented border crossers. He wanted to make Americans think; "How many people know where their food comes from?" he asked in the film's eventual program notes.[5] Young pitched the idea to the LA public TV station KCTV. Some $200,000 in further funding arrived in stages. Unlike *Nothing But a Man*, Young filmed *Alambrista* in the authentic locations. His small crew traveled some five thousand miles around northern Mexico, California, Arizona, and as far east as El Paso, Texas.[6] Although shot in and around the fields of the Southwest, and featuring genuine farm workers and immigration officials, professional—if unknown—actors played the key characters: Domingo Ambriz took the central role of Roberto, Trinidad Silva his friend Joe, and Linda Gillin the role of Sharon, a waitress who befriends the migrant. The only known face was Ned Beatty, who appears as a *coyote*, a facilitator of illegal border crossing, in this case to break a strike on his farm in Colorado. Minor characters included Edward James Olmos, hired for a tiny part in the film, who became the foremost Latino actor of the 1980s and '90s, and a regular collaborator with Young.

Young came to the film with a sense that the significant story *emerged* from the life he observed. He spoke of his role as a director as *allowing* his actors. He shot *Alambrista* sequentially to allow the film to gain its own momentum. He encouraged his cast to improvise within the framework of the script. The production soon gained an organic life and momentum of its own. This approach has been compared to that of a jazz musician. It was the sort of approach that terrified the certainty-hungry Hollywood studios.[7]

Filming began with the opening scenes in Mexico, under the scrutiny of a state censor, who eventually proved quite sympathetic. Even so the crew were asked to stop filming in Tijuana, over concerns that they might start "trouble." On the U.S. side of the border the immigration service cooperated with filming, recreating nighttime helicopter sweeps and farm raids for the camera. A scene shot at night on the streets of Stockton in which two drunks (played by Julius Harris and Edward James Olmos) taunt the Mexican migrants was played virtually for real. Olmos delivers a mocking: "Tote that barge...," a line from *Showboat*'s "Old Man River" that linked the undocumented Mexicans of the 1970s with the slaves of the nineteenth century and Hollywood's representation of them in film. As the two mocked the Mexicans as slaves of the twentieth century, the crowd became genuinely agitated. The crew hurried to film reactions before the situation got out of hand. On other occasions extras came to blows. A fight broke out during filming of a dance-hall scene, and Young found himself fending off an attacker who was armed with a six-inch lettuce knife.

The Content of *Alambrista*

At one level *Alambrista* is a reconstruction of experiences typical of an undocumented Mexican migrant worker in the United States. The film opens in northern Mexico as the wife of a poor farmer, Roberto, gives birth to a baby. Roberto, whose father had crossed over the United States and never returned, decides that he too must seek work north of the border. He crosses over, dodging immigration, and the audience experiences the United States through his eyes. He experiences much injustice—on one farm he and his fellows work all day, and then the farmer calls in the immigration department to arrest them all to avoid paying them. But Roberto also finds comradeship among the other workers.

After losing Joe in an accident while stealing a ride on a train, Roberto makes friends with a waitress. He ends up moving into her house. She takes him to a revival meeting. Despite/because of the language barrier they become lovers. But he is captured and deported by the INS. At this point the film moves into rather more formal narrative. Roberto crosses back into the United States to work as a strikebreaker in Colorado. In the fields he witnesses the death of a fellow worker who turns out to be his long-lost father. Discovering that his father had a second family in the United States he gives himself up and returns to Mexico. As he is crossing the border he sees a Mexican woman give birth clinging to a pole. The woman cries with happiness because her child won't need papers to be able to work in the United States.

The strength of *Alambrista* lies in its power to tell a story through Roberto's eyes. The American Southwest is rendered strange and alien; language remains a barrier as Roberto struggles to make himself understood and to understand. The strongest scenes of this alienation include his bewildered visit to a camp meeting in which he is baffled by the gyrating revivalist preacher, the scene where he seems lost in a department store, and a scene in the diner when, while "passing" as an American, a "good old boy" begins a long and involved story about his grandfather.

Arguably a weakness lies in the formal elements in the story. Young uses a standard *bildungsroman* format, with Roberto setting out on a quest. Like heroes from Oedipus to Luke Skywalker he finds that the whole trouble lies within the self—and his father. Once that inner confrontation has been resolved he is free to return. One must question the extent to which Young is here using the Mexican American experience as a vocabulary for exploring his own concerns. The degree to which it is primarily Young we find here is suggested when *Nothing But a Man* and *Alambrista* are set side by side. Both films develop a sense of community with scenes of eating, washing, and brushing of teeth; both show banter in the workman's space—no problem there. But in both films young men set out to make a new life, and come to a personal revelation having, quite by chance, been present at the moment of their absent father's death. Both protagonists watch ecstatic religious practices, but from the outside; both films show the mounting frustration of the protagonist, building to a moment of rage (spouse abuse in *Nothing But a Man,* a destructive spree in a junkyard in *Alambrista*). Seen from this perspective, *Alambrista* is a far more idiosyncratic text than it might first appear. There is of course a value in setting a universal "coming of age" story in the fields of California—public understanding of the predicament of undocumented Mexican immigrants was undoubtedly well served by *Alambrista.* The degree to which the body of the film rests on research and observation of conditions along the border saves this from being a *West Side Story*–style hot salsa poured over the cold eggs of the *bildungsroman* form.

But there are other places in which Young's presence as a storyteller is felt. If we compare the formal politics of *Nothing But a Man* and *Alambrista* we find that Duff and Roberto avoid active participation in the trades-union movement. In contrast to Ken Loach's recent *Bread and Roses* this is no recruiting poster for the trades union movement. Young may have admired Chávez, but he does not feel constrained to explicitly endorse the United Farm Workers. Chávez, like Dulce in Sicily or Martin Luther King in *Nothing But a Man* was the starting point, but Young's work seeks to advance the respective cause by stepping back and addressing the universal. Neither does the film suggest brutality on the part of the immigration authorities or police. Contrary to much Latino argument at the time these U.S. government agencies (who cooperated in filming) are shown to be as neutral as a force of nature: just doing their job. Young characterized his objectives in *Alambrista* as follows:

> This film is about people who pick the fruits and vegetables we eat, but because they are moving they don't have time to ripen themselves. Moving like that gives you the illusion of freedom. You think you are making choices but you're not. The film is also about divisions especially artificial divisions like borders. It's about someone trying to live with his heart in one place and his stomach in another. But you can't live like that, separated from your family and roots.[8]

Alambrista offers no political or religious answers. Young concentrates rather on a broad "humanism." He demands the audience recognize the "humanity" of the protagonist, and the injustice with which he is treated. Given the typical treatment of documented and undocumented Mexican American workers at the time in both American culture and American life, this was remarkable enough.

During the editing process of *Alambrista,* Young trimmed the early scenes between Roberto and his friend Joe, including an episode in which the two help a family of White migrants and are rewarded with a lift in their car. The scene establishes something of a commonality between Anglo and Latino working people, but also by implicitly referencing *Grapes of Wrath* locates *Alambrista* in a genealogy of American social commentary cinema. Other deleted scenes included Joe and Roberto selling their blood to a blood bank. These scenes have now been restored and help to develop an important dimension of the film: its humor. Young uses the humor of the scenes between Roberto and Joe to draw the audience into Roberto's story.[9] With fuller development Joe's death is felt all the more keenly in the director's cut. Young also deleted material from the second half of the narrative, including a scene in which Roberto goes to his father's house and meets a child—presumably his half brother—but goes away without identifying himself.

While editing the film Young also directed a second film with some Latino content: the screen version of Miguel Pinero's successful prison play *Short Eyes* (1979). Set and filmed in New York City's notorious Men's House of Detention (nicknamed "The Tombs"), like the play the film included a multiracial cast of ex-cons. The first director had so offended the ex-prisoner-cast during the first week of filming that they threatened to kill him if he turned up to work on Monday morning. Young embraced the challenge, recast the film, worked closely with Pinero to develop the screenplay, and completed the film. The film told the harrowing story of the fate of a known child molester (a *Short Eyes* in prison slang). Young completed both films at the same time.

Alambrista aired on KCTV and other public television stations in the "Visions" drama strand on Sunday 16 October 1977. Critics responded well. In the *New York Times* John J. O'Connor praised the "marvelously controlled expressiveness" of Domingo Ambriz as an actor and "stunning freshness" of Young's telling of "an old, old story." New York *Catholic News* noted: "Young has the eye of a poet in seeing beauty in even the most prosaic of circumstances: workers fanning out in the shimmering mist of dawn, water slowly filling an irrigation ditch."[10] Heartened, Young submitted both *Alambrista* and *Short Eyes* to the 1978 Cannes Film Festival. The festival declined *Short Eyes* because of the extremity of the violence and prison language, but accepted *Alambrista.* The film went on to be a critics' week selection and win the Golden Camera award for a first-time director. It also won "best feature" at the San Sebastian Film Festival later that summer. British critic Phillip Bergson praised it as "a gentle film of many qualities."[11] Martin Dowle in the *Scotsman* called it: "true to life . . . well made with a gripping story line."[12]

Over the following years *Alambrista* was developing a strong reputation on the art-house circuit. Janet Marlin of the *New York Times* (23 September

1979) praised the film's "unexpected intimacy" on the big screen. On 1 October 1980 Kevin Thomas of the *Los Angeles Times* compared the film to De Sica's *Bicycle Thieves* (with the INS green card as the equivalent to the bicycle) and noted that "Alambrista gives us the best idea yet of what it means to be a Mexican illegal," though he found the final birth scene "operatic." Reviewers of the re-release noted the complexity of Young's portrait of the U.S.-Mexico border problem as against the Charles Bronson action film *Borderline,* which depicted the border patrol as kindly cops and the immigrant problem as something that could be solved by tough police action against U.S.-based, White corporate traffickers.[13]

Young's Later Films

The twin success of *Alambrista* and *Short Eyes* opened commercial doors for Young. Robert Altman (whose style is anticipated in Young's camerawork in the 1960s) commissioned Young to direct his 1979 divorce comedy *Rich Kids.* Other mainstream films followed: the Paul Simon vehicle *One Trick Pony* (1980) and a comedy about a new pope locked out of the Vatican and forced to meet real people: *Saving Grace* (1984). In the 1990s Young even made a couple of biblical epics for Dino DeLaurentis (*Solomon and Sheba* and *Slave of Dreams—* both 1994). One of his most recent films is about the first westerners to observe the Panda, and was shot in China in the giant IMAX format.

Young has used these commercial projects to buy the opportunity to tackle issues closer to his heart, including rape in *Extremities* (1986) and mental handicap in *Dominick and Eugene* (1988). Some themes recur. Here the union organizer is portrayed as a lout—and a troubled father-son relationship is revealed.[14]

Young then addressed the Holocaust in *Triumph of the Spirit* (1989). This was the story of a Greek-Jewish boxer (played by Willem Dafoe) who stayed alive in the Auschwitz work camp by boxing for the entertainment of the Nazis. The film is notable for being the first shot on location inside Auschwitz; for tackling issues of both accommodation and resistance (it includes the inmates attacking one of the crematoria); and for including a Gypsy character, played by Edward James Olmos.

Through his work with Olmos, Young has kept alive the work of representing the Mexican American experience pioneered in *Alambrista*. In 1982 Olmos starred in Young's low-budget *Ballad of Gregorio Cortez* (for the PBS American Experience series). Young was again brought in to energize an existing production. The story focused on the celebrated Mexican American outlaw who famously eluded the Texas Rangers for weeks in 1901. Young told the story from the viewpoint of both Cortez and the Texas Rangers. In Young's version of the story Cortez's crime and flight are triggered by a tragic mistranslation. Cortez emerged from Young's account neither a rebel nor a criminal but a hunted human being. Young coproduced Olmos's directorial debut: the harrowing account of thirty years in the life of the Mexican American mafia: *American Me* (1992). Young directed Olmos in two family "dramas of the commonplace," *Roosters* (1993) about a Mexican American man's obsession with cockfighting and *Caught* (1996), about a love triangle in a Brooklyn fishmongers shop.

Meanwhile Young's son, Andrew, and daughter-in-law, Susan Todd, worked with Olmos on two documentaries, *It Ain't Love* (1996) on spouse abuse and *Americanos* (1999), a survey of the Latino contribution to contemporary American life and culture. Young and Olmos continue to work closely and are presently planning a number of further collaborations, including a historical film set during the Spanish conquest of Mexico and a biopic of a Mexican American hero of World War Two.

The 1990s brought some level of recognition of Young's work with the re-release of *Nothing But a Man* and the updating of his Sicilian film in *Children of Fate*. Young's awards have included recognition from numerous independent film festivals, including a Maverick award from the San Jose festival in 2000. *Alambrista* has continued to play at film festivals, and—thanks to a major grant from the Ford Foundation—is now reissued in a new director's cut with the present volume of supporting literature for use in classrooms. The film's central issue of humanizing the statistics of undocumented migration remains apposite of both sides of the Atlantic.

But more than this *Alambrista* now has added value as a historical document. It is more than a milestone in the representation of Chicanos. In 1999, during the preparation of the director's cut, the team working to produce educational materials about the film screened *Alambrista* to a group of farm workers at a community center on the outskirts of Palm Springs. Their overwhelming response to the film was to embrace it not as a window on the present situation but a piece of community history: a way of understanding their parents' experience. It may be flawed by the filmmaker's own psychological agenda (or allergy to a political one) but for the children of the people who lived through such conditions, it fills a silence.

Discussion Questions

1. How does Robert M. Young's choice of camera positions contribute to the impact of this film?

2. What is the function of the character Joe within the story?

3. Why do you think Young included the revival-meeting scene in the film?

4. The film ends with the massive coincidence of Roberto finding his father at the moment of his father's death. Does this undermine the film?

5. View one of Young's other films, for example *Nothing But A Man* or *Caught*. What does it share with *Alambrista*? Does it change your understanding of *Alambrista*?

Notes

1. Marlaine Glickman, "Sharp Eyes," *Film Comment* 24, no. 2 (March/April 1988): 32–37.

2. Gerald Peary, "Robert M. Young's Ordinary People," *American Film* 9, no. 7 (July/August 1982): 67–71.

3. Jim Davidson, "The Making of *Nothing But a Man*," *Common Quest: The magazine of Black Jewish Relations,* pp. 10–23.

4. The explanation follows the program notes issued in French at the Cannes Film Festival in 1978. BFI, London, *Alambrista* "micro jacket."

5. Ibid.

6. Young's associate producer from KCTV was Sandra Schulberg. Young had a coproducer, Michael Hausman. The rest of the crew included two brothers, Mike and Peter Barrow (grip and electrician respectively), an assistant cameraman Tom Hurwitz (son of Leo T. Hurwitz, the pioneer documentary filmmaker) and Young's son, Andrew, who served as the unit's still photographer.

7. Bill Shebar, "Celluloid and Synchrony," *Harvard Magazine* (January–February 1996): 52–55

8. Program notes (English), Cannes Film Festival in 1978. BFI, London, *Alambrista* "micro jacket."

9. This technique of strengthening emotional identification between characters and the audience prior to a tragedy is a staple of Young's films. In *Nothing But a Man, Alambrista, Caught,* and elsewhere in his work warming scenes in which characters dance together always prefigure disaster.

10. *Catholic News,* 13 October 1977.

11. Phillip Bergson, *Sunday Times* (London), 24 September 1978.

12. Martin Dowle, *Scotsman,* 28 August 1978.

13. Frank del Olmo, "Lights! Action! Border-crossings!" *Los Angeles Times,* 3 October 1980, p. 7.

14. Glickman, "Sharp Eyes," 32–37. Young described his impact on the story in the following: "I tried to push it as much as I could toward what is primal in the story, like the father beating his son, like the business between God and Jesus."

Robert M. Young and *Alambrista*

Howie Movshovitz

■ Let me start by saying that I've known Bob Young for many years, and that we've had many conversations about film in general and his films in particular. We're friends. We first met in about 1980 right after I saw *Alambrista!* I had seen *Nothing But a Man* when it came out in 1964 and I was nineteen, because my mother told me to see it, but I had no idea of Young's extensive documentary accomplishments. In 1982, when *The Ballad of Gregorio Cortez* was on the film festival circuit, we spoke at length about that film, and when I went home that evening, I realized that in the space of two hours, I'd just had about two years' worth of film education.

Young said several things that evening that seem to be like mantras for his work. He talked about how actors must not "indicate"; they must never signal to the audience what their character, the dialogue or the scene is "about." In other words, they must stay always in character, and allow meaning to come from the whole of the film without anyone telling the audience what to think or how to feel. Young also said that as a director and a writer it is his responsibility to create "situations," narratively and dramatically viable moments or events that reveal the essence of story and character. This principle is Young's variation on Hitchcock's famous comment that film is "life with the dull bits cut out."

Young also talked at length about lenses, colors, and camera movements. To understand and appreciate Young's filmmaking, it is crucial to realize that

Young comes to filmmaking first as a photographer/cinematographer, not as a novelist or playwright. He is primarily a visual artist and the core of his expression has always been visual.

For example, when Roberto (Domingo Ambriz) in *Alambrista!* tells his young wife that he intends to go north to find work, the shots in the sequence are far more about her than about him. In several shots, she dominates the foreground, and in several others, she's alone in the shot with only voice-over dialogue from him—showing the audience the sudden loneliness of her present and her future.

Young shot virtually the entire film with a hand-held camera. That kind of shooting causes a slight unsteadiness in the image, which instantly signals "real life" or "documentary," that the images in the film are taken on the run, that they're somehow unplanned and therefore—in the visual parlance of documentaries of the '60s and '70s—more "true" than steadier cinematography. More important, the hand-held camera also creates a general feeling of instability. As other essays point out, the title *Alambrista!* refers to the precarious state of a tightrope walker, and that very feeling resides in every visual image in the film.

In our long conversation about *The Ballad of Gregorio Cortez,* Young also talked about writing the screenplay. He said that early drafts essentially proclaimed, "Look what happened to this poor Mexican." Then Young looked at me and said, "Who cares?" Immediately he added, "Of course, we care, but that's not enough." His point was that the tearful story of unfortunate Mexican immigrant farm workers—or poor blacks in the American South, or Jews in Nazi Germany—has been told over and over. All one can do in the face of those chronicles of misery is to nod sagely and caringly, and the experience is over. Nothing's been shown, nothing communicated, nothing seen or learned. There must be something more at stake than the mere fact of wretchedness.

For instance, the Anglo Texans of *The Ballad of Gregorio Cortez* aren't simply racist jerks, and Gregorio Cortez himself is not just a poor Mexican. Cortez is smart, imaginative, sometimes combative, elusive, and capable of irony. Deputy Boone Choate (Tom Bower), who incites the Anglo population against Cortez, promotes his personal version of the precipitating event: horse thief Gregorio Cortez killed the sheriff in cold blood. But the film reaches beyond the clichéd tale of bad men chasing a good man because Boone Choate's character is at issue.

Choate is not simply a bigot. He's also a guy covering up his serious limitations as a translator with an appeal to ethnic hatred. His Spanish is inadequate. He doesn't understand the word *yegua,* and his failure helps to cause the shootout. Then that failure, in turn, opens the film into a number of interesting directions. Like Akira Kurosawa's famous *Rashomon,* which served as a model for Young, *The Ballad of Gregorio Cortez* becomes a film about versions of truth, how one's personality influences perception, and one's perspective on events.

In the same way, *Nothing But a Man* does more than intone the degradations foisted upon the young black couple. The young wife is the daughter of a prominent minister, who believes he must kowtow to powerful whites for the sake of his people and himself. The young husband is a laborer on a railroad section gang who's sick of bowing and scraping to white people. And so the class difference between the young marrieds, along with their different attitudes toward combating racism, bring the familiar racial family melodrama into new, more complex territory.

Alambrista! deserves immediate credit for simply showing audiences in the United States that there are in fact such people in this country. It's not necessary here to list the humiliations dumped upon Hispanic characters in American cinema. That's been done in a number of studies of images of Hispanics in film. It is important, though, to note that *Alambrista!* broke with that unhappy tradition. Unlike countless earlier (and later) American movies, *Alambrista! assumes* that the lives of Mexican immigrants to the United States are important and multidimensional, and that Roberto can do more than suffer with dull-eyed incomprehension—he can also run, think, and imagine. He can be sad, playful, angry, or forgetful. He can be judgmental, and he can even betray his wife.

But simply taking human beings seriously does not alone make a film significant. The achievement of *Alambrista!* is that the drama and the characters become interesting and meaningful beyond their specifics, beyond the characters' status as Mexicans or Mexican Americans or Anglo Americans or waitresses or farm workers. The film goes beyond the story of a young Mexican sneaking into the United States to do farm work.

In the same way, Michael Corleone or *The Godfather* is not interesting and significant because he's Italian, or because his father fled a murderous Mafioso and came here alone from Sicily. *The Godfather* films matter because they chronicle the life of a complex immigrant family and show how ancient and mythic patterns play out in that story. In the case of son Michael, the films imagine how a young man of intelligence and promise, who understands the trap that his family history represents, still gets trapped by his family's clichés and paranoias. Director Francis Ford Coppola took on profound and fundamental questions of America, and more than that, confronted the interrelated questions of insularity, culture, history, personality, power, and corruption.

So what makes *Alambrista!* a significant film is that in addition to acknowledging Roberto's ethnicity, the film makes Roberto and his experience important for all of us. *Alambrista!* is not an instructional manual on Mexican immigration for either Hispanics or other people; it's not medicine and it's not social work. It's art, socially committed art, but still a work of art that opens onto the land beyond the immediacy of its story, locations, situations, and characters to give all of those elements the power of metaphor.

Other writers in this volume speak far better than I can about how well *Alambrista!* portrays the social, political, and economic situation for people like Roberto Ramirez. Beyond those concerns, though, *Alambrista!* is a film about the conditions of strangeness and loneliness (unlike the constant crush of Corleones). The film casts its early scenes in Mexico as a graceful montage of soil, water, plants, family, and church, all supported by a single lyrical guitar. But as soon as Roberto heads north, the film severs him from those elements and rhythms of his life. To describe America, the film assembles often stuttering images of people running and hiding, helicopters with searchlights, police and highways. Instead of families there are groups of men; cooking is makeshift and the food itself is strange—as in Joe's (Trinidad Silva) playful lesson for Roberto in restaurant ordering: "Ham, eggs, coffee."

Perhaps the toughest experiences as an outsider come to Roberto in and around the restaurant in Stockton, California. Bob Young shoots the scene of the two ranting drunks outside the café with particular alienation. The camera moves so ungracefully, the images are so destabilized, that it's hard to know what's going on, and it feels terrifying. The sequence takes place late at night, faces loom like apparitions, and the backgrounds of the shots give the impression that life itself has lost its moorings. Roberto falls asleep at the café counter, a sleep so deep that he seems to lose forever his contact with home. He awakens confused and disoriented at the apartment of the young waitress, with whom he cannot communicate over the language barrier. Later he goes with her to the tent meeting, where the look on his face shows utter incomprehension at the antics of both the preacher and the congregation.

This religious convocation is certainly nothing like rural Mexican Catholicism, and the collective impact of these sequences marks Roberto permanently as someone dislocated profoundly—not just socially or linguistically. Roberto is as alienated as Camus's Stranger.

Bob Young is the one Anglo filmmaker in the United States who films characters of ethnic and racial minorities as if they were human beings, instead of exhibits in a zoo or circus. He does it in his best dramatic features—*Nothing But a Man, Alambrista! The Ballad of Gregorio Cortez,* and *Caught*—and he also does it in his documentaries—*Cortile Cascino* and *Eskimo: Fight for Life. Eskimo: Fight for Life* (1970), is about the last migration of a group of Canadian Inuit, and in 2001, when the Inuit feature *The Fast Runner* was released, I was stunned to see that thirty years earlier Young filmed Inuit people with the same intimacy—virtually the same shots!—as Inuit director Zacharias Kunuk and his cameraman, Norman Cohn, in *The Fast Runner.*

The Fast Runner is the result of what's called "indigenous filmmaking," a movement that began about 1980, when portable video became readily available. In a number of places around the world, filmmakers from industrialized countries and cities brought video technology to indigenous groups, on the theory that indigenous people had to "speak" for themselves. *The Fast Runner* and the work of Vincent Carelli in Brazil (among others) show that the ideas behind indigenous filmmaking work well. The movement is a direct, often politicized challenge to old-style ethnographic filmmaking in which outsiders come to remote parts of the world, observe native peoples from a proper anthropological distance, capture images in their cameras, and depart forever. Those films are then assembled and presented to audiences with narrations by the filmmakers that tell—that *determine*—what everything on screen means.

Indigenous filmmaking presents its peoples from the inside rather than the outside, and the cinematic (video) "language"—the visual intimacy that Nick Cull describes in his essay—is just what Bob Young has done all of his career. And it's how he films *Alambrista!* Young has a genius for understanding people different from himself, perhaps because in a fundamental way he does not see other people as strangers to himself. His genius, and the genius of *Alambrista!* is to make us see things the same way.

■

Discussion Questions

1. What do you consider to be Young's greatest achievement in *Alambrista*? Why did the film receive critical acclaim on its first release?

2. Why do you think *Alambrista* slipped from public view? Whose fault was this?

3. In what ways is *Alambrista* different from a commercial film made in a major Hollywood studio?

4. How would *Alambrista* be different if it were made today?

Notas en el Viento

The Musical Soundtrack of

Alambrista: The Director's Cut

José B. Cuellar

I. Introduction

I became involved in *Alambrista* when Davíd Carrasco phoned to tell me about his work with Edward James Olmos and Robert Young on the HBO documentary *Americanos—Latino Life in the United States.* He asked if I had seen Young's film *Alambrista* I told him that I had, and moreover how just days earlier I had been vividly reminded of it by a news video clip sent to me by activist Ricardo Sanchez of Seattle's Concilio for the Spanish-Speaking. It showed some of the deplorable living conditions of many migrant farm workers in the state of Washington.

At the time I was serving as director of the César E. Chávez Institute for Public Policy at San Francisco State University, and looking for ways to focus more attention on the past and present conditions of farm workers, plus the public issues and policies affecting them. I immediately thought of how *Alambrista* might well serve this purpose. We could screen the film for fundraising, and follow with a consciousness-raising forum focused on what things have changed and what have continued the same or gotten worse for workers in the fields.

The more we talked about it, the more I realized the great impression that *Alambrista* left on my concept of migrant *campesinos,* even though I viewed it only once in 1978. Before that, I really had no idea. The closest I came to the farm-worker experience were the few stories that my paternal grandparents, plus my father and his four brothers and sister, my *tios* and *tia,* shared with me about when they picked cotton and other crops as children in the south Texas fields. Mostly they impressed me with how hard they worked, how much they said their hands hurt, how much the hot Texas sun burned. I thought it interesting that they all told me they started by smoking the corn-husk tobacco cigarettes given them by my grandparents to keep the mosquitoes off their faces, while picking. By the time I was born in 1941, no one in my extended *familia,* and only a few families in my barrio, worked *las piscas* ('the pickings') for supplemental income. After graduating high school in 1959, I worked days as an apprentice topographical draftsman at Tobin Aerial Surveys, where my dad was a supervisor, and supplemented my income at night by playing second saxophone with the Dell-Kings, until I joined the air force more than a year later. I had no reason to think about farm workers.

It wasn't until six years later, after I moved to Stanton, California, to work as a club musician, and started using up my G.I. Bill education benefits by studying music full time at nearby Golden West College, that I noticed field workers more frequently, mostly from afar while driving past. Before that, I never had reason to think of them during my four years of military service or during my two years as a Las Vegas casino musician with various show bands. But the *movimiento* created by the historic César E. Chávez–led farm-worker march to the California capital of Sacramento on September 16th changed that, and soon had me petitioning, picketing, and learning to sing "De Colores," "Huelga en General" and "El Picket Sign" for *La Causa* alongside farm workers and other campus and community activists. I'm embarrassed to say nonetheless that more than a decade later my secondhand knowledge of the West Coast farm-worker circumstances was still mostly limited to what I learned from speeches of César E. Chávez, Dolores Huerta, Luis Valdez, and others associated with the United Farm Workers movement, and from Ernesto Galarza's *Spiders in the House and Workers in the Field* (1970). I learned enough about their real needs for better housing and health care, education and transportation, and reduced exposure to dangerous pesticides to be a UFW activist. I also learned how important artistic expression—*cancion,* mural, poem, poster, and *acto*—was to spreading support for the farm-worker movement.

Seeing *Alambrista* for the first time in 1978 made me even more aware of how little I knew about the actual circumstances of the undocumented farm workers, who remain unorganized and unrepresented. It made me realize how much more work was necessary to improve their conditions. It reaffirmed a number of primary public policy concerns for me: how to provide adequate housing for all farm workers, especially undocumented; what to do about strikebreaking and union-busting farm contractors who illegally use undocumented workers; and how to prevent exposure of nonunion farm workers to dangerous pesticides. Now it is obvious how viewing *Alambrista* only once caused me to become more involved in advocacy for undocumented and unrepresented farm workers. It reinforced my commitment to finding ways to meet their needs. It impressed me with the power of film, particularly this one.

Davíd told me that Bob Young really wanted to redo the film by cutting some overlong scenes and restoring others, plus giving it a new musical soundtrack more reflective of the farm-worker *cultura.* We agreed that, given contemporary technology, the costs of producing such a director's cut of the film was more affordable than ever before. Davíd already had a meeting scheduled with Bob in West Los Angeles later that spring, and invited me to join them after he heard what I had to say about *Alambrista,* and because of my extensive musical experience.

Since we first met in 1977, when I joined the faculty at the University of Colorado at Boulder, Davíd has observed and heard me perform everything from blues to salsa and from funk to *ranchera,* live with various groups, including Dr. Loco's Rockin' Jalapeño Band and Amorindio, at various venues from coast to coast. Davíd became convinced that my unique "anthro-músico" style contributed to the creative renovations that were redefining U.S. popular culture, and he attended our performances coast to coast and sometimes helped present Dr. Loco performances in Colorado and at Princeton University. He also analyzed my four critically acclaimed musical albums—*Con Safos* (1991), *Movimiento Music* (1992), *Puro Party* (1995), and *Barrio Ritmos & Blues* (1998)—and used them in his courses at Princeton and Harvard Universities as examples of what Chicanos call *la cultura* and *música fronteriza*. This made him aware that my comprehension of contemporary recording technology and my ability to work well with professional producers and performers have yielded outstanding results. And over the years, he has also listened to my lectures on various topics, and we have also talked about my eclectic experiences, transcultural tastes, diverse drives, and my language-mixing and genre-merging approaches to music generally, and to U.S.-Mexican borderlands music particularly. He has also long known of my passion for using music as a means of educating folks about the concerns and conditions of *la raza* in the United States. And now he knew of my passion for *Alambrista* This convinced him that I was the right person for the soundtrack before I knew it. Soon he convinced me as well.

After Davíd introduced us, Bob and I spent a long lunch at the UCLA student union talking about *Alambrista* and music. The three of us then devoted the rest of the day and evening to discussing in practical terms how we might make this director's cut dream a reality.

I asked about the possibility of screening *Alambrista* to raise concerns and funds for farm worker and day-laborer programs in San Francisco. In response, Bob told the story of how some years ago he gave his personal print of the film to Richard Marquez, a San Francisco activist who works with the homeless and other needy folk, like displaced farm workers, to use for fundraising. Bob also told of how much he was emotionally moved when he attended a screening of the film in a Mission District theater full of homeless folks who enjoyed it while they shared a meal. Before I left, he gave me a VHS copy of *Alambrista* to work with.

II. *El Método De Mi Locura* (The Method to My Madness)

Seven months later after we met with Bob, Davíd sponsored the first meeting with a group of interested borderlands scholars and activists who might serve as project advisors. We held it in Palm Springs, California, during the first weekend in December 1999, because by coincidence, I was performing at a significant borderlands event in a nearby community, the Indio Tamale Festival, and we wanted feedback on the film's value from a group of farm workers gathered that Saturday at the Valley Missionary Program in Coachella by Virgilio Elizondo's University of Notre Dame colleague, Daniel Groody, who was working with them.

At this meeting of potential project advisors, we discussed the positive reactions from what we might call our Coachella Valley farm-worker focus group. They generally felt the film was a valuable historical document showing the experiences of earlier generations, and illustrating some of the issues they face still. They encouraged us to go on with the project. Similarly the scholars and activists also agreed that the film had great educational potential at all levels and was worthy of support. At the same advisory group meeting, I agreed to put together a new soundtrack for the film using existing recorded music. Shortly after our meeting, Daniel Groody and others there sent me specific suggestions regarding songs and other aspects of the soundtrack.

With these in mind, I started by selecting songs or tunes with two criteria (one chronological and the other ecological), besides the obvious one of fitting the emotional and intellectual needs of the specific scene or scenes concerned. That is, they had to both be popular during the film's period, the mid-1970s, and represent the wide range of musical styles and variety of artists found along and across the U.S.-Mexican borderlands.

My first working list included Cornelio Reyna's "Te Vas Angel Mio" for the bus ride from Michoacán to Tijuana, Antonio Aguilar's "El Venadito" for the border crossing, War's "Cisco Kid" or my "Migra" for the border patrol's chase in the strawberry field, Buck Owens's "Streets of Bakersfield" or the Grateful Dead's "Truckin'" for the encounter with the Okie family scenes, Los Tigeres del Norte's "Banda del Carro Rojo" or War's "Low Rider" for the Cadillac-on-top-of-the-train ride, Santana's "Ain't Got Nobody" for the Stockton street scenes, Kris Kristofferson's "Help Me Make It Through the Night" for the love scene between the protagonist and the waitress, Vicente Fernandez's "Los Mandados" for the migra ride back to the border, Los Relampagos del Norte's "Que Tal Si Te Compro" for the slow waltz dance playing on the jukebox while the Chicano coyote is recruiting workers in the border bar scene, my compadre Francisco Herrera's "Saber Ante La Migra" for the border patrol nightclub raid, Jimi Hendrix's "Star Spangled Banner" for Roberto's junkyard rage-filled breakdown, and Bruce Springsteen's "Sinaloa

Cowboys" for the closing credits. But at our March 2000 advisory committee meeting, we all agreed that the royalty costs for the rights to use such existing recorded music on the soundtrack would cost much more than this project could afford. Davíd suggested that I consider producing a soundtrack of original recorded music instead, and I agreed.

III. *El Tema Principal*

It occurred to me almost immediately that the entire musical soundtrack of *Alambrista—Director's Cut* could be melodically rooted in the first inversion of the F major chord (A/C/F). I had carried this particular melody around in the back of my musical memory for more than three decades for a reason that was only now apparent.

It first came to me during fall of 1967 while I was running over some elementary piano exercises at Golden West College. In the middle of my practice, I picked out a very *mexicana*-sounding *melodia* that I had never heard before. There was something about it that had a *rancho* feeling. As I played it over and over, I remember thinking then that it had movie-soundtrack thematic potential, like *The Magnificent Seven* or something. But I had a completely different film in mind at the time. I thought of it as a theme for a film about a young ranchero coming of age in nineteenth-century northern Mexico. I had no idea how to really proceed with either the screenplay or soundtrack since I was just an undergraduate music student trying to learn elementary piano, so both ideas went on some mental backburner. Occasionally over the years, I recalled the melody for no apparent reason when I played around on the piano. But now it occurred to me as the potential musical cornerstone for the *Alambrista* soundtrack. I imagined the simple three-note melody could be imbedded in every tune of the soundtrack, in one form or another, thus serving as a triad thread from beginning to end.

That night I tried playing variations of the basic three-note melody on a variety of instruments—piano, saxophone, clarinet, and both silver and clay flutes—to hear which sounded best. The more I played it on my clay ocarina, the more convinced I became that it could work and that I really liked it because of its authentic *indio* sound.

The next morning, I took my ocarina to Bob's hotel room and played the theme for him. I tried explaining how I was going to use this melodic motif as the soundtrack's musical glue by imbedding it throughout the score. Although it was a pretty shaky performance and thin description, he was generally receptive, but didn't seem completely convinced. Yet he didn't discourage me. Instead, I felt encouraged by the quiet and gentle manner in which he shared some ideas he had for the new soundtrack, and his willingness to work with me.

I immediately went to work, reviewing the film and noting where we should replace existing music and where we should add new music. First, we decided to give the music a "raw" rather than "refined" finish, complementing the film's rather sharp (as opposed to soft) visual texture. That is, we decided not to musically polish the tonal and rhythmic edges to perfection. To the contrary, on some (e.g., the raunchy-style alto solo in "Ay Viene La Migra," the somewhat "sharp" soprano sax in the "Alambrista Cumbia," and the intentionally unrehearsed accordion melodic meandering on the national anthem) we sought to make the music particularly provocative by intentionally pushing the tonal and rhythmic margins.

Second, we felt it was also important to keep the musical soundtrack as lean yet layered as the film's story, acting, directing, and editing. So resisting temptation to include more rather than less, we maintained a minimalist approach to everything. We purposely kept the arrangements, harmonies, lyrics, melodies, rhythms, and tempos as simple as possible throughout.

Toward the same end, instead of recording with many musicians, we worked mostly with what is commonly known on the U.S.-Mexican borderlands as *conjunto-* (small group) style instrumentation (diatonic button accordion, saxophones, guitar, bass, and drum kit), in addition to the clay ocarina flute. We achieved the layering of melodies and tonal textures by first soloing this or that instrument or voice, with and without accompaniment, then computer editing the pieces together. We also sought to keep it simple yet connected by repeating various melodies over again as motifs in other scenes with different styles, tempos, or instruments. This is the melodic thread that weaves in and out. For example, we first state the *Alambrista* theme on the ocarina, then on the solo guitar, and later play it again with the full conjunto in norteño waltz style ("Esta Noche") featuring a dense accordion/alto sax soli in the middle, and then again in upbeat polka style for the "Alambrista Corrido," featuring improvised accordion adornments. On "Dead-Dog Tired in Stockton Blues, Part 1," we solo the slow-walking bass and play our low-down-and-dirty blues variation of the basic melody on the baritone sax. Then on "Dead-Dog Tired in Stockton Blues, Part 2," we feature California country-style slide guitar and Texas tenor-style sax solos. "Rite B4," the California country shuffle instrumental, features the Anglo country-style slide guitar with the Mexican conjunto-style accordion. "Right Before My Very Eyes" shares the same melody played at a slightly slower tempo, and with English and Spanish lyrics.

I should note that it became apparent fairly early in the process that in order to get the real-deal button-accordion conjunto sound, I was going have to learn how to play one. At first, I tried playing the parts on a Yamaha wind synthesizer using the sampled accordion sounds found in the Korg O5/W tone generator, but they didn't sound real. So after searching all over for several months, I finally found a Horner Club IB three-row button accordion in a San Francisco Mission District pawnshop. Knowing little about accordions, after pushing all the buttons to make sure they worked, and generally liking its sound, I bought it, only later to discover that it was an obsolete instrument no longer made or played. When I went to find someone to teach me how to play it, I found that everyone advised me to return it and get the Horner Corona II or Corona Classic accordion. But I couldn't return it, so instead I taught myself to play it and practiced enough so that I was ready to record the conjunto accordion parts on the soundtrack a little over a year later.

IV. My Raza/Ethnic Studies Paradigm

One of my principal motivations is to combine several creative threads of anthropological insight with the cultural grooves of my musical life. The Dr. Loco musical and educational projects have worked to combine these dimensions and I've worked hard to cultivate what I modestly call my Raza/Ethnic Studies Paradigm. This model, which has guided my activist scholarship over the past three decades, nurtured not only my personal perspectives and production efforts on the new soundtrack but the entire *Alambrista* project. The essential elements of this working model were first articulated and illustrated by Raza/Ethnic Studies precursors like Americo Paredes, Octavio Romano, Ernesto Galarza, and later developed by *colegas* like Juan Gomez-Quinones, Carlos Muñoz, Mario Barrera, Albert Camarillo, and Richard Griswold Del Castillo, among *muchos mas*. Here I have abstracted the five orienting propositions many of us adopted at the 1973 founding of the National Association of Chicano Social Scientists, as follows:

1. ...must be committed to scholarship that can contribution to Chicano liberation.
2. ...must be interdisciplinary in nature because the traditional disciplinary orientation...fragment[s] our research in a highly artificial manner, and obscure[s] the interconnections among variables that operate to maintain the oppression of our people.
3. ...should break down the existing barriers between research and action...[and] must develop close ties with community action groups.
4. ...must be highly critical, in the double sense of rigorous analysis and a trenchant critique of American institutions....
5. ...must place the Chicano community...within the context of those dominant institutional relationships...at the local... regional, national and international levels....Priority should be on the relationship between class, race, and culture... (Muñoz, 149–51).

By 2000, in an effort to make this methodological model more parsimonious and personal, I reframed these five propositions into the following four-point (community-centered, critical, holistic, and reflexive) paradigm (for a description of how I articulated this paradigm in the development of our Raza Studies program at SFSU, see Cuellar 2000). The following briefly summarizes this paradigm's four orienting principles and notes how it affected our work on the director's cut and its soundtrack.

First, our "community-centered" orienting principle urges deeply focused attention and action regarding those with great needs, like undocumented farm workers and day laborers, and emphasizes helping improve their life conditions. This operating principle directed us to take *Alambrista* to communities of farm workers and others, before and after completion of the film, for critical feedback and discussion of the issues raised. (For an earlier discussion regarding community-centered research, see Cuellar 1981.)

Second, our "critical" orienting principle leads us to confront, in positive and constructive terms, those elitist and dominant individuals, institutions, and ideologies that have negative and destructive effects on our global society. In terms of *Alambrista* this means specifically working to get those who most benefit from the continued unscrupulous use and abuse of undocumented farm workers and day laborers—such as greedy growers, scab contractors, strikebreakers, pesticide users, border patrol agents, and other law enforcement—to change their practices.

Third, our "holistic" orienting principle moves us to transcend the boundaries of traditional disciplines, collaborate across scientific and cultural borders, incorporate multiple methods and diverse perspectives, as well as to collect and construct findings, including qualitative and quantitative data gathered from multiple sources. It is crucial to recognize that raza/ethnic studies work to discover and organize new knowledge rather than see the world as a mirror of itself, as often happens when a single discipline or scientific approach operates without critical interlocutors. The holistic principle enables us to make analytic points, and to interpret their relative significance within a framework that integrates multiple theoretical perspectives (biological, sociological, ecological, psychological, culturological, chronological, cosmological, and espirituological). Therefore our holistic orientation emphasizes comparative analyses at all levels—from the interpersonal to the international, from the individual to the universal.

Fourth, our "reflexive" orienting principle, out of respect for the persona in the processes, encourages first-person presentation of selves. Our reflexivity thus steers our learning strategies in several specific ways. It encourages the public methodical exposure of our usually unstated assumptions and biases (specifically, those rooted in gender and generation, and geographic, ethnic, and economic statuses). It also insists that we learn to use life experiences continually as part of our intellectual craftsmanship, putting ourselves "in the thick of the action," as C. Wright Mills ([1959] 1971) emphasized, to examine and interpret it. Therefore, it also requires paying serious attention to the shifting hermeneutic of the "subjective insider/objective outsider" dialectic dilemma (for an early ethnogerontological discussion of this dilemma, see Cuellar 1979).

These four principles (*comunidad, crítica, totalidad,* and the *persona*) guided my choices in creating this soundtrack. I strove to create a *nueva Alambrista* experience by adding a sequence of combined compositions and arrangements, melodies and lyrics, harmonies and rhythms, instruments and voices that intensify the remarkable views of faces, body movements, and relationships revealed to us by Bob in his director's cut. I specifically searched for musical ways to both deepen and broaden how viewers appreciated Roberto's experiences of comunidad with Joe, the Okies, Sharon, and others whom he encountered. I also specifically melded musical sounds to screened gestures in ways that reinforced our crítica of how undocumented farm workers are treated in the United States. Most of all, I believed that our soundtrack music could help the film reveal even further the courage and concern, humor and honesty, tender vulnerability and beautiful humanity of farm workers with words articulating personalized perspectives on a variety of experiences from falling in love to being deported.

V. The Soundtrack

As soon as I received a VHS version of Young's final director's cut, I called in my musical collaborators—Francisco Herrera, Tomas Montoya, and Greg Landau—during spring 2001. A native of the borderlands, born in the California border town of Calexico, Francisco Herrera is my *compadre* (my daughter Ixchel's baptismal *padrino*/godfather) and a marvelous singer and imaginative songwriter, with whom I have worked on a number of projects. For almost five years, he and I performed nueva and classic canciones of love and liberation together in a group called Amorindio. Born in Wheatland, Wyoming, Tomas Montoya is a friend and an excellent guitarist with a wide range of musical interests and influences who can play a variety of styles and genres. He has made music with me for a number of years in both Dr. Loco's Rockin' Jalapeño Band and Amorindio projects, and I respect and admire his broad musical knowledge and experience. Greg Landau, also a close friend, has produced an impressive number of outstanding San Francisco–flavored recordings, including my own critically acclaimed 1998 CD, *Dr. Loco's Rockin'*

Jalapeño Band—Barrio Ritmos & Blues. His production knowledge and creative skills are invaluable assets. I was sure that together this team could create a superior soundtrack for the director's cut within the fiscal and time constraints we were facing.

In positive anticipation, Francisco, Tomas, and I started preliminary work on the melodies, harmonies, lyrics, and arrangements for the soundtrack in late January 2001, shortly after our funding proposal went to Ford Foundation. We met weekly to talk and play through some of our early ideas for the various sections of the score. Landau was brought in that following summer to help us develop and detail the good working version.

The director's cut that Bob sent included a "working" soundtrack with his musical suggestions for various scenes that we reviewed together a number of times, and we discussed everyone's suggestions. Given our well-developed outline, we were able to quickly reach general consensus on the details. At first, after I laid out the intros and parameters, we worked independently, each taking the lead on at least three of the tunes. Tomas assumed primary responsibility for the "Alambrista Cumbia," "Desert Cross," and "Rocky Road Rock." Francisco assumed primary responsibility for the "Alambrista Corrido," "Right Before My Very Eyes," and "Picket Sign" lyrics. Greg assumed primary responsibility for "Bajo el Tren," "Rite B4," and the "Star Spangled Banner (or José, Can You See?)." And I assumed primary responsibility for "Ay Viene La Migra," "Okie Dokie Shuffle," "Esta Noche," and "Dead-Dog Tired in Stockton Blues, Parts 1 & 2," as well as lyrical adaptations of "El Venadito" and "Adios California."

We then met for a couple of hours once a week in my home studio to work out the details of the tunes and lyrics together in various combinations. Generally, Tomas and I focused on the melodies and instrumentals, Francisco and I on lyrics and vocals, and Greg and I on the final arrangements. At various points in the process, we recorded and shared demo versions of the various soundtrack pieces with Bob, Davíd, and Al for critical feedback. By the end of summer 2001, we met more frequently as we rehearsed, refined, and finalized the soundtrack.

We finally recorded all the basic tune tracks with Brian Andres playing drums and hand percussion, Saul Sierra playing electric and acoustic bass, Tomas Montoya playing guitars, and me playing accordion and woodwinds, in Oscar Autie's recording studio in El Cerritos, California, over one long late

September weekend. I selected Brian and Saul for the rhythm section because of their impressive individual improvisational performance skills and their excellent ability to play a wide variety of styles in the pressure situation that is a real-time live recording session. The excellent quality of the musical sounds recorded in this session is testimony to both their musicianship and the engineering skills of Oscar and Greg.

I called this *conjunto* "Dr. Loco y Sus Tiburones del Norte" ["Dr. Loco and his Sharks of the North"], because no other *conjunto* has the name, and I liked the shark image. At another level, I thought it was consistent with the way we attacked all the different kinds of music we performed.

In an effort to stimulate spontaneous and creative responses to the film's emotive dimensions, we recorded several slightly different "live" versions of the tunes, while watching film segments on video monitors. Following Greg's lead, we then took these basic tracks and overdubbed the lead and harmony vocals by Destani Wolf, Francisco, Tomas, and me. Next we fixed glitches and added needed musical adornments such as Joe Goldmark's marvelous pedal steel guitar, plus other track sweeteners, like some additional live guitar and sampled percussion parts, in Greg's San Francisco studio, during October and November. Finally, the musical soundtrack was fixed, mixed, and set to the director's cut with the musical magic made possible by both the Final Cut Pro and Pro Tools computer programs during December 2001. After several finalizing music-to-film editing sessions involving Bob, we sent the finished soundtrack on hard disk to DuArt Studios in New York for the final film edit and placement in early January 2002.

VI. *Notas Musicales*

The following notes briefly detail the way we chronologically developed the soundtrack, from beginning to end, tune by tune, in the order of appearance. I include some notes on the motivation or intent, along with the complete lyrics and their English translation as needed.

El Tema del Alambrista

The *Alambrista* theme is introduced and developed on my small six-hole ocarina clay flute from the film's start with Roberto plowing to just before he opens the door on his daughter's birth scene. With it we wanted to stimulate some sense of the primordial roots that reach back to the indigenous by musically matching the essential elements visually represented here—rushing aqua water, plowed brown earth, hand-cultivated green beans. We play it again with similar intent for the scene in the Virgin's chapel where Roberto prays with his mother and she warns him just before he departs that he is leaving to never return like his father Alberto did years before. We bring back the ocarina-played theme for the last time near the end when Roberto finds his father dying in the fields.

The theme then appears in various musical forms at points throughout the film. Its first variations are developed on the solo Mexican-sounding guitar by Tomas Montoya, which we use to musically bind the next series of scenes—beginning with the moment Roberto opens the door on his daughter's birth scene and continuing to just before he enters the Virgin's chapel. We bring variations of this *guitarra mexicana* back several times at three important moments in the film, with the primary intent to emphasize Roberto's recollections, especially of his infant daughter. It plays in the background while Joe and Roberto finalize their travel plans, over beers, to go earn big bucks in Stockton. It plays again when Roberto tries to tell Sharon, the waitress who took him in, that he too has a little daughter in Mexico. And finally it plays during the scene at the end of the film when the young Mexican woman gives birth while holding on to a flag pole for dear life on the U.S. side of the border.

El Venadito

I thought the first verse of "El Venadito," a classic *corrido* that goes back at least two centuries, captures Roberto's essential wide-eyed innocence as he ventures down from his Michoacán hills to the streets of Tijuana, and across the *"alambre"* or wire fence into the United States. We changed the lyrics of the second verse to fit his "close encounter of the migra kind" with the helicopter-flying border patrol. The original third verse presented here, although not heard on film, perfectly prefigures his encounter-to-come with the fair-haired Sharon. Although also not heard on film, our closing verse anticipates Roberto's farewell as an alambrista.

Soy un pobre venadito que habita
en la serranía (repeat)
Como no soy muy manzito no bajo
a la luz del dia
de noche poco a poquito y a
tus brazos vida mia

I'm a poor little deer who lives
in the hills
Since I'm not very tame, I don't
come down during daylight
By night little by little and into
your arms my dear

Me subí al cerro mas alto para
devisar los planes (repeat)
Donde triunfan aguilillas no rifan
los gavilanes
Ni la migra Americana con sus
pinches aeroplanes

I climbed the highest hill to
see the plains
Where eagles triumph, hawks
don't rule,
Neither does the American
Immigration with its
chickenshit airplanes

Yo le pedi a una huerita que si me
lavaba un paño (repeat)
Ella me dijo que sí, sí señor
hasta lo baño
Pero vale mas temprano porque
tarde le hace daño

I asked a little blond if she would
wash my handkerchief
She said yes, yes sir I'll even
bath you
But better early because late
it might harm you

Ya con esta me despido, con un
solo hasta la vista (repeat)
Si con el favor de Dios dejo de
ser alambrista
Cuando cruce otra vez ya será
como turista

With this I say goodbye, with
only a "so long!"
If with the favor of God I stop
being alambrista
When I cross again it will be
as a tourist

To musically represent Roberto's movement north, we played "El Venadito" in the classic northern Mexican or norteño-conjunto style that blends the button accordion playing lead *(primera)* with the alto sax playing *segunda* (a harmonic third below) in a manner reflecting the stylistic influences of classic northern Mexican

188 ■ *José B. Cuellar*

conjuntos like Los Alegres de Teran. Francisco delicately sings both lead and harmony with subtle sensitivity.

Close Encuentro of the Migra Kind

"Ay Viene La Migra" is the alto-sax-*con-acordeon*-driven funky piece intended to instrumentally add a critical touch of ironic tension plus a taste of musical comic relief to the unsuccessful Immigration and Naturalization Service (INS) or border-patrol chase of Roberto in the tomato field. It definitely lets everyone know that Roberto is now on this funky side of the barbed-wire borderline. The intro to this warlike seventies-sounding laid-back U.S.-barrio-based groove plays a little later in Joe's head as he break-dances by the roadside while hitchhiking.

Órale . . . Okies

Bob added a set of scenes to his director's cut that he originally left out. These featured more of Trinidad Silva (*que en paz descanse*/R.I.P.) as Joe and allowed me to play music that intensified the visual treatment of their friendship that graces the film. Bob had an endearing sequence showing Joe and Roberto meeting up with an Okie family but he couldn't find the dialogue track. After studying the situational experiences, facial expressions, and body movements of this humorous but silent encounter, I found a way to musically magnify it.

I imagined that Joe said to Roberto something like, "*Órale . . . Okies*," when he first spotted them, and then taught Roberto that "okie dokie" in English translates as "*órale*" in Spanish. Watching the series of "silent" scenes featuring Joe and Roberto and the migrant "Okie" family in the beat-up overheated station wagon helping one another out on their way to Stockton led me to think, "Hey, they're shuffling around, having to move around, exerting a great deal of effort, and eventually even selling the tired blood out of their veins to barely make it from here to the next 'there.'" I decided the musical glue holding them together, "The Okie Dokie Shuffle," would be a California country groove that reflected the Steinbeckian soul of the state that spawned both Buck Owens's Bakersfield sound and the Grateful Dead's San Francisco sound. This seemed to be the perfect film moment for a musical transculturation bringing together the *mojados* or 'wetbacks' and the gringos or "okies." Toward this end, we combined Joe Goldmark's "San Francisco country" steel guitar solo along with my norteño-style accordion to instrumentally represent the musical merging of the Anglo and Mexican American traditions along the U.S.-Mexican border. As the finishing touch, we added our tongue-in-*cachete* lyrics that declare the *modus operandi* in simple two-part harmony:

> *You shuffle to the left*
> *You shuffle to the right*
> *You shuffle all around with all of your might*
> *When nothing you do ever turns out right*
> *That's the Okie Dokie shuffle.*

Rite B4

"Rite B4" is a slightly upbeat instrumental California country conjunto shuffle that, like the "Okie Dokie Shuffle," also combines steel guitar and accordion. We use it twice in the soundtrack. It first plays on the car radio as background for Roberto's Cadillac-on-top-of-the-train ride with Joe, and flows with the scenic rural landscape. Then its plays again on the jukebox as the White farm worker tells Roberto the story about his grandfather while sitting at the café counter. We used the same slightly upbeat "Rite B4" melody both times primarily because it serves as a mellow background for both the joking interactive conversation in Spanish between Roberto and Joe, and the funny one-way monologue in English. Secondarily, we wanted to musically underscore the ironically interesting similarity in both scenes of Roberto having to deal with the fact that there he was right before (therefore, the phonetic title "Rite B4") the cops, just to his left, at the end.

Bajo El Tren

We replaced the banjo piece that originally accompanied Joe and Roberto's tragic under-the-train ride to Stockton in the with our "Bajo el Tren," a finely electronically interwoven improvised piece that builds off the central theme by blending Brian's dynamically sensitive polyrhythmic interplay of rocking cymbals, snare, and tom-toms with the droning melody aggressively understated by Sierra on the bass with and without a bow, and various other sampled sounds, mingled with the roar of the rails and other sounds from the train's underbelly.

Dead-Dog Tired in Stockton

"Dead-Dog Tired in Stockton Blues, Part 1" starts with Sierra's deliberately slow walking blues bass line that musically marks Roberto's depressed stepping down the tracks into the darkness and cacophony that is Stockton late at night, after he discovers that Joe didn't make it with him. The haunting blues variation on the "Alambrista" theme played with a hanging dominant seventh note on the baritone sax remains in the background for the harrowing scene where the character played by Edward James Olmos harangues the early-rising farm workers by yelling derisively, "If the Mexicans are going to work, it must be my bedtime...," and fades out just before Roberto climbs into the back of a pickup truck with other farm workers to go pick grapes.

"Dead-Dog Tired in Stockton Blues, Part 2" opens with Joe's soulful steel guitar intro shortly after Roberto staggers off the old farm-worker bus and into the café. My gritty tenor sax solo begins just after he sits at the counter and improvises on the "Alambrista" theme by responding to Roberto's experiences from when he first sits down at the counter and then falls asleep. It builds to a free-blowing frenzy that starts just before he is robbed while passed out on the sidewalk in front of the cafe. It ends with the sax and steel guitar fading into the predawn darkness, as the Anglo American waitress and African American cook who saved Roberto from the mugging carry him off to her place. The intent here is to clearly indicate that Roberto now knows the blues.

Right Before My Very Eyes

For me, the most powerful love scene in *Alambrista* follows on the heels of the evangelical church scene, when Sharon looks at Roberto with delightful surprise and wide-open smiling eyes, and he responds in kind. "Right Before My Very Eyes" is the bilingual country love ballad that tries to articulate the astonishing feelings of attraction and affection that Sharon and Roberto seem to share from that moment. Bob said he wanted this to show how we all need love and the affection that comes with human touch, regardless of other circumstances. I wanted to show how the same loving situation probably had different meaning, significance, and value to each of them, and decided to express this bilingually by stating Sharon's sentiments in English and Roberto's *sentimientos en Español.*

After we first recorded Francisco singing both his and her parts, we decided it would be better to have a female singing the English verses. Our final version features Destani Wolf and Francisco representing each side of this brief love encuentro. Sharing the melody with "Rite B4" this country song features the following bilingual lyrics reflecting our imagined distinct desires of each.

Right before my very eyes
And much to my surprise
A look I've never seen before

Should I go or should you stay?
Will we see the light of day?
Will we wait until fate shows the way?

Entras en mi soledad	You enter in my solitude
Sonrisa alumbra mi oscuridad	Smile illuminates my darkness
Tu cuerpo cerca a mí	Your body close to mine
La verdad, te necesito	The truth, I need you
Aunque sea por un ratito.	Even if for just a little while
Tu pasión alivia mi dolor	*Your passion alleviates my pain*

Is it real, will it last?
Will you help me heal the past?
Why ask why, when only time will tell?

Should I go or should you stay?
Will we see the light of day?
Will we wait until fate shows us the way?

Tus labios sabor de flor	Your lips the taste of flower
Tus caricias con calor	Your caresses with heat
Me abren, siente mi ardor	They open me, feel my ardor
La verdad, te necesito	The truth, I need you
Aunque sea por un ratito	Even if for just a little while
Tu pasión alivia mi dolor	Your passion alleviates my pain

Right before my very eyes
Eyes that draw me to an open heart
A love that we might share

Again, we combined steel guitar and acordeon to musically represent the transcultural coming together of Anglo with Mexican. We wrote the last three additional verses because we wanted the song to play through Roberto's work in the cucumber field the next day. We left the last line in musical suspension, just like the relationship.

Alambrista Cumbia

Our "Alambrista Cumbia" musically marks the anticipated transition from the post office scene, where Sharon has just given Roberto a stunned look after learning that he is sending a money order to his wife, to the scene in the mexicano nightclub that follows. The cumbia, which originated in Colombia, has been a particularly popular dance among Mexicans along and across the U.S.-Mexican border since the early 1960s. Over the years, a Mexican variant of the cumbia has evolved along and across the U.S.-Mexican borderlands. We gave this moving accordion-centric instrumental a really evident *cumbia a la mexicana* two-four feel by matching the on-screen movements of the musicians playing and people dancing in the scenes with guitar and percussion accents.

Esta Noche

I was really impressed with the scene in the store when Sharon looks at the price tag of a kerchief she likes and decides not to take it, followed by the one when Roberto, who noticed her checking it out, takes it. Later, after they danced the cumbia, he pulls it out of his pocket and offers it to her. "Esta Noche" is a country-norteño-style waltz that we wrote to play from the moment Roberto hands Sharon the gift-wrapped kerchief that he bought for her and then romantically waltzes with her. It plays through his capture in a migra raid, and starts fading toward the end of the fourth verse, ending just before Roberto is booked and shipped back across the border. I especially wanted the last verse to be faintly heard as Roberto sits in the border-patrol van. These are the lyrics that came to me almost complete one evening after a rehearsal:

Esta noche te doy un pañuelo	Tonight I give you this kerchief
Pa' que vengas conmigo a bailar	So you can come dance with me
Tengo el corazon lleno de cariño	I have my heart full of care
Que con gusto te voy a regalar	That with joy I'm going to give to you

Esta noche te brillan los ojos	Tonight your eyes shine
Como espejos reflejan mi amar	Like mirrors reflect my love
Tu sonrisa como luna nueva	Your smile like a new moon
Escondiéndose quiere jugar	Hiding wants to play

Esta noche te baño con besos	Tonight I will bathe you with kisses
Cada estrella te voy a bajar	Each star I will bring down for you
Te decoraré todita con ellas	I'll decorate you completely with them
De pies a cabeza te voy a adorar	From foot to head I'm going to adore you

Esta noche soñaré contigo	Tonight I will dream with you
En tus brazos amaneceré	In your arms I will wake
Te amaré desde la mañana	I will love you from morning
Tarde tras noche siguiente tambien	To the afternoon after tomorrow night as well

Esta noche cantando declaro	Singing tonight I declare
Que te quiero, te quiero y que	That I love you, I love you, and so what
Esta noche juntamos esperanzas	Tonight we join our hopes
Que conmigo siempre llevaré	That with me I always take

My initial musical intent was for this tune to reflect the tremendous influence of Cornelio Reyna and Ramon Ayala on my writing and performance of norteño love songs since the 1960s.

Adios California

"Adios California" plays from the moment Roberto is seen riding the migra van back to the Tijuana border and continues through his signing up with the coyote to go work in the Colorado melon fields. This sequence in the film shows Roberto caught up in a ruthless revolving-door system that keeps deporting and recruiting desperate undocumented workers. "Adios California" underscores a combined sense of the work ethic, dispossession, and faith in God. Working from the "critical" principle of our raza studies paradigm we revised the lyrics to show the deported alambrista as driven by family love and deep desire to earn an honest living wherever he can get work. We lyrically adapted this borderlands narrative ballad or *frontera corrido*-style cancion by an unknown author to fit the film as follows:

Adios California	Goodbye California
No me voy me llevan	I'm not going they're taking me
Pero llevo tu presencia	But I take your presence
Si Dios me concede	If God will allow me
Muy pronto regreso	I'll return very soon
Aqui dejo mis experencias	I leave here my experiences
Volveré, volveré, volveré	I'll return, I'll return, I'll return
Esa feria me está llamando	This money is calling me
Estoy encerrado	I'm locked up
Perdí con las leyes	I lost with the law
Por andar de mojado	For being a wetback
Pero yo con gusto	But with joy I
Por mi familia	For my family
Voy a seguir camellando	Will continue working
Volveré, volveré, volveré	I'll return, I'll return, I'll return
Mis amores me están esperando	My loves are waiting for me
Si acaso el destino	If by chance destiny
Detiene a la migra	Stops the Immigration
Y no me corta los pasos	From shortening my steps
Yo sigo pensando	I keep thinking

Que pronto regreso	That I will soon return
No me importa los fracasos	I don't care about the failures
Volveré, volveré, volveré	I'll return, I'll return, I'll return
A luchar otra vez con mis brazos	To struggle again with my arms
Adios California	Goodbye California
Yo ya me despido	I now am departing
Me llevan para mi tierra	They take me to my land
Pero yo con gusto	But with joy I
Pa' ganar dinero	To gain money
Vuelvo a cruzar la frontera	I'll return to cross the border
Volveré, volveré, volveré	I'll return, I'll return, I'll return
Solamente que Dios no lo quiera	Only if God doesn't want it

Desert Cross and Rocky Road Rock

There are two guitar-driven instrumentals that we use to accompany Roberto on his reentry into the United States. "Desert Cross" is a densely layered meditative rock guitar solo *a la Santana* that frames the dangerous coyote-led desert crossing experience of Roberto and his coworkers. When we recorded "Rocky Road Rock," I asked the musicians to musically capture the sensations of surfing the Rockies for about thirty-six hours in the back of a large cargo truck with this guitar-powered punk surf piece that ends with a contemplative drum solo.

El Picket Sign

"El Picket Sign" is heard very briefly as Roberto and other illegal strikebreakers are fast trucked past the singing strikers picketing by the side of the road. This is a classic *causa* song that goes back to the grape boycott of the late 1960s. Although only the first two lines are heard on film, we adapted the classic UFW. cancion, sung over the tune of "Se Van El Caimán," with the following lyrics:

El picket sign, el picket sign	El picket sign, el picket sign
Lo cargo en Colorado	I'll carry it in Colorado
El picket sign, el picket sign	El picket sign, el picket sign
Mejor sueldos para todos	Better wages for all
El picket sign, el picket sign	El picket sign, el picket sign

Tenemos que organizarnos	We have to organize ourselves
El picket sign, el picket sign	El picket sign, el picket sign
Porque la union es la fuerza	Because the union is our strength
Salte de esos files	Come out of those fields
No pisques mas sandia	Don't pick more watermelons
Salte de esos files	Come out of those fields
No pisques mas sandia	Don't pick more watermelons
Mejor para'o con huelguistas	Better standing with strikers
Que empina'o con esquiroles	Than bent over with scabs
Salte de esos files	Come out of those fields
Únete con nosotros	Unite yourself with us
Salte de esos files	Come out of those fields
Únete con nosotros	Unite yourself with us
Porque trabajadores unidos	Because workers united
Jamás somos vencidos	Never are defeated
Salte de esos files	Come out of those fields
No rompas nuestra huelga	Don't break our strike
Salte de esos files	Come out of those fields
No rompas nuestra huelga	Don't break our strike
Salte con nosotros	Come out with us
Y mas pronto ganamos	And we'll win sooner
Salte de esos files	Come out of those fields
No dejes que te exploten	Don't let them exploit you
Salte de esos files	Come out of those fields
El coyote y el ranchero	Don't let them exploit you
Nunca pagan lo que deben	The smuggler and the rancher
	Never pay what they owe

Star-Spangled Rage (or José, Can You See?)

In the original film version, there is some rock-n-roll song playing on the radio in the junkyard background while Roberto emotionally explodes into what seemed a star-spangled rage. I wanted something more musically meaningful that critically underscores his physically painful realization that his hope-filled trip north had gone as sour as the taste in his mouth. This expresses several levels of loss. Roberto witnessed his long-gone father's death in the fields and discovered the miserable bus where he spent his last night alive in a Colorado junkyard, and how little his father had actually acquired, after many years of working in the United States. And he realized that these miserable food and living conditions are examples of how the "dollar" dreams of many alambristas often end.

I immediately thought of Jimmy Hendrix's Woodstock version of the national anthem playing in the background on a junkyard radio for this scene. From that it was easy to conceive of our acordeon version as a logical frontera extension. Our version starts with Brian's subtle drum solo building with Roberto's rage before my norteño-style acordeon tentatively (because I purposely did not practice playing it so that our one-take recording captures the "just figuring it out" feeling) states the melody that accompanies Roberto until his arrival at the border.

Alambrista Corrido

The "Alambrista" motif first heard on ocarina in that Michoacán field resounds at the end, only now on guitar as the border is crossed in both directions. The tema principal accompanies the unexpected birth of the baby boy as his mother desperately holds onto a U.S. flagpole for leverage. She has crossed the border going north so her son will be born an American citizen and not need papers to work. This border scene melodically segues into the polka-paced "El Corrido del Alambrista" that accompanies Roberto's walk away from the United States and into the closing titles. Our *corrido* poetically summarizes Roberto's odyssey to the United States and back, sung to an upbeat norteño version of our tema principal. Because the *corrido* was lyrically longer than needed for the film, the last two verses are not actually heard on the director's cut soundtrack. Here I use them to close these notes with a traditional touch.

Yo me fui de alambrista pa'l norte	I went as an alambrista to
Sin saber lo que iba encontrar	the north
En el rancho dejé a mi niña	Without knowing what I would
a mi esposa, y a mi pobre mama	encounter
	On the ranch I left my daughter,
	Wife and poor mother
Por la noche como venadito	By night like a little deer
De Tijuana a San Diego crucé	From Tijuana to San Diego
	I crossed
Casi a todos los pescó la migra	The Immigration grabbed
	almost all
Solo Dios sabe como escapé	Only God knows how I escaped
Como le hice yo no sé	How I did it I don't know
Pero aqui estoy pa' contarlo	But here I am to tell it
En el campo encontré otros pollos	In the field I encountered
	other chicks
Y con ellos las plumas deseché	And with them I lost my feathers
A ordenar ham and eggs	To order ham and eggs with
con sonrisa	a smile
Berto y Joe a mi me enseñaron	Berto and Joe showed me
en ingles	in English
Ese Joe fue pa' mi un gran amigo	That Joe was a good friend for me
Que pa' Stockton con	Who took me with him to
él me llevó	Stockton
Agarrados debajo del tren	Holding on below the train
Pobre Joe en los rieles quedó	Poor Joe stayed on the rails

Bien norteado en las calles
     de Stockton
De un asalto una mesera
     me salvó
Y por poco me quedo con Sharon
Que su casa y cariño
     me brindó
	Real disoriented in the streets
	     of Stockton
	From a mugging a waitress
	     saved me
	And I almost stay with Sharon
	Who her home and care
	     offered me

Corté uva y pisqué pepino
 	
Y una feria a mi esposa mandé
Pero en un baile me agarró
     la migra
De retache a Tijuana llegué
	I cut grapes and picked
	     cucumbers
	And some cash to my wife I sent
	But at a dance I was grabbed by
	     the Immigration
	To Tijuana I returned

Como viento bajo las estrellas
El desierto con otros crucé
Contratado por un gringo ranchero
Con coyote a
     Colorado llegué
	Like the wind below the stars
	The desert with others I crossed
	Contracted by a gringo rancher
	With a smuggler I arrived in
	     Colorado

Bajo el sol color
     cobre y sangre
Como un esquirol trabajé
Yo le pido perdon a
     la Virgen
Por el daño que a
     otros causé
	Below the blood- and
	     copper-colored sun
	As a scab I worked
	I ask for forgiveness from
	     the Virgin
	For the damage that I
	     caused others

Alli mismo encontré a mi padre *El la pisca el corazon le falló* *Nunca supo que estaba a su lado* *El hijo que él abandonó*	There is where I found my father Picking melons his heart failed He never knew that at his side Was the son that he abandoned

Palomita que vas pa' mi tierra	Little dove that goes to my land
Detrasito de ti vuelo yo	I'm flying right behind you
Voy de vuelta a ver mi familia	I'm returning to see my family
Entregarles todo mi Corazon	And give them all my heart
Es triste la cruzada de alambre	Crossing the border is sad
Aunque tiene aventura tambien	Although it also has its adventure
Va dejando atrasa su gente	You leave behind your people
Pa' venir a gana pa' comer	To come earn to eat
Ya con ésta, amigos me despido	*With this my friends I say goodbye*
Deseándoles todo lo mejor	*Wishing you all the best*
Preferible volver a mi tierra	*I prefer returning to my land*
Donde tengo amistad	*Where I have friendship and*
y calor	*warmth*
Tan Tán	*Tan Tán*

Discussion Questions

1. View a scene from *Alambrista* with the sound off and then with the sound on, and then try playing a sequence of the film with a sound track of your own choice. What difference does the music make?

2. What musical techniques does Cuellar use to contribute to the emotional impact of the film?

3. To what extent do Cuellar's musical choices deepen the cultural meaning of *Alambrista* as a document of border life?

4. Listen to the CD remixes of "Ay Viene La Migra," "Okie Dokie Shuffle," and "Alambrista Cumbia" and note your aesthetic and emotional responses.

5. View the music videos and note how the audio you didn't hear before augments your appreciation of the visual.

6. Critically assess how Cuellar's commmentary in the interview contrasts with his essay.

■

References

Cuellar, José. "Insiders and Outsiders in Minority Aging." *Minority Aging Research: Old Issues—New Approaches.* Edited by E. Percil Stanford, pp. 67–77. San Diego: Campanille Press, 1979.

———. "Social Science Research in the U.S. Mexican Community: A Case Study." *Aztlán* 12(1) (1981): 20–31.

———. "SFSU's La Raza Studies Paradigm: A Multidimensional Model for Multiethnic Latina/o Education Into 2YK." Special Issue: "Chicana/o Studies: An Academic Odyssey." Edited by Randall C. Jimenez and Maria C. Chinn. *Chicana/o Studies Paradigms: A Journal of Alternative Voices* 1(1) (2000): 23–46.

Galarza, Ernesto. *Spiders in the House and Workers in the Field.* Notre Dame: Notre Dame Press, 1970.

Muñoz, Carlos. *Youth, Identity, Power: The Chicano Movement.* New York: Verso Press, 1989.

Mills, C. Wright. *The Sociological Imagination.* New York: Oxford University Press, 1959, reprint 1971.

Dark Walking, Making Food, and Giving Birth to *Alambristas*

Religious Dimensions in the Film

Davíd Carrasco

In *Alambrista: The Director's Cut* we see and hear a powerful, profound, and humorous story about the human struggles of a Mexican undocumented worker who undergoes a painful and revealing odyssey. The combination of Robert M. Young's insightful cinematic eyes and José Cuellar's picante and soulful soundtrack have *recalled to life* this classic, award-winning film.

As the other essays in this volume show, there are multiple approaches to the film and the human sufferings it portrays. The film represents the complexity of farm-worker existence, which includes the themes of long-distance walking, exile, backbreaking labor, loneliness, temporary friendship, illegality, pesticides, labor struggles, sexuality, and death in strange lands. There are many ways to tell stories about Mexican immigrants coming and going to and from "el otro lado." My eyes are drawn to two threads that tie the film together for me: 1) the work and cultivation of food and 2) childbirth and family well-being. In my view these two threads weave the characters, structure, and narrative of the film together and take on religious dimensions. The word *religion* comes, in part, from the Latin *religio,* meaning 'to bind back and hold together' and suggests the image of a nexus. In this film, the central characters are held together by the work they do, the places they labor, and the friendships and families they love and serve. I like what the African American historian of religions, Charles H. Long, means by religion when he writes, "For my purposes, religion will mean orientation—orientation in the ultimate sense, that is, how one comes to terms with the ultimate significance of one's place in the world."[1] In *Alambrista,* Roberto, Joe, Sharon, and the others come to terms with their ultimate significance (in a world where they are treated as very *non*-significant) not primarily through the language or rites provided by the Christian faith or overt forms of religion (though they are important in the film) but through the *ways and places* they labor and relate to their families and friends, and their experience of human birth.

Another way to illuminate for the reader the religious dimensions of the creativity of the people in the film is to introduce the notion of *homo faber* or "Human as Maker of Place and Meaning." Examples of *homo faber* in human history include the making and use of fire; the construction of tools, weapons, and toys; the hunting of animals and the cultivation of plants; the production of new metals and wealth; the cultivation of new types of music, art, or languages; the production of laws; the generation of families, dynasties, and states; and the building of communities. In this notion, people become more effectively human through three types of "labor"—the work to bring new physical or cultural forms into the world, the labor of mothers to give birth, and the struggle of families to survive and thrive.

The film begins and ends with human births that reveal the painful outcast social condition of Mexicans and their lives as *homo faber.* The first birth, while initially a moment of quiet and humble joy, leads to Roberto's separation from his family so he can earn enough money for the baby to eat and be clothed. The second birth, which takes place literally on the Mexican-American border, dramatizes how the legal and social world of the Mexican American family and borderlands are split in two. As Roberto returns to Mexico in mourning and in disgust, a Mexican baby is born while his mother grips a flagpole crying, "He was born here, he won't need papers." These two "beginnings," one opening the film and the other closing it, show how these Mexican families are *oriented* toward crossing borders of poverty, labor opportunities, and U.S. citizenship.

We also see throughout the film how the spaces of labor and the consumption of food define the narrative of Mexican and farm-worker life from beginning to end. Homo faber in relation to food means 1) the physical work of growing, preparing, and eating food to gain access to the substances necessary to maintain human growth and health for the body as well as to earn a daily wage (on the part of the farm workers) and a surplus of money (on the part of the growers) but also 2) food as a metaphor for providing emotional, mental, or spiritual sustenance. There are numerous scenes of harvesting food from fertile green fields, of people eating on the run, in a café, and in a junkyard, showing how the places and work of food preparation and consumption locate farm workers in a *hyper-food existence.* The "place" of farm workers is the fertile fields owned by growers, mainly Anglo growers, yet the food the farm workers eat is humble, sparse, and without balance. Also, in this film the human relationships that provide some emotional and spiritual sustenance, if only temporarily, are intimately tied up with this culture of food.

Alambristas Making Family and Cultivating Plants

The combination of making food and making family appears in the first scenes of the film and recurs at crucial points. The film opens with water flowing in the rich Mexican earth between rows of plants, evoking the time of creation or the rhythm of a creation myth. A shovel held by Mexican hands carefully works the plowed earth so the water flows to where it is most needed as the musical theme, played by José Cuellar's ocarina (indigenous clay flute) suggests the mood of a primordial indigenous world. This physical labor intensifies as Roberto vigorously struggles and guides a horse and plow down rows of growing plants until he is loudly summoned, *"Venga a la casa."* He arrives to find that his wife has just given birth to a healthy daughter, who is being bathed by a midwife. These practices of cultivating the Mexican earth and regenerating the Mexican family reflect *homo faber* at the start of the film. *Alambrista* begins by showing the dexterity of Mexicans as workers who remake their world through farming, childbirth, and domestic care.

Soon after the happy birth of the baby, a quiet crisis develops in Roberto's household as he announces a need to *"cruzar por el otro lado"* to earn enough money so "we don't have to just eat potatoes all the time" and to ensure the baby will have clothes to wear. This painful separation reflects the irony of the Mexican *homo faber* because even though he is a sound and willing worker in the production of food for others, he barely has enough food to live or money to support his own family. At a moment of new orientation, new beginnings for his family, he is forced into a situation of disorientation, a temporary loss of his "center"—his home and family.

Alambrista Separation: Disorientation

The profound impact of this irony on Roberto's family is painfully revealed in a ritual moment when he and his mother are praying in a tiny local chapel on the eve of Roberto's departure. This chapel is located on an earthen hillside and is the first overt sacred space that reveals a major characteristic of farm-worker families—unwanted separation. Roberto and his mother are kneeling in prayer before a small alter with religious images and candles. Leaning against a statue of the Virgin of Guadalupe is a black-and-white photograph of Roberto's father, Alberto, who left the family some years ago for the United States, never to return. "No te vayas, hijo," his mother begs him out of fear that she will lose her son just as she has lost her husband. This quiet but tense exchange in a sacred place imbues Roberto's subsequent journey to the United States with a religious sense of loss and danger. Roberto tries to reassure his mother and wife and he awkwardly asks for their support for this journey to the United States in search of money for them to live.

This break with his family out of pressure to immigrate illegally into the United States is the common odyssey of over 8 million Mexicans. The priest Daniel Groody has recently written about the many dangers of this journey in his *Border of Death, Valley of Life: An Immigrant Journey of Heart and Spirit*. In a chapter called "A Crushed Heart" he summarizes this moment of separation:

> One of the most immediate human costs of immigration is saying good-bye. Only rarely do families emigrate together. Most often, the man is the

one who breaks from home, leaving his wife and children behind for eight months, a year or longer. "The most painful thing," said Juan, "is leaving the family behind, especially the children, but we do it in the hopes that some day we will have something in Mexico."[2]

Alambrista Walking

After making his way to the border on a bus that has the Star of David taped on its back window, Roberto is directed by a Mexican on the street to a hole in the *alambre,* the wire fence dividing the two countries. He dashes uphill and through the fence with other illegals and enters into a world of danger, uncertainty, economic exploitation, and backbreaking work. This vulnerability is echoed in Cuellar's musical choice of "El Venadito" (the little deer) in which the corrido cries:

With this I say goodbye, with only a "so long!"
If with the favor of God I stop being alambrista
When I cross again it will be as a tourista

At the very moment of his entry into the United States of America Roberto participates in a typical farm-worker "rite of passage" by walking quickly and furtively into what he hopes will be great opportunity. As some humanist geographers note, many forms of walking are disappearing from modern U.S. life, including the walk to work, the walk to the store, the walk to the park, and even the pleasure walk, though many North Americans walk as a workout.[3] For Roberto and the *alambristas* he meets, walking is the "in" mode of transportation at the very moment of becoming an immigrant and especially an illegal immigrant. These border crossers walk from a "familiar" landscape where they are legal citizens into an unknown territory where they are suddenly illegal. Daniel Groody writes about this moment of breaking from the familiar through walking or wading into a space where they will be hunted or hired.

In southern California, there are three main ways of trying to cross the border without passing through designated points of entry: through a fence along the border (those who do so are known as alambristas), across the border canals (known as mojados or braveros), or through the rugged terrain of the desert mountains and valleys. The immigrants make a dangerous crossing with few or no resources. No matter what the method, the three biggest threats come from immigration officials, smugglers (or coyotes), and the perils of the natural environment."[4]

Roberto is quickly threatened by the immigration officials and disoriented in the unmapped (though slightly marked by the footpaths of other alambristas) landscape. He and other alambristas are hunted by jeeps and a helicopter carrying border agents, who corner them in a dark canyon. Roberto slips away and now desperately alone hides through the night, a stranger in a strange land that has become like the underworld. Early in the morning he stumbles, literally, onto a group of other alambristas hiding in the bushes as dawn appears. This leads to the first food scene as Roberto is fed, both physically and emotionally, by these friendly and helpful men. The more experienced travelers share with him a makeshift breakfast in which they reveal two kinds of "maps"—a map of their diverse Mexican origins and cues on how Roberto needs to act around gringos and growers in order to survive. In this way, the scene of sharing food, where a used beer bottle serves as the *mano* to make tortillas, nourishes his body *and* his sense of self in a strange land.

We learn that these Mexican workers have traveled long distances from many parts and corners of Mexico to this temporary campground. They tell him they are from Michoacán (on the southwest coast), Zacatecas (in the north), Puebla (east central Mexico), Guanajuato (central Mexico), or as one says, "We're from everywhere." By word and gesture these many Mexicans transmit to him how to act, be silent, and focus on getting a job. He's instructed, "Don't ask questions … just say you want to work."

Alambristas Bent Over

Filled with food as well as some human sustenance, Roberto is next seen bent over picking tomatoes in the hot sun of California. This is the first of a series of scenes that reveal the backbreaking labor of alambristas in the United States, which is juxtaposed with the refreshing green fields in which they work and harvest tons of food for other Americans. Seen from a distance, as Young periodically shows us, these fields look beautiful and abundant and fill the screen with a sense of health and fertility. Close-ups, however, reveal another world that is "abundant" with bent-over laborers working quietly at dawn, sweating profusely in the sun in fields without sanitation, periodic financial rip-offs, loneliness and violence.

When *la migra* invades Roberto's first place of work, we see the desperate circumstances of these food laborers as Roberto races about, crawls on his belly in the dirt, and frantically hides so as not to be arrested and transported back to Mexico. In what may be the signature image of the dehumanized and marginalized condition of the Mexican farm worker, we see two human hands, shot from behind, gripping the top of a water cistern so as to avoid arrest. This scene is shot from Roberto's perspective so the viewer can begin to feel how his existence in this first job opportunity is clinging at the edge. Roberto has climbed down into a water tank, suspending himself with his hands, which are the symbol for what he has of human value in the United States. Young's perspective in this scene gives us an ironic view of *homo faber,* the human as worker and maker, showing us that the Mexican is valued only as "hands," without the attached head, face, body, or soul.

Cuellar has inserted a semi-comic funky version of "Ay Viene la Migra" as a wry comment on these moments of dehumanization, a way of saying, "Alambristas may be hiding, caught or deported but they aren't out of the picture." When Roberto emerges from the cistern, soaking wet in the midday sun, he challenges his employers, who had called the migra in to raid the workers so they wouldn't receive pay, for his wages. They drive off and leave him standing in the dust.

"Where We Live": *Lección Número Uno*

The physical, emotional, and spiritual dimension of food in the film is tenderly and humorously revealed through the formation of a friendship between Roberto and Joe in a scene called "Lección Número Uno." This significant friendship begins just after the migra raid, when Roberto is now seen bent over in a strawberry field where a more seasoned Mexican farm worker, Joe, teaches him some crucial survival skills. After a day of picking, during which Joe jokingly shows Roberto how to sneak strawberries into his mouth while working, Joe takes him to the migrant camp and shows him the chicken coop, which is "where we live." Then, through a series of symbolic gestures and a humorous dialogue Joe and another farm worker, Berto, show him how to enter a gringo café and order gringo food—"ham, eggs, and coffee." This powerful scene serves as a rehearsal and a microcosm for a number of later scenes in the film.

I am reminded of the anthropologist Mary Douglas's study of how symbolic activities associated with food contribute to the social identity of various peoples. She shows how the production, preparation, and consumption of food joined to a symbolic pattern of expressions play profound roles in the social construction of reality.[5] Among the symbolic actions Roberto learns from Joe and Berto are how to smile, walk, and talk in public gringo spaces. Most importantly he learns how to do these things within a Mexican style of moderation and charm. He is taught how to walk into a gringo café—upright head expressing confidence and with a measured smile on his face. He's told to smile but "not too much or they'll know you're illegal." He's instructed on how to sit in gringo spaces. It's important, Joe tells him, to cross your legs because "the gringos always cross their legs." He goes through the unfamiliar motions of mouthing three new words that will come to his aid later in the film—"Ham, eggs, and coffee." Joe tells him in Spanish, "What you want to order are beans and tortillas, but here in the United States it's ham, eggs and coffee." He's even taught, without his interest, to think of flirting with waitresses. This food game is a social rehearsal for a series of real situations Roberto will face in the future where he will have to express, symbolically, parts of his new identity.

This scene in particular appears to draw on the farm-worker theatrical tradition developed by Luis Valdez and the Teatro Campesino. Valdez has told us how the farm-worker theater developed a style of acting called "Actos" and not "Scenes." These "actos," which the Teatro Campesino acted out in camps, schools, theaters, and streets all around the United States and in many parts of the world, included four characteristics that direct the action of "Lección Número Uno": 1) bilingual dialogue, 2) dramatization of a social problem facing farm workers, 3) invitation to the audience to participate in the scene and especially with the resolution to the problem, and 4) a sense of humor. Bilingual dialogue appears for the first time in the film when Joe speaks both English and Spanish as he begins to teach Roberto how to smile. The problem of being a stranger in a strange land and ordering food in order to survive is humorously presented. And the viewing audience, in every screening I've seen, begins to relax when this scene is shown with its bilingual style, and it is at this point that laughter begins and the viewers begin to participate in the friendship between Roberto and Joe. What Robert Young has done in this transitional scene is to provide Roberto with a new sense of *orientation*—a new beginning in his friendships, his first words of English, and even knowledge of how to blow a kiss. This hypothetical drama around food, which ends with Joe and Roberto sharing a beer and hoping to earn *mucha plata* in the fields of Stockton, creates an aura of human warmth and thus hope in the film.

From Trickster to Low Rider

Roberto's cultural education and his existence as Mexican *homo faber* in America continues under Joe's tutelage as they hitchhike, befriend a stranded Okie family, give blood at a clinic to earn money, and invade a Cadillac being transported with other cars on a train. One of the crucial new scenes in the director's cut of the film is the Okie sequence, which José Cuellar ornaments with his splendid original composition "Okie Dokie Shuffle." Joe and Roberto help a stranded Okie farm-working family get their car going, loan them two dollars for gas, and share information and moments of laughter and mutual support. The viewers learn that farm working was a multiethnic reality.

A major mythic character in world religions is the trickster figure, a kind of culture hero who creates by rebelling against authority (the High God); often discovers or makes plants, fire, or other cultural elements; and is an excellent example of *homo faber*. Tricksters often emphasize their sexuality and often go too far in their challenge to authority or expression of their appetites and end up suffering serious injury or death. Elements of the trickster figure show up in a scene where Joe and Roberto hitch a ride on a train transporting automobiles. They get into a new Cadillac on the top tier of the train and for a few minutes seem to be riding a cloud of giddiness and fun. Roberto buckles up his first seat belt and plays with the electric window and Joe imitates how gringos hold their cigarettes. Then, Joe, who has already shown trickster elements in his endearing sense of humor, his ability to negotiate with the police, and his sly references to flirtation, begins to lose control and takes too big a risk. As the train carrying these two giddy farm workers on their imaginary trip to "Florida" glides down the track, a police car begins to shadow the train. Roberto becomes frightened but Joe, in a fit of rebellion and laughter, becomes louder and starts to blow the horn of the train, attracting the policemen's attention. Roberto panics while Joe has a cackling outburst, yelling out of the car window, "I love you, we love you, he loves you." Soon, the train engineer, alerted to his illegal passengers, stops the train and Roberto and Joe make a wild dash into the fields with the police in pursuit. As often happens, the trickster has gone too far in his enjoyment of his freedom and his defiance of authority.

Soon after, Robert Young gives new meaning to the term "low rider" when Joe and Roberto emerge from the fields carrying long nearly door-size pieces of wood. Joe shows Roberto how to rig up a wooden bed beneath the train so they can hitch rides to the next picking opportunity. As they start out on this ominous trip, Joe crosses himself and the two set off in these defenseless positions. Clinging beneath the train as it rushes to the next job, Joe slips under the train's wheels and is killed, leaving Roberto, once again, miserably alone. Stricken with shock and grief and remembering Joe's "lesson number one," he wanders into a nearby town. In his desperation he seeks some solace in a small café that becomes the center of the film for the next few sequences and that will soon become his temporary salvation.

Still stunned by Joe's death and the starkness of his situation, Roberto can barely articulate to an attentive waitress "ham, eggs, and coffee" and is helped by another Mexican who is bilingual. This scene, shot at night, among strangers following the death of his friend, communicates Roberto's desperation and we sense that food without friendship cannot nurture him.

From "Rent a Slave" to a Taste of Flower

Roberto's outcast condition and the nature of food labor for Mexicans are highlighted in the next scene, which could be called "Rent a Slave." Needing work to earn a few dollars to eat, Roberto joins a straggle of Mexican men waiting on the city street in the early morning darkness to hook up with a temporary job. Two drunks, played by Julius Harris and Edward James Olmos, stumble into the scene shouting insults at the waiting men, driving them to the edge of explosive violence. You men are "up-to-date slaves," screams one, and "rent-a-slave," yells the other. The Harris character, bobbing and weaving like a boxer in the ring, yells at the desperate men, "Ain't no future in pickin'. . . . That ain't what the American way of life is about. . . . Think about it . . . instead of bending over like a mule or something else. . . . " A fight nearly ensues but the message is clear. Roberto is now entering into an American way of life as a rent-a-slave.

In fact, he's next seen bent over in the fields with scores of other alambristas picking grapes. The heat, dirt, sun, and oppressive labor contrasts with a cornucopia of grapes being harvested. In this and other scenes Young chooses to film lush, ordered, green landscapes in which the abundance of food production by farm workers is juxtaposed with their own oppressive eating and living conditions. This scene of great physical efforts by Mexican workers ends with a close-up of a slow, seemingly endless cascade of green grapes falling into a truck, as if it were bounty from the sky, instead of from bent backs and blistered hands.

Completely exhausted, Roberto trudges off a bus and back to the café where, under the spell of Dr. Loco's "Dead Dog Tired in Stockton Blues #2," he first orders coffee and then collapses into sleep at the counter. As Loco's musical narrative builds to a free-blowing frenzy in the night, Roberto is helped outside and at first left on the sidewalk by the café's workers, a Black man and a White waitress named Sharon. Two street bums immediately move in to rob him, but the two café workers rush back to his rescue. Delirious with exhaustion and depression he is physically carried to Sharon's small, humble apartment where he sleeps on the floor through the night. Again we see that food culture, this time in the form of the café and its decent workers, one an Anglo, the other an African American, play pivotal roles in the film. This café becomes the first public space, beyond the fields, where Roberto can be relatively safe.

When Roberto wakes up on the floor of Sharon's apartment, dazed and not knowing how he got there, Sharon pulls out her waitress uniform to remind him of where they had met in Roberto's two previous visits to the café. Somewhere in the viewer's mind, the value, friendship, and warmth of "lesson number one" resonates for us in this scene. Hindered by language barriers, Roberto unsuccessfully tries to tell Sharon, who is feeding her infant daughter and caring for her younger brother, that he too has a daughter and wife in Mexico. She does not understand.

It may be a surprise to some that religion and sexuality often have a close relationship in culture. As the history of religions shows, sex and eroticism have important connections to religious ideas and religious ecstasy. The most overtly religious scene in the film leads to Roberto and Sharon's sexual liaison. She takes a cleaned-up Roberto to a charismatic tent meeting where a hollering, singing preacher delivers his version of another eating scene, the eating of the apple in the Garden of Eden, to a swaying, awakened, interracial congregation. Roberto appears curious but deeply puzzled, uncomfortable, even amazed at what he is witnessing as members of the congregation, including Sharon, swoon, sway, and fall into trances. The howling, prancing preacher works his congregation into a pitch of individual and collective feelings of ecstasy as Roberto looks on incredulous and amazed.

Whatever else this "holy roller" gathering meant to Roberto and Sharon, it leads in the next scene to their first sexual encounter. A moment with food plays a transitional role in this scene as well, which begins with Roberto and Sharon eating a meal she has prepared for them. She also feeds him coquettish glances and he responds with interest. They become intimate on his "bed" on the floor and the contrasting skin color of the two lovers is balanced by Dr. Loco's bilingual love song, which is surely one of the finest lyrical and musical examples of its kind. As Dr. Loco writes elsewhere in this volume, he wanted to write a

> love ballad that articulates the astonishing feelings of attraction and affection that Sharon and Roberto seem to share from that moment. Bob [the filmaker] said he wanted this to show how we all need love and the affection that comes with human touch, regardless of other circumstances. I wanted to show how the same loving situation probably had a different meaning, significance, and value to each of them, and decided to express this bilingually by stating Sharon's sentiments in English and Roberto's *sentimientos en Español.*

One image that links their different sentiments is expressed through the metaphor of taste—the "taste" of her "flower" that opens his desperate humanness to hot caresses and alleviates his pain. As their physical liaison takes place, these verses by Dr. Loco accompany the scene:

Tus labios sabor de flor	Your lips the taste of flower
Tus caricias con calor	Your caresses with heat
Me abren, siente mi ardor	They open me, feel my ardor
La verdad, te necesito	The truth, I need you
Aunque sea por un ratito	Even if for just a little while
Tu pasión alivia mi dolor	Your passion alleviates my pain

The musical rejuvenation and physical-emotional nurturing in this scene shows how the tasting of sex and love brings a new, and more pleasurable heat to Roberto's life and eases the confusion he is feeling. They are giving each other the sustenance of human affection.

Dissembling *Alambrista*

Roberto's life as *homo faber* extends to the work of learning more words in English and dissembling his understanding of the language in a scene where discovery of his illegal status in the United States is threatened. First, he returns to work in yet another field, a cucumber field that appears out of the morning fog and mist. Men and women bent over picking baskets of cucumbers under the eye of some field bosses is prelude to one of the most humorous and yet tense social scenes in the film. Roberto returns to the café for the third time and is sitting at the counter learning from Sharon how to ask for "apple pie and ice cream." Having just become comfortable with "ham, eggs, and coffee," this is something of struggle. It is, in a sense, "Lesson Number 2," only now at the hands of Sharon, who playfully teases him unintentionally into a situation of social risk. Seated on one side of Roberto is the actor Jerry Hardin, who delivers a boisterous soliloquy about uppity bosses and his own family. Speaking in intense, animated cadences of colloquial English, Harden unleashes a narrative embroidered with profanity, with references to disease, hunting, and guns, and peels of laughter. Roberto timidly responds with looks and nods as though he understands this soliloquy so as not to appear out of place and give away his ignorance of the language and his status as an illegal. At the height of this soliloquy a policeman enters and sits on the other side of Roberto, eyeing him and his responses to Hardin's verbal artistry. Sharon slips by and perhaps not paying attention to the social danger Roberto is facing, asks him again what he wants to eat and he states, "ham, eggs, and coffee." Soon, she brings him apple pie and ice cream. The viewer sees and feels the rock and the hard place that Roberto is in—on the one side a crescendo of a cackling story in vernacular English and on the other a law officer who at any moment could grab Roberto and disrupt completely his newfound friendship and opportunity. For me this represents another stressful dimension of the work of the alambristas, which is deciphering and negotiating situations of social awkwardness and legal danger.

Thirteen Unlucky Steps to a Migra Bus

A terrible dimension of food cultivation is revealed in the next scene when Roberto takes on a job as a flagman with a pesticide company. We also witness the evolution of his social identity through the donning of a different "costume" or set of clothes. The irony of the situation is that while his spirit is rejuvenated by having a new, better-paying job, he has entered into the most lethal atmosphere of farm work, pesticides. He's given a new uniform, nicer than any clothes he's ever had, and taken to the edges of thriving green fields where he's taught how to walk thirteen steps along the edge of the field, stop, and wave his flag at an oncoming helicopter spraying pesticides. Then, he takes thirteen more steps down the line so the pilot will know where to drop the next load of poisons. Roberto has no idea that he's being poisoned by his new job-that his life as *homo faber* is becoming infused with *la Muerte*. Instead, he returns to Sharon's house proud, smiling and showing off his new uniform and the promise of higher wages. Not understanding but admiring his new outfit, she asks, "You're working at a car wash?"

With his pocket money and some new clothes, he and Sharon go shopping together and he notices her interest in a scarf that she decides against buying because of the cost. Quietly and without her seeing, he purchases the scarf for her and prepares to give it as a gift later in the day. Then, in a scene that makes the viewer squirm, Roberto attempts to send a money order back to his wife in Mexico through the help of Sharon and an interpreter at a post office. Through a bilingual exchange Sharon learns the truth—that Roberto is married and has a family. Through masterful camera work and the poignant gestures of the two actors, we are drawn into her hurt and his confusion as glances of misunderstanding pass between them.

All seems forgiven, however, in the next scene in a cantina that switches, in minutes, from sweetness to heartbreak. Roberto and Sharon dance happily together in a crowd of swaying Mexicans and he surprises her with the *pañuelo*. Again, Dr. Loco illustrates the emotional power of this scene with the right musical moves. He inserts the song "Esta Noche," which begins with the words,

> *Tonight I give you this kerchief*
> *So you can come dance with me*
> *I have my heart full of care*
> *That with joy I'm going to give to you.*

And just at the moment when we are relieved that these two lonely people have overcome their misunderstanding and understood something vital about the nature of their relationship, its depth and limits, Roberto is ripped away and Sharon is stunned and left standing alone on the dance floor. Someone yells that the alambristas are being hunted by the migra and the only escape is out the back door. Roberto rushes out for safety only to be corralled along with other alambristas into a migra van and transported back to the Mexican border, never to see Sharon again. *Esta noche* becomes a dark night of painful separation and loneliness.

Peripatetic Mexicans

What follows are a series of scenes that reveal the peripatetic condition of farmworker existence. *Peripatetic* comes from a Greek word and means 'to walk up and down' or 'to tread'. It refers to the practice of walking or traveling about and also reflects the itinerant condition of walking from place to place in search of work. Peripatetic also refers to the spatial flows of commodities like foodstuffs. From Roberto's first sprint through the fence into the United States to his long walks with Joe and his furtive, desperate hustle back to the border after this first deportation, he represents what Paul C. Adams calls the "dark peripatetic." This is the walking of outcasts along the edges, on unmarked pathways and in the secret shadows of legitimate society. Another scholar defines the dark peripatetic as "a fevered, haunted, misdirecting, unilluminated and unilluminating walking."[6] This is the walking of outcasts, whose desperate forms of mobility in darkness, along unmarked but secretly traveled pathways, reveal an alternate map of human orientation and movement. Adams writes

> The dark peripatetic motif signifies that the bonds of society have been torn, or a character's identity is beginning to dissolve or both. Walking is, on this account, an ominous excursion: out of doors, out of society, out of community, out of normal reality, and perhaps even out of life itself.[7]

Roberto's ominous excursion (one might say his entire journey has been an ominous excursion) begins when he walks back across the dusty ambiguous border into Mexico and right into the hands of two coyotes who are looking "for numbers of bodies" to smuggle back into the United States. Ned Beatty appears as the head coyote, telling his Mexican assistant in a darkened bar, "I want the labor…bodies, numbers of bodies amigo. That's where you make your money." Roberto joins a group of alambristas who agree to pay $200 each out of their wages after being transported to Colorado to *levantar el melon* where a farm-worker strike is going on.

The alambristas are seen sneaking in the dark along back roads, skirting a trailer park, zigzagging along the border fence and out into vaguely marked pathways in the desert. The dark peripatetic condition, the condition of being put outside of society and perhaps life itself, is best exemplified when Beatty's character lashes out at his Mexican counterpart for allowing a woman with a baby to travel to their nighttime rendezvous point, "I don't care what you do with her. You can take her back with you or turn her loose on the road." Being turned loose on the road is the peripatetic metaphor for what Roberto and all farm workers experience, fear, and struggle to overcome.

Roberto and his fellow alambristas are soon on the road for a thirty-six-hour ride stuffed in the back of a hard-bed truck. Arriving at the junkyard meeting place, they are pulled out of the canvas truck as if from a huge tomb on wheels, barely awake with life.

Like Father, Unlike Son

Roberto's next field of food appears just before sunrise as the alambristas are confronted with *huelguistas,* or striking farm workers, holding up signs and chanting pleas to not enter the field. Once inside, a long carpet of watermelons becomes the stage for another sad revelation. Roberto and his cohorts are working intensely to pick and throw watermelons onto trucks while highschoolers are bused in to make up for the reduced field hands during the strike. While Roberto is seen earnestly heaving watermelons in the sun, the students see this backbreaking work as an opportunity to play games of catch, breaking some of the melons in the process. Then, Roberto hears a commotion nearby where an older farm worker named Alberto Ramirez has been stricken with a heart attack. Walking apprehensively in this field of fruit he comes upon and kneels down near the dying body of his father, who is being attended to by other pickers. It is too late, as his father dies next to a partially loaded truck of watermelons and they never have a chance to communicate.

In a state of shock and sadness Roberto is taken to the place where his father lived with other farm workers, in an abandoned school bus. A kind coworker of his father shows him Alberto's bunk, his worn suitcase, and its contents, including a book in English, a toothbrush, a fifty-dollar money order for a woman, pictures, and some letters. As a fly lands and crawls on his face Roberto learns that his father had a second wife elsewhere in the United States to whom he sent money. The heartrending irony of this situation is shown in Roberto's face and we recall the beginning of the film when Roberto and his mother were praying in the family chapel in front of his absent father's picture. The value that his father held for the family was symbolized by its leaning up against a statue of the Virgin of Guadalupe. His mother had said to him, "*No te vayas hijo . . .* your father never returned." We recall that Robert tried to send a fifty-dollar money order to his own wife back in Mexico and we sense that he understands that he is now faced, in stark and lonely terms, with the same destiny—dying while working in a watermelon field, while Anglo teenagers play with fruit, far from his wife and children. He realizes he has to make a choice—to stay and probably live a life like his father in an abandoned school bus or return to his family in Mexico and start over again.

The pain and pressure of this situation is dramatized in the penultimate scene when Roberto explodes in rage after tasting what he thinks is rotten food in the makeshift junkyard kitchen. The rotten taste mirrors his rotten situation—he has a dead father and a dead future before him in a land of plenty. As Roberto repeatedly screams in pain about the food, he sobs and says, "I don't want to be here, I want to go home." The larger irony of Roberto's crisis is reflected in Dr. Loco's rendition of Jimmy Hendrix's Woodstock version of the national anthem used to punctuate this scene.

Roberto is next seen hitchhiking alone on the road. A cop stops and politely transports him back to the border. As the police car moves south Roberto gazes out at green irrigated fields and trucks overflowing with tomatoes—the fruit of farm-worker labor and the scene of their daily lives but an abundance that is not for him or his kind.

The profound, pathetic sadness and irony of the work of alambristas is crystallized in the last scene at a border-crossing station. As Roberto and his cohorts are waiting to walk back into Mexico, a young Mexican woman in child labor rushes over the borderline, grabs onto a flagpole, and begins to give birth. This birth recalls for us the birth of Roberto's baby, which began this story, only here at the concrete border station joining two countries the scene is rowdy and frenetic. As onlookers drive by and stare, the woman, aided by two other Mexican women, gives birth to a boy on the concrete. Through joyful tears she sighs, "He was born here. He won't need papers." While this birth of a new U.S. citizen is taking place, Roberto's face is filled with sadness, exhaustion, and disbelief. He then joins a line of Mexican men walking back into Mexico where we expect he will soon rejoin his family.

As the film-ending corrido shows us, Roberto has painfully come to terms or at least become aware of "the *divided*-ultimate significance of his place in the world." This ultimate significance is divided because his life and imagination are both in the United States and in Mexico. In the United States he dwelt for a time in a world of hyper-food-labor where his father died as a stranger to him in a field. In Mexico his family lives in what looks to be eternal poverty but at least there is a living family he can work to nurture. He has come to this understanding through this journey of labor *and* labors. His identity is that of *homo faber*, the human as a worker and maker. He has labored in the fields, struggled to find friendships and affection, and undergone the ordeal of humiliation, deportation, and the deaths of his friend Joe and his long-lost father. He worked honestly, intensely, and with hope. And his journey to and from the United States was framed by two other labors tied to moments of separation—the labors of the Mexican women giving birth to babies and future hopes.

These patterns of work, birth, and immigration, while filmed in 1977, are recalled to life in 2003 through the ingenious collaboration of Robert Young, José Cuellar, and the Alambrista Project and represent several key dimensions of the immediate future of U.S.-Mexican relations. In this essay I've tried to show the religious dimensions of Roberto's odyssey by highlighting the three types of work that give structure to the film, the work in the fields, the labor that creates new lives, and the struggle to make friendship and family. Dr. Loco sings it best, showing the alambrista as *homo faber*, the human worker who cultivates life.

I cut grapes and picked cucumbers...
Like the wind below the stars
The desert with others I crossed...
I ask for forgiveness from the Virgin
For the damage that I caused others
You leave behind your people
To come earn to eat
I prefer returning to my land
Where I have friendship and warmth.

■

Discussion Questions

1. Watch the film and notice at least three scenes where a religious icon or ritual plays a transitional role. Describe how this icon or ritual action leads, in the very next scene, to a significant transformation in Roberto's life. For example, the image of Guadalupe in the chapel is followed by his journey to the U.S.

2. Carrasco suggests that there is a religious dimension to the work in the fields and the labor of having babies in the film. What does he mean by "religious dimension," and do you agree or disagree with his interpretation? Should discussions of religion among Mexicans be confined to church activities?

3. At the end of the film, Roberto returns to Mexico. This can be interpreted in religious terms as the "return to origins" in order to have a new beginning. But we don't know what happens to him. Take a half hour and write the next scene in the film so that it expresses your vision of Roberto's destiny.

■

Notes

1. Charles H. Long, *Significations: Signs, Symbols, and Images in the Interpretation of Religion* (Aurora, Colo.: The Davis Group, 1999).

2. Daniel G. Groody, *Border of Death, Valley of Life: An Immigrant Journey of Heart and Spirit* (Lanham, Md.: Rowman & Littlefield Publishers, Inc. 2002), 17.

3. See Paul C. Adams, "Peripatetic Imagery and Peripatetic Sense of Place," in *Textures of Place: Exploring Humanist Geographies,* ed. Paul C. Adams, Steven Hoelscher, and Karen E. Till (Minneapolis: University of Minnesota Press, 2001), 186–206.

4. Groody, *Border of Death*, 19.

5. Mary Douglas, *Purity and Danger; An Analysis of Concepts of Pollution and Taboo* (New York: Praeger, 1966).

6. Adams, "Peripatetic Imagery and Peripatetic Sense of Place," 196.

7. Ibid.

About the Contributors

David Carrasco is an historian of religions whose bestselling *Religions of Meso-america: Cosmovision and Ceremonial Centers* (San Francisco: Harper & Row, 1990) is taught in many Chicano Studies and Religious Studies courses. He is also the editor-in-chief of the award-winning *Oxford Encyclopedia of Meso-american Cultures: The Civilizations of Mexico and Central America* (New York: Oxford University Press, 2001), and author of *City of Sacrifice: The Aztec Empire and the Role of Violence in Civilization.*

Nicholas J. Cull is professor of American Studies at the University of Leicester, where he directs the Centre for American Studies. He is a historian of the media who has written widely on film history and the history of propaganda in Britain and the United States. He is presently completing a history of U.S. propaganda overseas since 1945.

Albert Camarillo is a professor of History and is the Miriam and Peter Haas Centennial Professor in Public Service at Stanford University. He is the author of seven books and dozens of essays and articles on Mexican Americans and other ethnic groups in American history. Three of his books related directly to Alam-brista and the history of Mexicans in the United States: *Chicanos in California: A History of Mexican Americans in California* (San Francisco: Boyd & Fraser Publishing Co., 1984); *Chicanos in a Changing Society: From Mexican Pueblos to American Barrios in Santa Barbara and Southern California, 1848-1930* (Cambridge, Mass.: Harvard University Press, 1996); and *Not White, Not Black: Mexicans and Ethnic/Racial Borderlands in American Cities* (forthcoming, 2004).

Richard Griswold del Castillo is a professor and chair of Chicana and Chicano Studies at San Diego State University. He is the author of *The Treaty of Guadalupe Hidalgo: A Legacy of Conflict* (Norman: University of Oklahoma Press, 1990); *La Familia: Chicano Families in the Urban Southwest, 1848 to the Present* (Notre Dame, Ind.: University of Notre Dame Press, 1984); *The Los Angeles Barrio, 1850-1890: A Social History* (Berkeley: University of California Press, 1979); *César Chávez: A Triumph of Spirit* (with Richard A. Garcia; Norman: University of Oklahoma Press, 1995); and *North to Aztlán: A History of Mexican Americans in the United States* (with Arnoldo de León; New York: Twayne Publishers; London: Prentice Hall International, 1996). He is married and has six children and six grandchildren.

Daniel Groody, CSC, is currently an assistant professor of Theology and the director of the Center for Latino Spirituality and Culture at the Institute for Latino Studies at the University of Notre Dame. He is a Roman Catholic priest and a member of the Congregation of Holy Cross who has spent many years working in Latin America, particularly along the U.S.-Mexican border. Groody is the author of *Border of Death, Valley of Life: An Immigrant Journey of Heart and Spirit* (Lanham, Md.: Rowman and Littlefield, 2002).

Bill Ong Hing is a professor of Law and Asian American Studies at the University of California, Davis, and founder of the Immigrant Legal Resource Center. He is the author of *To Be an American: Cultural Pluralism and the Rhetoric of Assimilation* (New York: New York University Press, 1997) and *Making and Remaking Asian America through Immigration Policy, 1850-1990* (Stanford, Calif.: Stanford University Press, 1993).

Teresa Carrillo is an associate professor of Raza Studies, College of Ethnic Studies, San Francisco State University. In her teaching and research, she specializes in Latino politics with an emphasis on immigration, and transnational connections in the Americas, and Latinos as political actors in constant interaction with local, national, and transnational political forces. She is the author of *Working Women and the "19th of September" Mexican Garment Workers Union: The Significance of Gender* (East Lansing: Michigan State University, 1989) and "Cross-Border Talk: Transnational Perspectives on Labor, Race, and Sexuality," in *Talking Visions: Multicultural Feminism in Transnational Age,* ed. Ella Habiba Shohat (Cambridge, Mass.: MIT Press, 1999). Carrillo is currently working on a book titled *Watching Over Greater Mexico: Governance of Mexico's Ten Million Citizens Abroad.*

Cordelia Candelaria is a professor and chair in the Department of Chicana and Chicano Studies and a professor of English at Arizona State University. She is the author of *Chicano Poetry: A Critical Introduction* (Westport, Conn.: Greenwood Press, 1986), and the editor of *Multiethnic Literature of the United States: Critical Introductions and Classroom Resources* (Boulder: University of Colorado, 1989).

Howie Movshovitz is Director of Education and a curator at the Starz FilmCenter in Denver, which is affiliated with the University of Colorado, Denver. He has been a film critic at Colorado Public Radio for nearly thirty years, and a contributor to National Public Radio's "Morning Edition" for sixteen years. Movshovitz also teaches film classes at the University of Colorado, Denver.

José Cuellar (aka Dr. Loco), is a professor of Raza Studies at San Francisco State University. His recordings include *Movimiento Music,* by Dr. Loco's Rockin' Jalapeño Band (1992); *Con Safos* (1991); *Puro Party* (1995); and *Barrio Ritmos & Blues* (1998).